Presented to

with the warm

regards of its

author.

June 3, 1942?

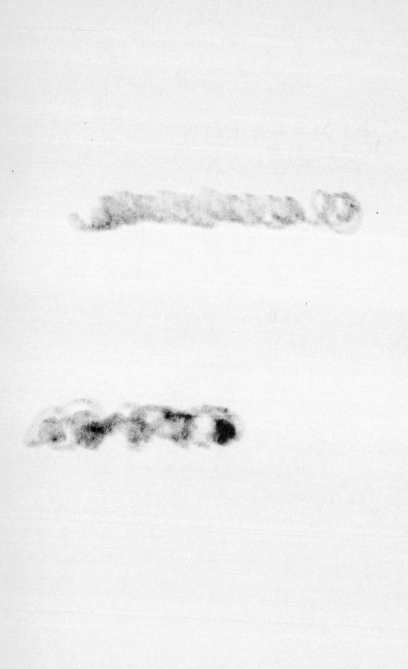

PEMBERTON

Defender of Vicksburg

General Pemberton during the war

PEMBERTON

Defender of Vicksburg

BY

JOHN C. PEMBERTON

WITH A FOREWORD BY

DOUGLAS SOUTHALL FREEMAN

CHAPEL HILL

THE UNIVERSITY OF NORTH CAROLINA PRESS

1942

PRINTED IN THE UNITED STATES OF AMERICA BY SEEMAN PRINTERY, INC.,
DURHAM, N. C.; BOUND BY L. H. JENKINS, INC., RICHMOND, VIRGINIA

TO

Vicksburg

FOREWORD

BY DOUGLAS SOUTHALL FREEMAN

THE STUDENT of war is too fond of successful strategy and tactics. He loves to have a seat in Hannibal's tent the night before Cannae, or to look over Marlborough's shoulder as the Duke plans Blenheim. So spoiled by victories a professional reader may be that he will get a mistaken conception of risk, of the influence of chance, and of the narrowness of the line between success and failure. The scrutiny of lost battles is not defeatist any more than interest in the offensive necessarily leads to rashness. If the observant soldier only would realize it, he may learn as much from the analysis of a campaign that went wrong as from a similar review of an operation that vindicated the plans of a great leader.

Particularly is this true, I think, of the major engagements of the War between the States. Lee, Grant, "Stonewall" Jackson and Sherman have not been studied too much; but Pemberton and Banks and Bragg and Buell have been studied too little. Of all these men, John C. Pemberton has had least attention, even at the hands of those of Grant's biographers who failed to see that they did not add glory to the winner at Vicksburg if they depreciated Grant's adversary. Pemberton was a technically proficient soldier, and in his theories of artillery he was well ahead of most of his contemporaries. To what extent his difficulties were due to his own temperament, and how far they were traceable to the prejudice of the South against Northern-born Confederates, it is difficult to say. Certainly the doubt some Southerners expressed concerning the loyalty of men who sacrificed everything for the cause of states' rights was as pronounced as it was shameful. On a par with some South Carolinians' avowed distrust of Pemberton was D. H. Hill's continuing suspicion of Josiah Gorgas, who had not only devotion but also an administrative capacity scarcely rivaled in the South. Both Gorgas and Pemberton had the unswerving support of Mr. Davis, but in Pemberton's case, even as early as the Spring of 1863, the confidence of the President involved as much liability as advantage.

Pemberton was hampered, further, by the distance of his command from Richmond. Beyond doubt, commanders remote from the Confederate capital were not watched closely or restricted daily, but their occasional orders from the Commander-in-Chief were based sometimes on alarming misinformation. Given little direction, these officers got poor direction at that. Armies south of Charleston and west of the Appalachian divide appear, also, to have had worse equipment and to have received less attention as respects current wants than did the Army of Northern Virginia, though Confederate forces in the West and in the Gulf States had sufficient horses and usually had fair rations while their comrades nearer the Potomac went often without.

The final difficulty of Pemberton was Joseph E. Johnston, the most fascinating of all the Confederate commanders because the most enigmatic. Johnston was a generous superior, a carping equal, an impossible subordinate. Generous today, he would be exacting tomorrow. Affection and jealousy were combined in feminine, rather than in masculine proportions.

Reasonable and patient in one mood, he was irascible the moment he felt his prerogative challenged. As equable a commander as Lee had difficulties with Johnston. Between Johnston and a man of Pemberton's temperament, chained to the defence of a fixed position of strategic importance, what possibility of coöperation was there? Lacking Johnston's unrelaxing and persistent help, what could Pemberton expect other than the fate that befell him?

These considerations of distance, of equipment and of contrasting personality and capacity on opposite sides of the lines at Vicksburg must have intrigued many students. I know they have baffled as well as intrigued me. For that reason, when I learned that my friend John C. Pemberton of New York—*exul immeritus!*—had the unpublished papers of his Grandfather, I besought him to embody them in a biography of General Pemberton, which would include a new and thorough study of Vicksburg. As I knew well the author of this volume, I did not feel caution akin to that which Thackeray once admonished us to exercise concerning widows' biographies of their husbands. I believed that the exact reasoning so admirably displayed by Mr. Pemberton in the practice of the law would be employed in his analysis of Vicksburg. That belief has been vindicated. The result of his researches is much the fairest, as well as the fullest study of that tragedy from the viewpoint of the principal Confederate actor. In the spirit of the drama, having spoken this prologue, I step back and signal the gentlemen of the Chapel Hill press to raise the curtain.

ACKNOWLEDGMENTS

MY THANKS are due to Dr. Douglas S. Freeman for persuading me to undertake this biography and for generously providing it with a Foreword; to my secretary, Eleanor Haeselbarth, for her unvaried patience and accuracy; to Basil C. Walker, Fletcher Pratt, the Honorable John B. Brunini, Colonel R. E. T. Riggs, U. S. Infantry Reserve, and John Lindsay Morehead for encouragement and advice; to my brother, Frank Pemberton, for much of the difficult Charleston section; to Dorothie Bobbé, Charles M. Kinsolving, and Captain Alfred Dodd Starbird, Engineer Corps, U. S. Military Academy, West Point, for reading the manuscript; to Colonel Girard Lindsley McEntee, U. S. Army, Retired, for his introduction to Captain Starbird and to West Point; to R. S. Wilkins, Esq., Boston, Massachusetts, for lending the original of a letter from Pemberton to Davis; to Major General Frank Ross McCoy, U. S. Army, Retired, for permission to use a valued letter respecting the Vicksburg Campaign; to Colonel William Couper, Executive Officer, Virginia Military Institute, for the use of a hitherto unknown letter reporting a conversation between Pemberton and Secretary of War Seddon; to Mrs. Dunbar Rowland for her gracious consent to the use of material from her husband's *Jefferson*

Davis, Constitutionalist; to Dorothy Perry Hammond for significant Sherman data (and the reminder that Sherman's only defeat was at the hands of Pemberton); to Zona K. MacPhee, of my publisher's staff, who helped mightily with the painstaking revision of this story in manuscript.

To the following authors and publishers I am grateful for their generosity in permitting me to quote from copyrighted publications: Robert S. Henry and The Bobbs-Merrill Company (Henry, *Story of the Confederacy*); Harris Dickson and The Crowell-Collier Publishing Company (article in *Collier's,* March 19, 1938); D. Appleton-Century Company, Inc. *(Battles and Leaders of the Civil War);* Dodd, Mead & Company (B. H. Liddell Hart, *Sherman, Soldier, Realist, American,* Copyright, 1929, by Dodd, Mead & Company, Inc.); Houghton Mifflin Company (John Fiske, *The Mississippi Valley in the Civil War*); Little, Brown & Company (B. H. Liddell Hart, *Great Captains Unveiled*); Liveright Publishing Corporation (Emil Ludwig, *Napoleon*); Longmans, Green & Company, Inc. (G. F. R. Henderson, *Stonewall Jackson and the American Civil War*); William Morrow & Company, Inc. (Armand de Caulaincourt, *No Peace with Napoleon!* Translated by George Libaire, Copyright, 1936, by William Morrow & Company); Old Hickory Book Shop (Howard Swiggett, ed., *A Rebel War Clerk's Diary at the Confederate States Capital*); Random House, Inc. (B. H. Liddell Hart, *Through the Fog of War*); D. S. Freeman and Charles Scribner's Sons (Freeman, *The South to Posterity* and *R. E. Lee*); John W. Thomason, Jr., and Charles Scribner's Sons (Thomason, *Jeb Stuart*); The State of Wisconsin State Historical Society (William F. Vilas, *The Vicksburg Campaign*).

CONTENTS

ILLUSTRATIONS

MAPS

PEMBERTON
Defender of Vicksburg

CHAPTER I

Historical Position

THERE HAS NEVER BEEN a biography of General Pemberton notwithstanding "he probably had the most difficult task that fell to the lot of any general in the Confederate army, excepting Lee alone."[1] In Grant's *Memoirs,* written more than two decades after Vicksburg, this peerless soldier records for history his view that Pemberton's surrender with the largest body of troops up to that time on the continent sealed the fate of the Confederacy.[2] More recent military studies find Vicksburg's capture to have been the greatest feat of the war.[3] But despite the role of Pemberton as Grant's antagonist for mastery of the South's Gibraltar, Grant facing replacement and repulse until the last, Pemberton has remained a man unknown, except to family and to those who were his friends. We have not far to seek for answer: he failed! So doing, he but earned the bitterest distinction; he surrendered Vicksburg on the nation's anniversary of independence, while Grant became "The Man of Destiny." The wobbling Union exulted: "The Southern States were cut in two.... Grant's victory had finally opened up the Mississippi River." Even the somber Lincoln was not proof against a rare feeling of elation. Writing lyrically to J. C. Conkling, a trusted friend, he penned his now familiar letter, opening with the celebrated passage, "The Father of Waters again goes unvexed to the sea."

Lieutenant Colonel Vilas, who was with the Wisconsin Volunteers during the operations around Vicksburg, wrote of that surrender that it would become "a question for historical debate whether any justification remained for further resistance of the Union arms."[4] Many now consider Vicksburg more decisive than Gettysburg.[5] But few were the unsuccessful commanders on either side who failed to seek their prompt exoneration from press and public. Pemberton had only one request: that the President convene a Court of Inquiry to pass upon his Vicksburg conduct. Nor had he long to wait for answer. President Davis at once replied from Richmond:

"To some men it is given to be commended for what they are expected to do, and to be sheltered when they fail by a transfer of the blame which may attach; to others it is decreed that their success shall be denied or treated as a necessary result and their failures imputed to incapacity, or crime. . . . I have been taught by a disagreeable experience how slowly the Messenger of Truth follows that of slander. The Court which has been ordered to inquire into the campaign in Missi. & E. La. will I trust develop the real causes of events, and give the public the means of doing justice to the actors."[6]

This promised chance for vindication never came to Pemberton. Hard-pressed Southern armies clamored for their leaders—in the field. None could be spared to square the past, the present loomed too urgent.[7]

Not long before his death at Shiloh, Albert Sidney Johnston wrote his chief at the Confederate capital: "The test of merit, in my profession, with the people is success."[8] So tested, Pemberton for the most part stands in history as a man condemned. But there still remains untold his story of those days of desperate crisis and ultimate defeat.

In the estimation of Virginia's historian, publicist, and journalist, Douglas Southall Freeman, "General Pemberton was one of the great men of the Southern Confederacy...a gallant and gifted man who paid as great a price for his devotion as circumstances ever exacted of an American."[9]

Whence, and from what stock, came this warrior for the South—a "blunderer" to some, "great man" to others? Strange to relate, he called the second city of the North home and birthplace. Pembertons had settled Philadelphia in 1682 with the Quaker William Penn.

Yet, little less unusual was Samuel Cooper's case: New York man, full general, and ranking officer of the Confederate armies.* And what of David Farragut, the Tennesseean, who in the end was promoted first Admiral of the Union navy?

In a recent study of the Southern struggle for independence, a brilliant Southern author has said: "If a man's deserts are to be measured by his sacrifices no man deserved more of the Confederacy than Pemberton, who gave up his thirty years of career in the Army and his own people to follow the right as he saw it...."[10]

But even with such estimate of Pemberton, none has yet essayed the telling of the Vicksburg epic, except in light of afterknowledge. The time is more than due for the integration and publication of the Pemberton MSS, monographs, correspondence, and reports. Thereby, judgments formed by scholars and the public may undergo modification in appreciable degree. It is Robert Henry's matured conclusion that, "On the military side, value would be greatly heightened if all critics used so admirable a method as that of Freeman in his re-creation of the campaigns of Lee, wherein events are

---

* The following Northerners, by birth or ancestry, served with the Confederacy as generals: Cooper, Pemberton, G. W. Smith, Ripley, French, Blanchard, Lovell. Baldwin, Gorgas, and Pike.—Howard Swiggett, ed., *A Rebel War Clerk's Diary at the Confederate States Capital*, I, 33, 42, 89, 178, 221, 222, 245, 270, 286.

shown as they appeared to Lee at the time—that is, as scattered fragments, broken scraps of information, reliable and unreliable, which had to be pieced together as a basis for conclusions and decisions. Justice to the military commander who must walk in the 'fog of war' requires the application of some such difficult and painstaking method in the study of campaigns."[11]

CHAPTER II

Family and Early Life

OF THE EARLIEST Pembertons, Phineas was the first of any prominence. Coming to this country in 1682 from Radcliffe Bridge, near Bolton in Lancashire, England, he accompanied his father Ralph Pemberton and William Penn, with whom he settled in Bucks County, Pennsylvania. In those unhappy days, the Quakers—including the Penns and Pembertons— were sorely persecuted in Lancashire for their religious tenets.

Phineas was a distinguished man, "the ablest as well as one of the best men in the Province," in William Penn's own words. He shortly became well-to-do and held countless public offices, Penn later generously presenting him with a splendid property, now known as Bolton Farm, an estate of more than four hundred acres. Coming down through Phineas' descendants (he left a numerous family), Bolton was willed near the end of the nineteenth century to a collateral relative, Effingham B. Morris, late President of the Girard Trust Company, Philadelphia. Upon Mr. Morris' death in 1937, his heirs presented this rich rolling farm land (close by Fallsington) to the University of Pennsylvania, by which it is now owned.[1]

John Pemberton, father of General Pemberton, was born in Philadelphia, April 9, 1783. Before reaching twenty he

married Rebecca Clifford of the same city. When he died at
the age of sixty-four in 1847, the *Pennsylvanian* said editorially:

"John Pemberton, Esq., was one of the most influential
members of Friends. As a man, he was just, high minded
and honorable, enthusiastic in his feelings and speech; he was
much beloved by all who really knew him, and the circle was
a large one. A personal friend, and ardent admirer of the late
General Andrew Jackson, whose character of mind his own
very much resembled, he accepted from him without solicitation, and held, the post of Naval Officer at Philadelphia,
through all the time of that gentleman's administration."[2]

General Pemberton's mother, Rebecca Clifford (Pemberton), bore her husband thirteen children, of whom General
Pemberton was the second-born. Ten of her sons and daughters lived to reach maturity, and she saw five of them bring
up their own large families. Tall, and conspicuously blond,
she was by many thought a beauty. Always the head of her
household of temperamental children and grandchildren, the
Fine Lady would impressively remind the family's young
blades that "in Revolutionary Days the ancestral home at Third
and Chestnut streets was financial headquarters of those leg-
endary figures—Hamilton, Jefferson, and Robert Morris." The
anxious mother indulged the illusory hope that these noble
specters might temper celebrations often deemed to be "un-
mannerly, and out of keeping."

Lieutenant General John Clifford Pemberton, Confederate
States Army, was born August 10, 1814, in the city of Philadelphia. In early life he enjoyed every advantage which the
educational facilities of the time afforded. To supplement the
usual schooling of that day, his father employed private tutors
for his better instruction in Latin and in Greek, and to his
proficiency in these, especially in the study of Latin authors,
he owed much of the literary enjoyment of his later years.[3]

When he had attained his full height, Pemberton stood five feet ten and one-half inches in his stocking feet; and until the very day of his death, near sixty-seven, he remained as slender and erect as when in the prime of life. So dark brown were his eyes they appeared the color of his hair, which, except in earliest youth, was rather more black than brown. Though of a family markedly reserved—"never was there so reticent a family as ours," remarks a daughter—Pemberton was quiet, rather than untalkative. He was fond of congenial company, studious, and a favorite with women; they admired his good looks and erect bearing. To some of his contemporaries, and occasionally in the army, he was known as Jack. But such intimacy was not general, for there was in him a certain stern-ness, a suspected preference for having casual acquaintances keep their distance. Hardy and tough, he could always march and ride with the youngest troops or oldest veterans. This ability he used to good advantage in Indian, Mexican, and Vicksburg days to follow.

Entering West Point, July 1, 1833, Pemberton remained throughout the four-year term, graduating near the middle of his class of fifty. In 1843 his indomitable opponent of later years—Ulysses Simpson Grant—likewise graduated "near the middle." Moreover, both Pemberton and Grant were at their best in mathematics and in horsemanship.

Conspicuous among Pemberton's West Point classmates were these who would rise to high Confederate command in the brothers' war, later to divide them: Robert Chilton, who would go South to become Lee's first chief of staff; Jubal Early, to rank as a Lieutenant General and, as such, to com-mand the last invasion of the North; Arnold Elzey, who as a major general would be charged with protecting Richmond from Federal raids; William H. T. Walker, to attain distinc-tion as a major general in J. E. Johnston's army. Another classmate was Braxton Bragg, to rank as one of the Confederacy's eight full generals.* But all in all, William W. Mackall, the brigadier who served as chief of staff to both Bragg and J. E. Johnston, was Pemberton's closest friend in the class.

Counted in the group of 1837 graduates who took the Union side were John Sedgwick and Joseph Hooker, major generals both. In May of 1863 Sedgwick nearly saved the day at Chancellorsville for classmate Hooker, only to have old "Fighting Joe" routed in the end by the rush of Stonewall Jackson's men.

At West Point, during Pemberton's cadetship, but of a different vintage, were—besides those mentioned—a further number who sided with the North: Henry Halleck, who late in '62 became general in chief of all the Union armies; William Tecumseh Sherman; John Pope; and George Thomas from Virginia, "The Rock of Chickamauga." Well-known Southerners (not classmates), then cadets, were Pierre Gustave Toutant Beauregard, Richard Ewell, and Lloyd Tilghman, killed near Vicksburg prior to its siege. These future generals were schooled and spanned the years together at the Point.[4]

Upon Pemberton's graduation, he was appointed second lieutenant in the Fourth Regiment of U. S. Artillery. He was at once ordered to Governor's Island, New York, where he served as post commander. A linguist fluent in modern as well as in ancient languages, reared in nearby Philadelphia, and accustomed to New Yorkers' ways, Pemberton found the Governor's Island assignment pleasant, though brief. That same year he served in the Florida wars against the Seminole Indians, though acknowledging "he saw no flash of enemy guns in Florida until 1838."[5] Subsequently, during the Kansas and Utah troubles of the succeeding period, he commanded as

---

* In this order of seniority: Samuel Cooper, Albert Sidney Johnston, R. E. Lee, J. E. Johnston, P. G. T. Beauregard, Braxton Bragg, E. Kirby Smith, John B. Hood, youngest of the full generals, aged thirty-three.—*Photographic History of the Civil War* (New York, 1911), Vol. X; also Freeman, *R. E. Lee,* I, 559nn.

captain on border service, and later did a brief tour of duty on the Canadian boundary. Here it was the young lieutenant's good fortune to serve under Albert Sidney Johnston, a soldier whom many felt to be without a peer in all the army.

In the pre-war span the uncommon number of Pemberton's widely separated posts happily varied the then numbing monotony of eventless army life. By count, his different stations totaled a round twenty, spread, as they were, along the borders of Florida, Kansas, New York, Pennsylvania, New Jersey, Virginia, and Minnesota.[6]

It was in 1842, while in garrison at Fort Monroe, Virginia, that Pemberton met Martha Thompson, his future wife. She, with many others, had come for the social "goings on," so popular at Old Point Comfort in those days.

Martha Thompson, called Patty, was the daughter of William Henry Thompson and Mary Sawyer (Thompson). The Thompsons were Norfolk folks, while the Sawyers were North Carolinians—Elizabeth City, born and bred. At this time, the Thompsons owned and operated an extensive line of ships plying from Charleston and Norfolk to well-known French and English ports. In the early 1800's some of these valuable cargo vessels were captured by Napoleon's navy, an embargo having been placed on trade with Britain. Claims under the so-called "French Spoliation Acts" for the loss of this shipping are still pressed by Thompson heirs.

The most distinguished ancestor of Pemberton's wife-to-be was Elbridge Gerry, a signer of the Declaration of Independence. Lineage such as this almost consoled Pemberton's family for his proposed marriage outside Philadelphia, though none could deny that marriage to a Philadelphian was his birthright.

The Virginia bride hardly reached the groom's shoulder. She stood five feet two. At this time Martha Thompson is described as having brown hair, unusually fine teeth, and "very handsome gray-brown eyes." The family considered her a beauty (all families seem to feel they have one), and certainly she was exceptionally lovely, both in feature and expression. Throughout her life she was a devout church member of the Protestant Episcopal Church. To Pemberton's family a southern girl was a strange animal, and the visit to Martha's relatives, planned by his sister Anna, "was about like an excursion into darkest Africa." Nevertheless, Martha, once married, soon won over the entire clan "up North" and, forsaking her own people (until the war), became as thorough a member as though born one of the elite. Shortly before the death of her father-in-law, the bride dutifully wrote to him. They had never met, nor were to. The Patriarch, after perusal and a proper interval, announced "he was sure she was a lovely little girl and of good sense. She wrote well, and there was a propriety in her letter he liked to see." The marriage took place January 18, 1846, at Norfolk. She was then twenty-two, the groom already thirty-four. The bride later bore five children to her husband and lived for a quarter of a century after his death. In 1907 she died quietly in New York at the age of eighty-one, that city having been her home for many years.

CHAPTER III

Mexico and the Frontier

Mexico

PEMBERTON'S YEARS in garrison duty at Trenton, Carlisle Barracks, pathless Texas, Detroit, New Orleans, Forts Brady, Mackinac, and Pickens were all without incident of uncommon interest or later consequence. His first chance for distinction came in Mexico. Here, as aide-de-camp of Major General William J. Worth, Pemberton participated and was twice wounded in the assaults preceding the capture of Mexico City. He took part in the battles of Palo Alto, Resaca de la Palma, the siege of Vera Cruz, Monterey, Cerro Gordo, Churubusco, Molino del Rey, the storming of Chapultepec, and the capture of Mexico City. On September 23, 1846, he was brevetted captain for "gallantry" in the several conflicts at Monterey; and major, September 8, 1847, "for gallant and meritorious conduct in the battle of Molino del Rey."

In the first month of war with Mexico, September, 1845, a lieutenant in his earliest twenties had joined the small, efficient army of General Zachary Taylor, at Vera Cruz. There, attached to General Worth's unseasoned forces, he found another junior officer with like claim to a considerable obscurity. Transferred under hurried orders from Monterey to Mexico City, General Taylor's chunky young courier was greeted on arrival by a stranger somewhat his senior. Introductions followed, but brought not the slightest enlightenment to either. It was first acquaintance for Pemberton and Grant.[1] No monument marks this desert spot; neither fame nor adversity had yet touched either man. But of a later meeting Winston Churchill has written: "An upright cannon marks the spot where a scrawny oak once stood on a scarred and baked hillside, outside the Confederate lines at Vicksburg. Under the scanty shade of that tree, on the eve of the Nation's birthday, had stood two men who typified the future and the past. . . ."

A further reminiscence of Pemberton and Grant in Mexico comes from a London correspondent: "Do you remember Pemberton?" said General Grant. "Well, Pemberton was in Mexico, and a more conscientious, honorable man never lived. I remember when an order was issued that none of the junior officers should be allowed horses during the marches. Mexico is not an easy country to march in. Young officers not accustomed to it soon got foot-sore. This was quickly discovered, as they were found lagging behind. But the order was not revoked, yet a verbal permit was accepted, and nearly all of them remounted.

"Pemberton alone said, No, he would walk, as the order was still extant not to ride, and he did walk, though suffering intensely the while. This I thought of all the time he was in Vicksburg and I outside of it; and I knew he would hold on to the last. Yes, he was scrupulously particular in matters of honor and integrity."[2]

In Mexico City, when it seemed likely there would be haggling over the revised treaty as ratified by the United States Senate, a large group of the officers, including many who were to meet in 1860-64, viz., McClellan, Fitz-John Porter, Franklin

Pierce, Lee, Grant, and Pemberton, got together and formed "The Aztec Club of 1847." This was, and remains today, the only patriotic society ever to have been founded in the enemy's country and capital.[3] Though Grant and Lee were members, Lee kept no remembrance of "the untidy young captain who was one day to dictate the terms of surrender Lee had to sign at Appomattox,"[4] and at Vicksburg take the measure of Pemberton.

Mexican experience proved valuable to all the Army; though even "Lee did not return from Mexico a national figure, in any sense."[5] Pemberton emerged a brevet-major, Grant a brevet-captain.

At the close of the Mexican War, the legislature of Pennsylvania on May 20, 1849, passed a series of "resolutions" expressive of "profound" regard and admiration for the good conduct and heroic courage displayed by certain officers of the army, natives or citizens of Pennsylvania. These resolutions were, with the following letter from the Governor, transmitted to the officers designated by that body.

"To MAJOR J. C. PEMBERTON,

Fourth Regiment Artillery, U. S. Army.

"*Sir:* The Legislature of Pennsylvania, appreciating the distinguished services rendered by you in the late war with Mexico, and desirous of commemorating, by an appropriate and enduring memorial, the just estimate of a grateful people of your meritorious conduct and heroic courage, unanimously passed the foregoing resolutions with a request that they should be transmitted to you. In complying with the desire of the Legislature, I avail myself of the occasion to unite with that department of the Government in the expression of my profound admiration of the bravery and good conduct which signalized your services in several sanguinary battles, and which, while conferring enviable distinction on yourself, merit your country's warmest gratitude.

"I have the honor to remain,

Truly your friend,

WILLIAM F. JOHNSTON."[6]

FORT LEAVENWORTH, KANSAS

Except for the family's oft repeated reminiscenses of Pemberton, we know few anecdotes of his frontier life.

At Leavenworth in those days a "command" was a preposterously small number of men, two or three companies at most. Pemberton's troops here were elements of the Fourth Regiment of U. S. Artillery. At that time serving as infantry, they would soon be marched on foot from Leavenworth to Fort Kearny in New Mexico. Although called a fort, Kearny in reality was only a small depot (under Brigadier General Stephen W. Kearny) set up to furnish supplies for troops passing through.

In Kansas, as in Mexico, Pemberton made sharp point of marching with his troops, experience convincing him the example was good for discipline, discouraged straggling, and greatly helped the men's morale. In those lonely parts, most Indians met with on the march were equipped so wretchedly it took but the smallest number to scatter or to control them. Nonetheless, they often pressed alarmingly close around the isolated settlements, so that recurrent fears were felt for the safety of those unavoidably distant from the garrisons.[7]

There was a beautiful parade ground at Fort Leavenworth, also a fine military band, many officers, and many families. Hence it was that Pemberton's children had numbers of their own age with whom to play and a wide variety of excitements. Young bachelors abounded, keeping alive gaieties of various kinds, dancing, dinner parties, much as in town back East. (The family recalls that Major and Mrs. Hancock, in particular, did constant entertaining.) Much of the time, however, Captain Pemberton was absent on endless Indian affairs. Generally he took with him his small six-year-old son John—to the boy's hardy delight and pride. Then, on September 6, 1858, with much subsequent musical celebration of the event, Anna, the youngest of the five Pembertons, put in her appearance: the regiment's first Leavenworth baby.

Moving orders inevitably arriving, Pemberton and his family made part of the tedious prairie trip to Minnesota by covered wagon. Daily, they skirted Indian parties on stealthy hunting expeditions for game, or for enemies.

It so happened that, milk in those days being a risky affair, Anna, still very much a baby, had her own special cow in tow. Starting with the Pemberton entourage from Leavenworth, and furnishing the daily food supply in exemplary fashion, she was undisturbed, even when the party eventually took a creaking Missouri River boat. But when held up close to shore one day, "Sukey" took advantage of her opportunity and scrambled up the steep banks to freedom, defying pursuit; and that was the last seen of her.

Fort Ridgely, Minnesota

A small frontier garrison was Fort Ridgely in 1859. That year there were no more than six or seven families, and three or four young playmates for the even younger Pembertons; no music, except drum and fife corps. For around six months the thermometer was down to 31 below zero. Meanwhile the river was frozen solid and the snow too deep to wade through.

During the fall, Indians came in scores—with every variety of game: geese, turkeys, ducks, grouse, quail, swans, not to mention venison.

The garrison at Ridgely was a poorly equipped affair: wooden quarters with no heat except a central stove and inadequate smaller stoves in such bitter weather. No chapel.

The Captain's wife played on a stiff melodeon in the parlor

of one of the officer's quarters, where a half-hearted audience
gathered to hear the Episcopal service and a soporific dis-
course. One day Mrs. Pemberton fainted with the effort required in working the treadles.

The physician was rarely in condition to minister to the
ailing. In fact, on one occasion his libations almost cost the
life of a young woman, the wife of Lieutenant George H.
Weeks (afterwards quartermaster general of the Union army),
whose first baby was born in Fort Ridgely. At the time of
her confinement, the doctor was *hors de combat* and could not
be brought to a sufficiently normal condition to take charge
of the case. As there was no nurse in the place, Mrs. Pemberton, with the aid of a sergeant's wife, spent a night of
anxiety over a desperately ill woman, delivering her of a stillborn son.

A large annex to the kitchen, where quantities of wood
were stowed away for winter use, served as "refrigerator."
Overhead, the rough beams of the annex hung with game
enough to last till spring.

No army child of those days could ever forget the continual
files of stalking Indians, their gaily colored blankets and feath-
ered heads emerging through the waist-high prairie grass,
their strings of game birds (strapped across their shoulders)
reaching the ground. It was always picturesque, but un-
canny. No Indian ever smiled, nor betrayed more than
passing interest. The Sioux tribe wore a particularly savage
aspect at all times. Their scalp dances, close by the garrison,
were indeed fearsome performances. The wife and children
of the victim would stand in the center of a ring of whooping
devils, the dying warrior's locks dangling from a wire frame
at the end of a long pole.[8]

Moreover, tragedies occurred now and then to the troops
of the garrison when they resorted to whisky to keep warm.

The sutler's store, quite a distance from the fort, was forbidden after dark; but the order was at times disobeyed. A rebelling noncom in Pemberton's company undertook to walk there one severely cold night. Next day, he was missing. He was missing all winter—for there was no searching that ice-encrusted snow. When a thaw set in, the poor Corporal's boots were discovered, but of him—nothing. They threw his boots across the saddle of his horse. Fellow soldiers soon followed to a dead march, a melancholy sight. A childish heart beat fast, and tears poured down the cheeks of one little girl watching from a window. She covered her ears with her hands as the seemingly heartless comrades double-quicked on their return from the burial—to the lively strains of "The Girl I Left Behind Me."[9]

In their isolated position, frozen-in and without direct communication with the great world, mails were slow and delivered at long intervals. The daily papers, *Harper's,* and *Leslie's Illustrated News* were old by the time they reached Ridgely. Nevertheless, they were new with alarming news of gathering war; and all troops were soon held in readiness for a call to the seat of trouble.

Pemberton's Company, F of the Fourth Artillery, was the first of the garrison to receive orders to hasten east to Washington.

Looking backwards, as the troops speedily pulled up tents and emptied barracks, Pemberton could regard the past eventless years (occupied chiefly with Indian affairs) as having afforded him much valuable opportunity for close study and practice of artillery. Study and practice alike were to serve his future well, at Charleston, Vicksburg,[10] Richmond, and "in the defense of Petersburg, [where] he recklessly exposed himself in the handling of his guns...."[11]

CHAPTER IV

Why Pemberton Went South

WHEN PEMBERTON was last in Philadelphia, his family had known him as the merest boy. For the most they recalled a carefree lad, thrilled with the prospect of a soldier's career. There would be Indians, Mexicans, maybe even Englishmen and Frenchmen to war upon. Now, in 1861, when war loomed North and South, Captain Pemberton was in a truly troubled state. Perhaps he recalled a hot sultry day in 1831 when he and two other Philadelphia striplings played the "Battle of New Orleans" for the hundredth time. Then, the baby of the group, George B. McClellan, hadn't been much good except in the role of "English prisoner," while the two older ones, Pemberton and George Gordon Meade, uniformly fought for turns to take the victor's part—that of Andrew Jackson. Pemberton had the same Northern heritage as did his playmates of those years before, and Andrew Jackson had been his earliest hero. But in the South he now counted his dearest, his wife and children. There, too, were his heart and sympathies, deep-rooted since earliest manhood.

Pemberton's family were fully aware of his Southern feelings, and his brother Henry (who detested horses) hurried astride a balky critter to Harrisburg. From there he rode all night to Washington with unsmiling sober-faced Captain Pem-

berton, pleading with this Philadelphia family's first Rebel not
to take the "fatal step." His brother's arguments weighed
heavily with him, but Pemberton never wavered in his view
that the South was right. Though he could not blind himself
to the grief and mortification he would bring to his devoted
mother and to all his family, he determined to give up "his
thirty years' career in the Army and his own people to follow
the right as he saw it."

Pemberton tendered his resignation from the United States
army on April 24, 1861. Instead of receiving an immediate
acceptance, he was requested to call upon General Winfield
Scott; and in the interview which resulted Scott impatiently
argued the case with him, endeavoring to persuade him to
remain with the North. In a few days the General promised
him a colonelcy.[1] Even Robert E. Lee had not achieved pro-
motion from the rank of captain (except by brevet) in eighteen
years or more.[2] Moreover, Pemberton had just received unexpected news concerning two younger brothers. That day
Andrew and Clifford joined the Union cavalry, the Philadelphia City Troop.

To General Scott's proposal Pemberton replied that his sympathies were wholly with the South, that he was surprised at
his overture and at the delay and trouble the authorities, contrary to all custom, were occasioning him. Finally, after repeated solicitation, he demanded as his right that his resignation should be at once accepted and requested that the acceptance be addressed to him at Richmond. For this city he left
Washington on April 26, 1861. Thus Pemberton took the
plunge, for such before long it proved to be.

Mrs. Pemberton's family, too, divided North and South.
Imogene Thompson, her sister, married Benjamin Pollard
Loyall, an ensign on the Confederate *Merrimac* at the time
of its historic battle with the *Monitor*. In turn, one of Loy-

all's sisters married David Glasgow Farragut, while another sister became the wife of Alexander Mosely Pennock. Detailed under Captain A. H. Foote to take over the building of gunboats at St. Louis for the Mississippi, Pennock's flotilla was subsequently to succeed in running past the land batteries under Pemberton's command at Vicksburg.

How can we account for Pemberton's espousal of the Southern cause while friends of boyhood and two blood brothers took up Union arms? Jubal Early, Lieutenant General of the Confederacy, West Point intimate and classmate, and a friend of thirty years' standing before the war, answers crisply: "I can only add to what Dick Taylor says that as a young man at West Point, Pemberton was noted for his liberal and States-rights sentiments, and for his affiliations with the young men of the South."[3]

General Early was referring to what Lieutenant General Richard Taylor had earlier written of Pemberton: "His first station was in South Carolina, and he there formed his early friendships. The storm of 'nullification' had not yet subsided, and Pemberton imbibed the tenets of the Calhoun school. In 1843 or 1844 I met him for the first time on the Niagara frontier, and quite remember my surprise at his State-rights utterances, unusual among military men at that period.... Later, he married a lady of Virginia, which may have tended to confirm his political opinions.... Certainly he must have been actuated by principle alone; for he had everything to gain by remaining on the Northern side."[4]

Further answer also comes from Pemberton's eldest son and namesake, a lad of twelve at Vicksburg's siege.

"General Pemberton was, from earliest manhood until the close of his life, a firm believer in the doctrine of State sovereignty, and was at no time in harmony with the advocates of a paternal government.

"In the spring of 1833, being then in his nineteenth year, he conceived the idea of entering the United States army, and, unassisted by any outside influence, made application by letter to General Jackson (then President) for a cadetship at West Point. This he received almost by return mail, the prompt reply being probably due to the friendship which General Jackson always entertained for his father."

Of Pemberton's war sentiments, of his divided family loyalties and background—why he went South—we have but one further family record. Pemberton's mother, in a letter to her favorite daughter-in-law, showed with touching pathos the ties which held her son to the North, and those stronger ones which led him to cast his lot with the South.

"Yours of the 20th, dear Carry, has just come to me and though I wrote to you yesterday, yet I know you are both anxious to hear all. Your husband got home this morning, but alas he brings but faint hopes—he says that nothing but John's affection and feeling for us, prevents him from resigning—his ideas of duty and honor are all the other way, and he is perfectly honorable and open in all he does—his feelings are well known to his brother officers—if your husband had not gone to him, he would probably have resigned this first night he got there—but he begged and pleaded with him, telling him how we all should suffer if he did it, and he has postponed it for the present—at least did not act upon it while he was there—As long as he remains, he will do he says, anything he is ordered to, excepting going to attack and fire upon Norfolk—if he is ordered to do *that,* he would resign at once—he is perfectly willing to stay and protect "Wash.," in which he says the Government is right. The first day John got there, he was sent for to the War Department and received orders to go and seize some steamboats, which were at the wharves—he collected his men, marched them some distance off and then ordered them to load their muskets, and told them what it was they were going

to do, and if anybody opposed them, they were to fire
upon them—they set off in a quick run, jumped on board
the boats—John seized the rudder and the boats were
theirs—he was selected for this service, expressly to try
him, he knew it—and was perfectly willing to perform
any duty, except going to Norfolk—John is most dread-
fully distressed and worried, *on our account*—for his heart
and views are that the South is right and we are wrong—
he says Patty's family (that of his wife) have never spoken
or written on the subject to him—but while your husband
was there a letter came to John from Patty, in which she
says "My darling husband, why are you not with us? Why
do you stay? Jeff Davis has a post ready for you"—in
answer John spoke of the hard position he was in and
enclosed the letter which I had written to him, in order
that his family might see what a sore thing it was for
him, so to grieve us all—your husband also wrote to Patty,
in which he used every argument to convince her what
a serious thing it would be for John's future, and besought
her to advise him remaining with the Government.

"I have been more wretched in this horrid state of sus-
pense than words can tell. I feel that if this grief and
mortification *must* come upon me, that I must accept it,
and submit to it—we have done all we can—John firmly
believes it would be the most honorable and right—'tis
only for us he hesitates.

"I have a great fear now, that so many of the officers
knowing John's sentiments, they may take some summary
steps with him, and dismiss him before he resigns. Of
the two cases, that would be the worst. Some begin to
think that after all, there may be no fighting—pray
Heaven it may be so.

"Do let me hear soon again—love to Harry

> Your poor worried
> Mother."[5]

CHAPTER V

Richmond and Charleston

ON A BRIGHT spring morning in 1861, a recent Captain of Artillery—'Old Army'—stepped down from the cars just arrived in Richmond. Unfamiliar scenes opened to his eye, and strangers were everywhere afoot. Except for passing through on way to Fort Monroe in 1842 and '48, this was Pemberton's first introduction to Richmond. The curious and those on government business flocked in crowds around the new arrivals just come from Washington. By dint of endless questions and several coppers to tempt small Negroes on the way, Pemberton at last succeeded in reporting to headquarters of the Army of Virginia.[1]

It was the twenty-sixth of April, 1861. Pemberton found that Joseph E. Johnston (later a full general), and John Bankhead Magruder (later a major general) were not more than seventy hours in advance of his arrival. "His resolution to come to Virginia, having been taken long before hand, and being well known to his associates in the old Army, he was detained only until that time by nothing but the remoteness of his station at Fort Ridgely, Minnesota, and the deliberation evinced by his adopted State, Virginia." For it was not until Lincoln's call to arms that Virginia, in those last days of April, ultimately withdrew from the Federal Union.

Formalities of greeting concluded, Pemberton, Johnston, and R. S. Garnett (later a brigadier general, former commandant at West Point and first general officer to meet death in battle) tendered their services simultaneously to the State of Virginia.

Pemberton soon learned his first commission, dated April 28, 1861, was to be that of lieutenant colonel in the active forces of Virginia. Johnston, now become a brigadier general, arranged Pemberton's rank as well as his assignment to himself as adjutant general. All of this had been before Pemberton reached Richmond.[2] He was immediately assigned the responsible work of organizing the artillery and cavalry of the state, with headquarters at Norfolk—though still a member of Johnston's staff.[3] Jeb Stuart's biographer tartly describes Pemberton's first problem in this wise: "The matter in hand was the organization and training of the volunteer masses which were coming forward; and it was necessary to find somebody who would take charge of the horsemen. Nobody wanted the job. The road to glory was considered to lie with the infantry, or with the artillery; not with the mercurial units of mounted men. But somebody had to take charge of them, because they insisted on fighting, if at all, on horseback. And Stuart, as reluctant as the others, felt that it was a time for personal sacrifice. . . . He looked the recruits over and chuckled. . . ."[4]

No matter how the task appeared to Stuart, first to *assume* it was Pemberton. He handed over the horsemen to Jeb only when ordered the following May to artillery duty under Lee and Johnston, who were then mightily concerned about Norfolk. For "to give up Norfolk was to lose all hope of creating a Navy to cope with the Federal seapower."

It was during these same packed days of double duty for every Norfolk soldier that the *Monitor* and *Merrimac* collided at Hampton Roads; while at nearby Smithfield, Imogene

Thompson, her sister Mrs. Pemberton, and her children, as one betrayed their anxiety for Imogene's fiancé, an ensign on the *Merrimac*.

Here also, General Lee in November communicated to Pemberton his appointment as brigadier in the Provisional Army of the Confederate States, explaining that he (Lee) had had Pemberton's commission detained in order that it might be so dated as to give him his proper rank. Likewise in this same year Pemberton cast in Norfolk, in ratification of the Ordinance of Secession, the first vote ever given in his life.

On the morning of November 29, 1861, Pemberton reported for duty to General Lee at Charleston. The famous Virginian, in the eyes of Charlestonians, had not lived up to his great reputation. Critics agreed as one that he had been a disappointment. Nonetheless, he had been tendered a ready reception, and though "his reticence concerning his military plans was generally remarked . . . the fact that he was the son of a distinguished defender of South Carolina [Light Horse Harry Lee] made a most favorable impression apparently on every one, with the sole exception of General Ripley."[5]

Nor were the prospects for Lee's popularity improved when it was learned that he was to have a Northern officer as his second in command. At that time General Beauregard was the idol of this section of the South and they would not be happy until they had *him* back again.

Pierre Gustave Toutant Beauregard, the "beau ideal" of the Confederacy, and a native of Louisiana, had graduated from West Point, second in his class, a year after Pemberton. He was indeed a romantic figure, and his fame had spread throughout the land when his command fired on Fort Sumter. This step the North regarded as the opening of the war. Perhaps it was.

When Pemberton reached Charleston, he was not surprised.

Warning had been given him in Richmond that Charleston was a casual, complacent sort of place—full of gentlemen. As Jonathan Daniels has ruefully reported, "there were only two kinds of South Carolinians, those who had never worn shoes and those who made you feel that you had never worn shoes."[6]

Populace and civil authorities in Charleston—the Simons, Rhetts, and Gadsdens, backed up by Governor Pickens—soon wanted to talk over Pemberton's plans for defense. When he curtly declined discussion of the Department's defensive measures not yet disclosed, distrust and, soon, dissatisfaction followed.[7] The cool impartiality with which he treated high and low alike speedily caused a stiffening of backs amongst the city's people of importance. Thereafter, all local co-operation proved conspicuous by consistent absence.

General Lee, also, "had avoided, and very cautiously refrained from any discussion of his plans in Charleston." To be sure, it was not an unfamiliar practice for a commanding officer. Had not Andrew Jackson himself, Pemberton's nominator to West Point, been found secretive and lacking in a proper spirit of co-operation by the gentry of New Orleans when panic swept that city in 1815?[8]

Before long, Lee, now a full general, was called to Richmond, March 2, 1862, and Pemberton succeeded to Lee's command, embracing the entire coast from South Carolina to Florida.[9] Soon Pemberton let it be known he intended to dismantle and abandon Fort Sumter, "as being of no protective value to the city."[10] At this there arose such angry outcry that the sound of it reached Richmond almost as swiftly as it sped through the streets of startled Charleston. Though later events were to furnish complete vindication of this decision, they did nothing to still the present storm.

Some idea of the difficulties facing an officer at this time can be gathered from the fact that Governor Pickens, after a long

conference, was able to agree on a compromise—no more—
with General Lee. It was at this period that Lee confided to
his wife, "It is so very hard to get anything done."[11] And
while Lee was here "struggling with inertia, incompetence,
and a multitude of troublesome duties, the Confederate cause
elsewhere suffered two disasters. On February 6, Fort Henry,
on the lower Tennessee River, was captured by a Federal army
under a general who then came prominently into the news
for the first time, Ulysses S. Grant."[12]

In those troubled months the new commanding officer's
difficulties were added to when his wife became desperately
ill after the birth of a child. The attending doctor was a
certain George Rhett, of the powerful South Carolina family
of that name. Pemberton, in great distress at the serious illness
of his wife, could nevertheless find little time to spend with
her, so harassed was he in effecting the measures considered
necessary for the protection of his Department. In this unhappy state of mind, he met by merest accident an old friend,
then stationed as an army doctor in the city. In his grief, and
forgetful of the professional proprieties, Pemberton asked the
army doctor to attend Mrs. Pemberton and determine whether
anything might be done to save her. Dr. Rhett took loud
and instant offense at this unintended slight and declined to
have anything further to do with the case.[13]

Nor was this the sole aftermath. In that hot summer, ice
was so scarce that Pemberton had ordered the entire supply
set aside for, and rationed out to, the local hospitals. With
his wife apparently at the point of death, he unhesitatingly
ordered a small amount of ice sent beyond the city to his house,
in an effort to relieve the high fever from which Mrs. Pemberton was suffering. Another of the Rhetts, who owned one of
the Charleston papers, immediately seized upon the incident.
Ignoring Mrs. Pemberton's illness entirely, he contented him-

self with publishing the charge that Pemberton was sending ice to his own house while the sick and wounded in the hospitals languished from its want.

Nor were Pemberton's multiple responsibilities at this period lightened by the embargo he placed on trading with the enemy in cotton. This action was in accordance with orders from the Richmond government, and he accordingly enforced it to the fullest extent possible. Smuggling was very generally practiced from the port, and a handsome revenue derived by many privileged persons was at stake. Lieutenant General Richard Taylor, old Zachary Taylor's son and brother of Jefferson Davis's first wife, subsequently wrote feelingly of this trafficking with the enemy: "Our people were much debauched by it. I write advisedly, for during the last two and a half years of the war I commanded in the State of Louisiana, Mississippi, and Alabama, the great producing States. Outpost officers would violate the law, and trade. In vain were they removed; the temptation was too strong, and their successors did the same. The influence on the women was dreadful, and in many cases their appeals were heart-rending. Mothers with suffering children, whose husbands were in the war or already fallen, would beseech me for permits to take cotton through the lines. It was useless to explain that it was against the law and orders, and that I was without authority to act. This did not give food and clothing to their children, and they departed, believing me to be an unfeeling brute.... It is with no pleasure that I have dwelt on the foregoing topics, but the world can not properly estimate the fortitude of the Southern people unless it understands and takes account of the difficulties under which they labored."[14]

Unruffled by the chatter and antagonism, Pemberton, fortunately for Charleston, went ahead as though nothing were amiss. The lack of confidence and co-operation exhibited by the local authorities had no effect on his operations, but he was not as successful as Lee had eventually been in winning some meed of local approval.

The past months had been for him, as for Lee, "a period of preparation for action, rather than action itself, but it was a preparation of the most valuable sort." Pemberton was instrumental in the construction of the Charleston defenses, which held out until February 17, 1865. They were largely his work in spite of the fact that Beauregard was subsequently accorded almost the entire credit therefor. Even Jones, the Rebel War Clerk at Richmond, could not ignore this in his rather grudging diary entry. "Beauregard says Fort Wagner, which has made such a successful defense on Morris Island, was located by Gen. Pemberton, and this is evidence of some military skill."[15]

During his Charleston stay of nearly a year, Pemberton had succeeded to the command of twenty-five thousand men, scattered on a line of some three hundred miles. This constituted practically the entire Atlantic seaboard of the South.

Years later Pemberton thus summarized his South Carolina accomplishments: "I was in immediate command and defeated the enemy at Port Royal Ferry, in South Carolina, on the last day of January, 1862, while a Brigadier General; and while in command of the Department of South Carolina, Georgia and Florida, conducted the operations and made the dispositions which resulted in the repulse of the enemy on James Island, in June, 1862."[16] Nothing here of his having constructed the formidable Fort Wagner and Battery B, later to be so warmly praised; nor of his having commanded for months one of the largest areas and greatest number of men within the Confederacy; nor yet of time's proving the accuracy of his military judgment respecting Fort Sumter's vulnerability.

Protesting against the brevity and modesty of this and other reports by Pemberton, there came later a letter from Colonel William Preston Johnston, son of General Albert Sidney Johnston. The Colonel, a graduate of Yale of '52, became after the war professor of history at Washington College during Lee's presidency and, after some further time, president of Louisiana State University. To Pemberton he said, in part, "You under-value the weight of your character and reputation; the discriminating have always done you justice; even the prejudiced will eventually do so."[17] Yet Charleston felt there was too much steel in the soul of Lee's successor, that there was in him the stuff of which military dictators are made.

Meantime, Governor Pickens continued to register his displeasure. It emphasizes the weakness of a confederacy and accentuates the insuperable obstacles facing Jefferson Davis— that he was compelled to spend so much of time and effort soothing the brittle feelings and cajoling the governors of his associated states. And how easy it is for modern authors to criticize the President for not exercising an authority that by the very nature of the confederacy he never possessed.

To Governor Pickens on August 5, 1862, Davis wrote: "Regarding the removal of the present commanding General [Pemberton], I am desirous of obliging you, and would be glad also to secure the services of Genl. Pemberton elsewhere. ...I have tried to get a competent officer, whose assignment to the position would be satisfactory, and will not relax my efforts to that end. My own confidence, however, in Genl. Pemberton is such that I would be satisfied to have him in any position requiring the presence of an able General."[18]

Again, ten days later and at more length, the President wrote the South Carolina governor:

"Your letter of the 10th inst. has been received. I have recently had a long interview with Genl. Pemberton, and received a full exposition of his views relative to the defence
of the coast of South Carolina. I find that his determination
to hold the city of Charleston is as fixed as you could desire
it to be, and that the measures he has adopted to that end are
in a good state of progress, and promise to be effective. The
obstructions to the harbor, so far as completed, have been tested
with favorable results, and when finished would seem to be
sufficient, in connection with proposed batteries and the Forts,
to prevent vessels from entering....I have requested Genl.
Pemberton to have a conference with yourself and, if it be
desired, with the council, in order that he may communicate
to you, as he has to me, the defensive arrangements that have
been prepared and projected.

"With every desire to gratify your wish for a change in the
commander of the Department, the matter has been attended
with much difficulty....

"The General who would fulfill the requirements of the
position must be an officer not only experienced in Infantry
and Artillery service, but also generally acquainted with Engineering. The education, elementary and practical, of Genl.
Pemberton in the old army and our own service has given him
this requisite knowledge. I do not now find it practicable to
send in his place another General who would equally well
answer for the command. He is, besides, thoroughly acquainted with the condition of the Department, and feels an
interest in the works that are in progress for its defense which
would have to be acquired by a new commander.

"I hope, after a conference with Genl. Pemberton, and when
you are more fully acquainted with his plans, that you may
have the same confidence in his ability and good judgment

that has made me willing to entrust him with so important a command, and feel secure that all the aid you may give him will be well and zealously applied to the defense of a harbor of great and increasing value to the Confederacy, and of a city for the successful resistance of which we have a desire heightened by the malignity which makes it the special object of attack and would doom it to destruction."[19]

General Beauregard was now restored to health and South Carolina was clamoring for the return of the man whom she regarded as almost her own.

In the same month, George W. Randolph, Confederate Secretary of War, wrote to Pemberton from Richmond. (Randolph, a grandson of Thomas Jefferson, had given Pemberton many evidences of his confidence and esteem.) In his letter, August 28, he confided that Governor Pickens' antagonism had not diminished in the slightest degree, despite the President's pleas for co-operation with the local commander. As a result, Randolph went on to say, "General Beauregard, having reported for duty, has been ordered to assume command of the Department of South Carolina and Georgia.... Governor Pickens still continues, and if anything becomes more vehement in his remonstrances against your continuation in command. We have turned a deaf ear to them, being satisfied that you were doing everything that could be effected. But if any misfortune should occur it will be impossible to obtain a fair judgment of the case and it will be imputed to you in spite of all proofs to the contrary. I think it will very much lighten your responsibility without impairing your capacity for usefulness for General Beauregard to be assigned to the Supreme command, and I hope and believe that he will not interfere with the execution of your plans. General Beauregard has not yet signified his acceptance of the command but I presume that he will not decline it."[20]

The logic of the Secretary's letter was, of course, unassailable. Moreover, what could Pemberton, a Northerner, accomplish with a governor in whose opinion not even General Lee was a fit person to be entrusted with the defense of Charleston and Savannah?[20a]

In the first week of October, 1862, Beauregard arrived to assume command of the southeastern coast, and Pemberton, now promoted to lieutenant general, moved on to his new headquarters at Jackson, Mississippi. His efforts and abilities apparently had earned some final and official recognition in his elevation with Stonewall Jackson, James Longstreet, William J. Hardee, Leonidas Polk, Theophilus H. Holmes, and E. Kirby Smith.[21] Commenting on Pemberton's departure, the Charleston *Mercury* (which was not Dr. George Rhett's paper) remarked editorially:

"Soon after the fall of the Port Royal batteries, and the invasion of our seacoast by the enemy, Gen. Pemberton was sent to South Carolina, in lieu of Gen. Van Dorn, whom the South Carolina delegation had applied for, to come with Gens. Evans and Gregg—three officers of repute for daring and activity. From that time until last week, Gen. Pemberton has had a command here—at first as a Brigadier; and then, upon the departure of Gen. Lee to Virginia, as Major General commanding the Department. His stay in South Carolina has been characterized by long months of arduous, incessant labor and devoted energy, and, in that time, although little known when he came here, he has established the reputation of an accomplished and thorough soldier. He has associated his destinies with us, lived with us, and served us faithfully, and we deem it due to his ardent and unremitting exertions to express our appreciation of his merits as an officer, and our regrets that he has judged it necessary to leave us under existing circumstances. We had hoped that he would have lent to Gen. Beauregard the assistance of his knowledge and energy towards the defence of our coast and city.

"As a young man, upon the fields of Mexico, and as a member of Gen. Worth's Staff, Gen. Pemberton long since achieved for himself the reputation of a most dashing and gallant soldier. And at the outbreak of the war, he bore in the old Army of the United States the character of an able officer and strict disciplinarian.

"Gen. Pemberton, like Gen. Ripley, was not a 'popular man.' His habitual reserve and occasional brusqueness of manner forbid. Yet to those better acquainted with him and his labors, against prejudice and misconception, he won greatly upon their confidence and esteem, and leaves many warm friends in South Carolina. His independence and directness are marked characteristics, worthy of appreciation. For he is a soldier—a thorough soldier—and the character of the soldier has stamped itself upon his whole mind and bearing. His energy of character, keenness of perception, quickness of thought, promptness of action and earnestness in preparation, with the professional knowledge and practical experience he possesses, cannot fail to render him an officer whose services will carry strength in the field wherever he may be assigned.

"He has the cordial good wishes of a large portion of this community in his future career."[22]

To Pemberton, in later months and years, the successful defense of Charleston must have been a source of pride and satisfaction. Fort Sumter, upon which the Northern fleets poured an unremitting fire, in time cracked and collapsed; meantime the Federal pounding of adjacent forts settled down to nothing more serious than deadlock.

Not till after the fall of Vicksburg did Pemberton receive the following letter, but for the sake of its Charleston subject matter, it is quoted here and now.

"HD. QRS. CHIEF OF ARTILLERY
James Island, Sept. 17th, 1863

"LIEUT. GENL. J. C. PEMBERTON,
Atlanta, Geo.

My dear General: Your heroic defense has had all my admiration enhanced by your silent endurance of so much obloquy.

"... It has been my pleasant duty to pay a tribute to truth and justice, by meeting the numerous attacks made on you among people you strove so hard and so unpopularly to defend. Fort Sumter, the dismantling of which you have been accused to have counseled, is utterly and completely dismantled and laid in ruins by the enemy, and still Charleston is not his; and it is not his because of Wagner, which you constructed, as you did Battery B, the obstructions and works of the inner harbor, now stronger because (in a great measure) of the guns taken from Sumter, of which ten ten-inch Columbiads, due to your personal endeavors in Richmond, contributed so largely to the repulse of the 7th April, and are contributing now to hold the enemy at bay. Although a friend of General Beauregard, whose merit I recognize, I am still more the friend of truth, and hope that these lines, even from so humble an individual as myself (though, nevertheless, better acquainted with the defense of this Department since the day of secession than anyone else), may prove to you that malignity and slander, if public, are not universal....

"I remain, General,
Very truly and sincerely
Your obedient friend and servant
A. J. GONZALES

Colonel and Chief of Artillery
Commanding Infantry on James Island and Maine"[23]

Colonel Gonzales, married to a South Carolina low-country lady, was the Cuban patriot who so nearly succeeded in enlisting General Lee's services in an abortive Cuban rising of the early 1850's.[24]

As for Pemberton in those last Charleston days—no man to bandy responsibilities under the fierce pressure of the war— he could and did conscript the city's aid; not so its sympathies. To Charleston he appeared "A man severe and stern to view." Now he went to carry heavier burdens. Was he again to swim against the stream; or would those Southern soldiers to whom once more he came as total stranger, and from the North, give him the best that was within them? Such was his due. Confidently he stepped forward to the sunshine of Mississippi and to serve a more generous people—even in disaster and defeat.

CHAPTER VI

Background of the Vicksburg Campaign

ALMOST IMMEDIATELY it became evident that Pemberton's paramount task would be to keep Grant (and his able lieutenants, Sherman and McPherson) from placing the Federal army on high ground in the rear of Vicksburg. So long as this was possible, Vicksburg was reasonably secure. But if Grant should somehow get across the river—lower down—Pemberton saw clearly the further duty this would place him under: the destruction of the invaders, driving them back, or so delaying them that their lack of a base of supplies would force retirement. All along, Grant would be greatly assisted by the Union navy under Farragut and Porter. On the other hand, Pemberton at no time would have heavy enough guns to oppose, much less to block, either Farragut's or Porter's passage. Moreover, the strength of Sherman alone would at all times nearly equal Pemberton's. Could Pemberton afford to rush at Grant below, leaving Sherman above—to move to any point selected for attack and be thereafter free to walk unopposed into the stronghold's unprotected center?

To stop both Grant and Sherman was, in Davis's opinion, of enough import to the South to warrant Pemberton's risking the loss of an army—an opinion which he held both before and after the event. On March 11, 1864, he wrote to Pemberton: "I thought and still think that you did right to risk an army for the purpose of keeping command of even a section of the Mississippi River. Had you succeeded none would have blamed; had you not made the attempt, few if any would have defended your course."[1] "Davis' order to Pemberton to hold Vicksburg was certainly strategically sound. The proof of this is that when Vicksburg fell the Confederacy commenced to fall apart—and if Pemberton had gone wandering off with Johnston, the Confederacy would have fallen apart that much sooner."[2] But no more than others does the author know the true answer to such a loaded question of military strategy. Whether Davis's conception of the problem faced by the Confederate commander at Vicksburg is historically tenable may always remain an open question.

Beyond a doubt the command entrusted to Pemberton at Vicksburg was the most difficult, if not the most important, that fell to the lot of any general, except Lee, in the Confederate army.[3] Why was Pemberton chosen to assume this tremendous undertaking so vital to the whole Confederacy's success? T. J. Wharton, who was attorney general of Mississippi at the time of the Vicksburg Campaign, says he went to Richmond, and a day or two after the Federal troops entered Jackson, Mississippi, he had a conference with President Davis. In the course of the conversation he mentioned several generals who the people of Mississippi thought should have been assigned to that important command instead of General Pemberton. Among those he mentioned were Lee, Jackson, J. E. Johnston, Longstreet, and others. Mr. Wharton says Mr. Davis "assigned reasons why none of the officers I named could be detached from their commands. He said he entertained a high opinion of General Pemberton's capacity, but was careful not to act upon his own judgment without consultation with others. He consulted distinguished officers who had belonged to the United States service long before the War, and in his anxiety to have their unbiased judgment withheld any expression of opinion as to the proper man for the place. I recollect distinctly that he said he asked General Lee and General Cooper (Adjutant General) to recommend some one whom they considered suitable for the position; that he consulted them separately, neither knowing that he had spoken to the other on the subject, and the reply of each was that General Pemberton was the man to command at that point. He mentioned others whom he consulted but whose names I do not remember." Mr. Wharton continued: "The President seemed particularly anxious to know whether the appointment of General Pemberton was acceptable to the people of the State. On that point I said: 'Mr. President, your question admits of no evasion. Do you wish me to speak candidly?' He said, with emphasis, 'I do, sir.' I replied that, speaking first for myself and from my observation of him, I had been most favorably impressed by him; that he brought me a letter of introduction from him (Mr. Davis) when he assumed command of the army; that and the fact that he had frequent occasion to consult me as the law officer of the State, in his anxiety to secure the hearty co-operation of the civil authorities, established intimate relations between us; that I had never seen a more laborious and painstaking officer, or one who devoted more attention to the minutest details pertaining to the army under his command; that while many of our citizens doubted his loyalty to the cause, more from the fact that he was of Northern birth than anything else, I believed that there was not a man connected with the government from himself as President to the lowest magistrate, nor in the army from General Lee to the humblest private, whose heart was more deeply interested in the success of our cause than that of General Pemberton."[4]

The commander whom Pemberton came to replace was Major General Earl Van Dorn. Born near Port Gibson, Mississippi, September 17, 1820, six years after Pemberton, Van Dorn's parents on his father's side emigrated from Holland in the 1700's. The mother of the chivalrous cavalryman was the stately niece of Andrew Jackson's wife, Rachel Jackson. Here was still another tie to the old president who had appointed Pemberton to West Point. Although Van Dorn's father was of Northern birth and a graduate of Princeton, he soon moved to Virginia and later pushed on to Mississippi. There he became a lawyer and in his later years a probate judge. When the suave and sparkling Earl reached eighteen, the Judge procured his appointment to the Military Academy, which he entered in 1838, one year after Pemberton's graduation. The two men fought side by side in Mexico so that when Pemberton came as successor, he and the dashing cavalier were no strangers to each other by reputation or acquaintance. In the earliest days of the war Van Dorn had been appointed major general of the Mississippi state troops in succession to Jefferson Davis.

Prior to Pemberton's arrival, Van Dorn had proclaimed martial law east of the Mississippi. This, he explained to the people, "was the will of the Commander." Though he was a Mississippian born and bred, his action excited such a storm that President Davis found it necessary to supersede the cavalryman. Civil and States' rights crippled the Confederate army throughout.

Upon Pemberton's coming to relieve him, Van Dorn was put in charge of all the cavalry thereabouts, an assignment for which he was well fitted by temperament and training. He burst into Holly Springs, some months later, wrecking General Grant's winter stores and effectively crippling the projected campaign against Vicksburg.[5] Soon, though, Van Dorn was killed in a private quarrel at Spring Hill, and Bedford Forrest was placed in command of his cavalry. Forrest, who rose to become a lieutenant general without having had a day of military experience before the war, was first recognized as a military genius by a British army man, Garnet Wolseley.[6] As will appear, Forrest's brief period in Pemberton's Department was characteristically packed with action and result.

When Pemberton arrived at Jackson to assume his new command, he found the President had paved the way for him with Mississippi's governor, J. J. Pettus. To Pettus the President had written from Richmond, September 30, 1862: "Major Genl. Pemberton goes directly to Jackson to command in your section. He is an officer of great merit and I commend him to your kind consideration. His Department will be Mississippi and Louisiana, East of the River."[7]

Disregarding his Northern background and heritage, the Vicksburg press soon greeted their new commander most handsomely. Said one local newspaper of Pemberton within a few weeks of his arrival: "In view of the fact this department had been so extremely unfortunate in its Commanding Generals previous to the appointment of General Pemberton, the people and the army were very much indisposed to give their confidence to any General who brought not the prestige of great victories gained on the field of battle. The idea had prevailed that the Government failed to appreciate the vast importance of preserving this important region from the capture of the enemy, and that we were to be put off and imposed upon with one-horse Generals until the enemy had succeeded in placing us under his hoof. It requires something more than ordinary generalship something more than ordinary tact, energy and administrative capacity, to repair the tremendous errors of the past, and save us from the doom that now so threateningly looms up before us.

"In General Pemberton we have a man worthy of trust and confidence. Free from ostentation, an indefatigable and untiring worker, he has traversed the whole department, and overlooked all our works of defense. He proceeds with an activity and a dispatch which has completely gained the implicit confidence of all. Where work is needed, he has done it at once. He has no favorites. His whole mind is absorbed in the great business before him. It is said of him that he has no use for a man except to work him; and if he finds that he has about him one unfit for the performance of the duty expected of him he allows no false notions of courtesy to control his action, but drops him at once, and fills his place with some one who knows how and is willing to work.

"Gen. Pemberton was assigned to this department with the strongest endorsement that a commander could receive. The President, when consulted on the subject, said to a friend that he had looked over the whole field, and knew of no man better qualified for the great duties of the post than he. Gen. Lee also expressed the same opinion. It should be remembered that aside from the intense interest which the President feels in the cause itself, that all his worldly interests and home ties are wrapped up in the defense of this Valley from the marauding Yankees, and he would not be apt to send a man in whom he did not repose the most perfect confidence. This high endorsement, we are happy to say, has been fully sustained by his course since he assumed command. It is indeed, strange how quickly Gen. Pemberton has succeeded in inspiring the most implicit confidence. Brief as has been his command he has brought order out of chaos, and if after the well-nigh fatal blunders of his predecessor it is possible to defend ourselves against the Yankees we believe he will do it."[8]

Soon a rival paper, not to be outdone by its competitors in Vicksburg, carried the following laudatory editorial respect-

ing their Northern defender: "When Gen. Pemberton first
came west to assume command of this department, he was
comparatively unknown. As an unknown and untried man,
so far as the western public was familiar with his official action,
he labored under some disadvantages, having reference to
what is understood by acceptability and popularity. He succeeded one commander, in South Carolina, who was much
trusted and beloved—General Beauregard; and he came among
us at a time when affairs in this military department were in
a very awkward and critical condition. Much had to be done,
with limited means of doing it, and with vital consequences
depending upon its accomplishment. It is but an act of simple
justice to record what seems to be a common, universal, judgment upon the merit and efficiency of Gen. Pemberton's administration, that the projection and execution of the proper
defenses of the Mississippi River, and perfecting those already
planned and partially completed, accomplished by the ceaseless, untiring personal efforts of this commander, justly entitle
him to the confidence and gratitude of the country. With the
practiced eye of a master—the science of an engineer—he surveyed the ground at Vicksburg—at Port Hudson—and at other
points, and determined at a glance what was necessary, what
was practicable, what was possible—the problem being to render our positions impregnable and set the assailants at defiance. Having solved these questions in theory, Gen. Pemberton exerted all the practical, matter of fact energy required
to translate the conceptions of intellect into stern and terrible
and fear-inspiring realities. It is this species of energy alone
which laughs to scorn the obstacles to success and accom-
plishes great results. Work—work—work—is the enchanters
wand. Labor, action, effort, will remove the hindrances to
the accomplishment of the mightiest designs. Is Port Hudson
secure? Is Vicksburg impregnable? Do we hold the great

river against all assault? Is Gen. Pemberton a meritorious
agent in this vital result? Then has he achieved much for the
Confederacy, and has written his name on the imperishable
records of the Mississippi. We have not the honor of a personal acquaintance with the commander whom we feel gratified to notice; and our remarks are a voluntary tribute to worth
and official merit. Honor to whom honor is due."[9]

Still a third paper in the beleaguered city rallied to its commander's side: "The energy displayed by the officers of the
various departments in this command merit the highest com-
mendation. Since the appointment of General Pemberton to
this command order has been brought out of chaos, and new
life, new energy infused into the army and the people. Whatever may be said of the inexperience of General Pemberton
as an officer in the field, he has given ample evidence of rare
military administrative tact, and proved himself a superior de-
partmental commander.

"The officers of the Department have performed their duties
faithfully. They have often worked day and night; and instead of entering complaints for what they have failed to do,
let us remember that no small work has been accomplished.
But the people are called upon to help. They must co-operate
with the authorities or the army supplies will fail in a most
critical juncture. Provisions are still needed—corn is needed,
and those having a surplus must be willing to dispose of it at
a fair price. If all do their duty, the army will be well fed
and well clothed."[10]

The editor's comment as to Pemberton's "inexperience in
the field" is a fair sample of the then prevailing view. But
Pemberton was not alone in having had little line or field experience. Until Lee was in Mexico "he had never aimed a
weapon at a foe in more than twenty-two years of military
duty." In fact, when Lee left Texas in 1861, "he was with his

own soldiers only fourteen months and with other troops a little more than two months. That constituted his experience as a line officer prior to the time he resigned from the United States army." When the war was near the end of its first half year, "cynics," writes Lee's biographer, "affirmed that his reputation was based on an impressive presence and an historic name rather than on ability as a field commander."[11] Whatever their ability as field commanders, the experience of Pemberton and Lee was much the same through the war's first year. There was, moreover, another similarity: ". . . the troops Lee led during the Seven Days were not a united force, accustomed to working together, but consisted of four separate armies, met together for the first time on the field of battle";[12] the instruments of war at Pemberton's disposal at Vicksburg could with equal truth be so described.

Months after Pemberton's coming to Mississippi—as Grant approached their city—Jackson papers of May 3 were as warm as those in Vicksburg in support of Pemberton. Said one editorial: "It would be idle to say that our State and country was not in a position of great peril. Yet, strange as it may seem to our readers, we have never felt more secure since the fall of Donelson. The enemy will never reach Jackson—we are satisfied of that. Our fortifications are progressing finely— reinforcements are pouring in—new companies and regiments for the trenches and local defense are rapidly forming. With all these additional advantages not counted upon a short time since, our defense may be regarded as doubly sure. The fact is, we feel very sanguine as to the result. Gen. Pemberton, assisted by vigilant and accomplished officers, is watching the movements of the enemy, and at the proper time will pounce upon him. Let us give our authorities all the assistance we can, and trust their superior and more experienced judgment as to the management of the armies. We know that we have a force sufficient, if properly handled, not only to defeat but to rout and annihilate Grant if he ventures far from his river base. We understand that Gen. Pemberton is confident of success. We have no cause to doubt either his sagacity or skill. Let any man who questions the ability of Gen. Pemberton only think for a moment of the condition the department was in when he was first sent here. No General has evinced a more sleepless vigilance in the discharge of his duty, or accomplished more solid and gratifying results. Last year, when Gen. Pemberton assumed control of this department, we were menaced by 150,000 Federals. Yet, with not more than 25,000, he so manoeuvred his little band that this immense host was kept at bay. He managed to hold Vicksburg and Port Hudson and to stop the enemy's advance from North Mississippi. With the exception of the recent raid of Grierson—for which he is not culpable—we have had all success. We now have a force equal to the enemy's, and we have reason to be hopeful. For our part, we are perfectly willing to trust to the plans and execution of our Generals. They know more than we do. Our duty is to assist them to our utmost ability and trust to them. Let every man do his duty."[13]

In the main, Pemberton may be said to have had an excellent press in Vicksburg and in the Mississippi capital where were his headquarters. But the editor was a bit too "sanguine" in his opinion that all was well with Vicksburg and Port Hudson. Reinforcements had come, it is true, but Grant was receiving reinforcements to a far greater extent, and help had to come to Pemberton from other sections of the Confederacy. Would the President order reinforcements to Pemberton from Virginia and elsewhere? Could a new government, "dependent on the support of sovereign states," afford to create the impression that Mississippi's Vicksburg was being defended at the expense of the other Southern states? For the "Southern states were allies, not a united nation, and the conduct of military operations was subject to nearly all the difficulties, save language, that weaken most alliances."[14]

Columns of description could not illuminate more vividly this paradox of states' rights—the object of, but an obstacle to, independence—than does the case of Governor Joseph E. Brown of Georgia. Brown was the "chief malcontent of the southeastern states,"[15] and to him "Georgia was his country; its direct defense on its own soil, his chief obligation; the maintenance of a government at Richmond, with the help of Georgia rifles in far off Virginia, merely secondary—a local point of view which affected many another leader."[16] With disastrous consequences to Vicksburg, this local point of view also sadly affected Lee. "Even of Robert E. Lee, perfect in his subordination to the civil government of the Confederate States, it might be said with much truth that the country he defended was Virginia."[17]

"The influences that were to thwart the efforts of the administration in later attempts to effect large-scale concentration were already operative [June, 1862] and had to be taken into account," says Freeman. This was true when Davis was to call on Lee for divisions to reinforce Pemberton at Vicksburg. Lee replied promptly to the government's urgent call and gave three reasons why he could not spare even Pickett's lone division for Vicksburg, then hourly in increasing desperation. Else might Pickett never have known that day at Gettysburg where his fabled charge became the South's very bid for life and independence.

In Lee's eyes the proposal to send Pickett's division to Vicksburg "represented a choice between holding Virginia and holding the line of the Mississippi, and he so advised [Secretary of War] Seddon by telegraph. Then he wrote a fuller answer, to be transmitted by mail. In this letter he mentioned the possibility that if the Army of Northern Virginia were weakened he might be compelled to withdraw into the defenses around Richmond."[18] Lee's reason number two for advising against the suggested reinforcement of Pemberton was that before Pickett's division could arrive at Vicksburg, the necessity for its presence there might have passed.[19] Yet the third, and last, reason for Lee's views against relief in Mississippi was the most extraordinary: He said, ". . . by that time . . . the climate in June will force the enemy [Grant] to retire."[20] Perhaps others might be forced to surrender, or might feel impelled to move to different fields of war in deference to the climate, but Ulysses S. Grant, never! Still was this a name near meaningless to Lee.

Lieutenant General D. H. Hill, always a stubborn fighter, and wholly devoted to Lee, nevertheless was outspoken in criticism of his revered leader's neglect of Vicksburg. Nor in later years did he change this earlier judgment, still protesting in 1875: "The Federals had been stunned by the defeat at Chancellorsville, and probably would not have made a forward movement for months. A corps could have been sent to Mississippi. Grant could have been crushed, and Vicksburg, 'the heart of the Confederacy,' could have been saved. The drums that beat for the advance into Pennsylvania seemed to many of us to be beating the funeral march of the dead Confederacy."[21]

But never did Davis falter in his support of Pemberton, nor rest in his search for Vicksburg reinforcements. "Vicksburg, the nailhead that held the South's two halves together, must be saved."

The President alone could possibly lift the Confederate States out of the paralyzing delays that side-stepped relief at Vicksburg, since in those hours few heeded the ancient warning of Washington, "The independence and liberty you would possess must be the work of co-operative efforts, that common dangers and sufferings may be overcome."

In the face of the darkening prospects, Davis did not despair. He resolutely made his bid for assistance, both near and far afield. But from Lee, Johnston, Bragg, Holmes, and Kirby Smith, on their respective fronts, came back the same answer: no men could be spared for Vicksburg. Soon Grant had an army of one hundred thousand men under his command, of whom seventy thousand were in front of Vicksburg where Pemberton's twenty-eight thousand stubbornly defended themselves. The rest of the Union forces faced eastward, determined to prevent Johnston's or any other troops from raising the siege that shortly followed.

Making but scant headway, Davis nevertheless kept at his ceaseless search and efforts for collaboration—and for relief at Vicksburg for Pemberton. These excerpts from his correspondence tell the story and make their own appeal:[22]

Davis to Senator Phelan (October 11, 1862).—"Major General Pemberton was sent to Jackson and . . . I submitted for the advice and consent of the Senate the nomination of Genl. Pemberton to be Lt. Genl., having confidence in his ability to make the most of the means for the protection of Missi. &c. &c."

Davis to Pemberton (December 7, 1862).—"Are you in communication with Genl. J. E. Johnston? Hope you will be reinforced in time."

Davis to Lee (December 8, 1862).—"[Pemberton's] force is much less than that of the enemy, but I have the most favorable accounts of his conduct as commander. . . ."

Davis to Seddon (December 18, 1862).—"General Johnston will go immediately to Mississippi, and will, with the least delay, reinforce Pemberton by sending a division, say 8,000 men, from the troops in this [Chattanooga] quarter."

Davis to General Holmes (January 28, 1863).—"The loss of either of the two positions,—Vicksburg and Port Hudson—would destroy communication with the Trans-Mississippi Department and inflict upon the Confederacy an injury which I am sure you have not failed to appreciate."

Davis to the Hon. William M. Brooks, Marion, Alabama (April 2, 1863).—"I selected General Pemberton for the very important command which he now holds from a conviction that he was the best qualified officer for that post then available, and I have since found no reason to change the opinion I then entertained of him.

"If success which is generally regarded in popular estimation as evidence of qualification be so regarded in his case, I am surprised that General Pemberton's merits should still be doubted. With a force far inferior in numbers to the enemy, menaced by attack at several points widely distant from each other, with no naval force to meet the enemy's fleets on the Mississippi and its tributaries, by his judicious disposition of his forces and skilful selection of the best points of defense he has repulsed the enemy at Vicksburg, Port Hudson, on the Tallahatchie and at Deer Creek, and has thus far foiled his every attempt to get possession of the Mississippi River and the vast section of country which it controls.

"I think that he has also demonstrated great administrative as well as military ability. He has been enabled to subsist and clothe his army without going out of his own Dept....

"With reference to the fact that General Pemberton was born at the North being alleged as a justification of distrust in his fidelity to our cause, I can imagine nothing more unjust and ungenerous.

"General Pemberton resigned his commission in the U. S. army on the secession of Virginia—his adopted State.—He came at once to Richmond and was ... immediately appointed to a field commission. He afterwards entered the service of the Confederate States in which he has risen from step to step to his present position. In addition to the other proofs which he has afforded of his devotion to the cause of the Confederate States, I may add that by coming South he forfeited a considerable fortune."

Davis to Pemberton (April 21 and 22 [?], 1863).—"Anticipating your wants of heavy guns, I have endeavored to provide for them and will continue as far as practicable to supply you.... If your requisitions are not complied with promptly advise at once by telegraph.... Have you tried the use of fire rafts, to be set adrift from the Cove, at upper batteries of Vicksburg, to float down the river, when boats are attempting to pass? Covered with pine or dry cypress, they would be dangerous to passing vessels and at least would serve by lighting the river to aid the gunners in their aim. Have you tried anchoring fire rafts in the river on dark nights?"

Davis to General Johnston (April 30, 1863).—"General Pemberton telegraphs that unless he has more cavalry, the approaches to North Mississippi are almost unprotected and that he can not prevent cavalry raids."

Davis to Pemberton (April 30, 1863).—"Have telegraphed to General Johnston in reference to your want of cavalry. Am trying to get you some from South Alabama."

Davis to Pettus (May 2, 1863).—"Can you aid General Pemberton by furnishing for short service militia or persons exempt from military service, who may be temporarily organized to repel the invasion?"

Davis to Pemberton (May 7, 1863).—"General Beauregard insists that he cannot spare more than the five thousand men sent. I hope he may change his view. The prisoners taken at Post of Arkansas will be sent to you as soon as practicable. ...Four thousand arms have been sent to Col. Stockton. Will endeavor to send more if more are required to arm the militia furnished to you.... Am anxiously expecting further information of your active operations. Want of transportation for supplies must compel the enemy to seek a junction with their fleet after a few days absence from it. To hold both Vicksburg and Port Hudson is necessary to our connection with Trans-Mississippi. You may expect whatever it is in my power to do for your aid."

Davis to influential citizens of Columbus, Mississippi (May 8, 1863).—"The repulse of the enemy at Charleston relieving our immediate necessities at that place, call was made for eight or ten thousand troops to be sent to reinforce Genl. Pemberton.... [He] has my full confidence, and will, I think, in the progress of events entirely justify the faith with which he has been received by the people of Mississippi."

Davis to Pemberton (May 12, 1863).—"I have impressed upon the Governor the necessity to aid you by calling out all who can render even temporary service, and have ordered arms and ammunition to meet wants which will thus be created. The efforts to supply you with cavalry have not been successful, but it may be that you can get mounted men from volunteers of the country. The reinforcements sent to you should now be arriving. In your situation much depends upon the support and good will of the people. To secure this, it is necessary to add conciliation to the discharge of duty. Patience in listening to suggestions which may not promise much is sometimes rewarded by gaining useful information. I earnestly desire that, in addition to success, you should enjoy the full credit of your labors. We look anxiously and hopefully for the next intelligence of your campaign."

Davis to Pemberton (May 13, 1863).—"To save time and give the exchanged prisoners opportunity to prepare for active service in Mississippi hereafter, a temporary exchange was made for an equal number of Genl. Bragg's army. They must be on their way and should very soon be with you."

Davis to Pemberton (May 23, 1863).—"Your dispatch of the 19th received. I made every effort to reinforce you promptly, which I am aggrieved was not successful. Hope that Genl. Johnston will soon join you with enough force to break up the investment and defeat the enemy. Sympathizing with you for the reverses sustained I pray God may yet give success to you and the brave troops under your command."

Davis to Johnston (May 28, 1863).—"The reinforcements sent to you exceed by say seven thousand the estimate of your dispatch of 27th inst. We have withheld nothing which it was practicable to give. We cannot hope for numerical equality and time will probably increase the disparity."

Davis to Lee (May 31, 1863).—"Genl. Johnston did not, as you thought advisable, attack Grant promptly, and I fear the result is that which you anticipated if time was given.... It is useless to look back, and it would be unkind to annoy you in the midst of your many cares with the reflections which I have not been able to avoid. All the accounts we have of Pemberton's conduct fully sustain the good opinion heretofore entertained of him, and I hope has secured for him that confidence of his troops which is so essential to success."

Davis, in a paper written on February 18, 1865, enclosed in a letter to Senator Phelan (March 1, 1865).—"When General Grant made his great demonstration on Vicksburg, General Johnston failed to perceive its significance.... He arrived, as he reported, too late.... After the investment of Vicksburg, General Johnston remained inactive near Canton and Jackson, stating his inability to attack Grant notwithstanding very urgent requests to do so.... After both Vicksburg and Port Hudson had been captured without one blow on his part to relieve either,... [Johnston] permitted Grant again to con-

centrate a large force, against the third and last section of that
Army.... No sooner had the enemy commenced investing
Jackson than General Johnston pronounced it untenable....
Not only was Vicksburg forced to surrender with its garrison;
but Port Hudson with its garrison had been captured, when
he was able to relieve it, but abstained."

Pemberton was to surrender Vicksburg July 4, 1863. A year
earlier, "The downfall of the Confederacy by midsummer was
a distinct possibility. Johnston and Lee were both alive to this
danger, but they took fundamentally different views of the
best method to meet it."[23]   So was it to be with Pemberton and
Johnston at Vicksburg. West Pointers all, their study of Napoleon plainly warned of the danger of investment in a fixed
position—standing a siege. Nonetheless, sieges were at times
inevitable, the outcome not.

"On June 26 [1862], McClellan's army of 105,000 effectives
had been like a sharpened sickle, ready to sweep over Richmond. His outposts, five miles from the city, could see its
highest spire. The farthest Union infantry had been less than
eight miles from the capitol itself."[24]   Yet two weeks later,
Lee was able to report that the siege of Richmond had been
raised. The siege of Knoxville, the siege of Chattanooga were
likewise "raised." European history furnishes countless older
examples: Orleans (1429), Nancy (1477), Vienna (1683),
Poltava (1709), Tournai-Fontenoy (1745).

Nine days before the fall of Vicksburg, Lee was far from
despairing of the outcome, as he wrote the President: "...I
still hope that all things will end well for us at Vicksburg.
At any rate every effort should be made to bring about that
result."[25]

Pemberton, for his part, was confident "every effort would
be made to bring about that result," as he informed Johnston
(May 18, 1863): "I have decided to hold Vicksburg as long

as is possible, with the firm hope that the Government may yet be able to assist me in keeping this obstruction to the enemy's free navigation of the Mississippi River—I still conceive it to be the most important point in the Confederacy."[26]

On the eleventh of June, 1863, Johnston was to telegraph to Richmond: "I have not at my disposal half the troops necessary to relieve Vicksburg. It is for the government to determine what Department, if any, can furnish the reinforcements required. I cannot know here General Bragg's wants as compared with mine. The Government *can* make such comparisons."[27] And on the fifteenth: "I consider saving Vicksburg hopeless."

To this last dispatch from Johnston, Secretary of War Seddon would reply on the sixteenth: "Your telegram grieves and alarms us. Vicksburg must not be lost, at least without a struggle. The interest and honor of the Confederacy forbid it. I rely on you still to avert the loss. If better resource does not offer, you must hazard attack. It may be made in concert with the garrison, if practicable, but otherwise without. By day or night, as you think best." And again from Seddon to Johnston on the twenty-first: "Only my convictions of almost imperative necessity for action induces the official despatch I have just sent you. On every ground I have great deference to your judgment and military genius, but I feel it right to share, if need be to take, the responsibility and leave you free to follow the most desperate course the occasion may demand. Rely upon it, the eyes and hopes of the whole Confederacy are upon you, with the full confidence that you will act, and with the sentiment that it were better to fail nobly daring than, through prudence even, to be inactive. I look to attack in the last resource, but rely on your resources of generalship to suggest less desperate modes of relief. . . . I rely on you for all possible to save Vicksburg."[28]

"Vicksburg must not be lost, at least without a struggle....
it were better to fail nobly daring than ... to be inactive." But
for Johnston to save Vicksburg would require the kind of
daring shown by Lee a year earlier when Lawton and his
troops were rushed off from Richmond to reinforce Stonewall
Jackson in the Valley; and of such "an act of daring, Johnston
was by nature incapable in either thought or execution."[29]

Upon General Johnston's recovery from wounds he received
some six months before at Seven Pines (outside Richmond) he
had been assigned (November 24, 1862) to the command of
a geographical Department which included Tennessee, North
Carolina, Georgia, Alabama, and Mississippi. According to
President Davis's wife, Johnston was "very averse to leaving
Virginia."

At this stage of the war Mrs. Davis and Mrs. Johnston were
extremely intimate friends; hence it was natural for Mrs.
Davis to call upon General Johnston and his wife before the
General left Richmond. According to Mrs. Davis, "General
Johnston seemed ill and dispirited." In answer to a hope expressed by her "that he would have a brilliant campaign," General Johnston replied, "I might if I had Lee's chances with the
army of Northern Virginia."[30]

CHAPTER VII

Grant's First Attempt to Capture Vicksburg

SOUTH OF Memphis, the next bluff encountered on the eastern bank of the Mississippi is the hill fortress of Vicksburg, some four hundred miles below. Not only was Vicksburg the first high ground below Memphis, it was in 1862 the one and only rail and river junction to be found between New Orleans and Memphis. Furthermore, opposite Vicksburg, across the river and on the west bank, another railway line lead into Shreveport, important commercial center in western Louisiana. Thus Vicksburg had an immense commercial value, a great defensive value, and an inestimable moral value to the Confederacy. For months to come, Vicksburg alone "blocked the Union fairway . . . and controlled the bloodflow along a vital economic artery."

The considerations that brought Pemberton and his army to defend Vicksburg kept them there. First was the President's view that Vicksburg and Port Hudson must be held to insure the Confederacy's connection with trans-Mississippi. Second was the view that it was right to risk the loss of an army for the purpose of keeping command of even a section of the Mississippi River. Moreover, the commander himself believed that Vicksburg was the most important point in the

Confederacy, and it was his firm hope and belief that the government would be able to assist him successfully.

When he assumed command of the Department of Mississippi and East Louisiana in October, 1862, Pemberton at once perceived the magnitude of the undertaking at hand. The Army of Northern Mississippi, under his predecessor Van Dorn, had been defeated a short time before at Corinth; it was sadly demoralized as a consequence and required thorough reorganization. Plainly, in the quartermaster, commissary, engineer and ordnance corps confusion reigned without distinction. No semblance of system prevailed; the entire Department was in distressing chaos. From this disorganization order gradually emerged. Promptly, chiefs of the various corps were appointed, and through their untiring exertions, under aid and direction of Pemberton, the Department was truly reconstructed, remodeled, and substantially supplied.[1] Many of Pemberton's staff subsequently vouched for the speedy revolution that took place under his administration. Holly Springs, Port Hudson, Vicksburg, points separated by hundreds of miles, were repeatedly and prudently surveyed by Pemberton and his staff; as a result, artillery works were everywhere pushed forward to completion with unfamiliar speed.[2]

Coincident with Pemberton's appointment to Vicksburg in October, 1862, Grant was formally put in command of the army opposing; and he was given the particular task of opening the Mississippi from the north. "The Yazoo and its tributaries, some of which were really cross-cut channels between it and the Mississippi, offered several 'back ways' to Vicksburg, but all of them difficult to negotiate with steamers and impossible overland."[3]

Grant's first plan was to take his main army down the railroad, south from West Tennessee to Jackson and across to Vicksburg; and at the same time to send Sherman down the

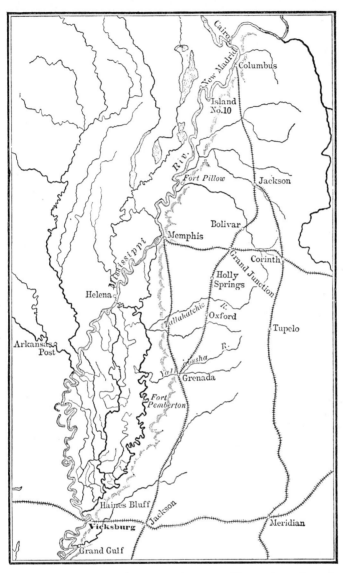

Vicksburg and the country above it, illustrating Grant's first attempt against the city. From Fiske, The Mississippi Valley in the Civil War.

river with a fleet of transports, convoyed by the gunboat flotilla of Rear Admiral Porter. Sherman, after a conference with Grant at Grand Junction (where the Memphis and Charleston and the Mississippi Central railroads cross), returned to Memphis on December 8. He at once began preparations to put about twenty thousand men on river steamers and proceed down the Mississippi, to Helena, Arkansas. There he planned to pick up about twelve thousand more troops and go on into the Yazoo. An attempt would be made to effect a lodgment on the north side of Vicksburg at Chickasaw Bluffs.

On the eighteenth of December Major General J. A. McClernand came to Grant with *his* orders to take command of the river forces against Vicksburg. Grant telegraphed to Sherman at Memphis to hold up his departure, but Sherman was already away down the river.

"Grant's main base for his overland movement was at Columbus, Kentucky, using the rail line from that point south to Holly Springs, Mississippi, where a great secondary base was established. Two days after Sherman had sailed away from Memphis to make his attack, relying on co-operation from the land forces coming down the railroad, things began to happen in General Grant's rear, such things as forced him to give up the land movement entirely."[4]

By advancing along the upland through Mississippi, Grant hoped to draw out Pemberton's army and, if he could defeat it, reach the Confederate defenses on the land side. In the event of his own defeat, however, Grant would not be left without a line of retreat and base of supplies. Moreover, this plan accorded with Grant's pet theory—that the so-called strategic points of an enemy were not the true objectives to seek, but rather the enemy's army and its destruction.[5] This accomplished, any desired point, thus inadequately defended, was open to easy seizure. Pemberton, however, eluded this trap. He designated Van Dorn to make a surprise attack on Grant's intermediary base at Holly Springs. And this shattering cavalry expedition against Grant's rear proved such a shock to the invaders that the Confederates were enabled to destroy a million dollars' worth of Union stores.[6]

On the day before Van Dorn's raid "General Forrest had got on Grant's rail line, at Jackson, Tennessee, and started north toward Columbus, Kentucky, capturing garrisons and supplies, burning bridges and trestles, wrecking track. It was a common complaint of army commanders on both sides that cavalry could not be relied on to get down off their horses and do the hard heavy work necessary to wreck a railroad track so that it would stay wrecked, but Forrest's men were not orthodox cavalry. By Christmas of 1862, after a week's work, they had made the railroad from Jackson north useless for the rest of the war."[7] The raids of Van Dorn and Forrest, coming at the same time, convinced Grant that he could not rely on this line to supply the needs of his advancing army, and compelled him to make a change of plans. This first attempt of Grant's ended with his withdrawal to Memphis. There he must have had ample opportunity to reflect on the fallacy of any campaign involving the maintenance of a line of communications over two hundred miles long—in the face of cavalry commands such as Van Dorn and Forrest were able to muster—time and time again. Forrest's men, alone, had cut over sixty miles of railroad and telegraph lines on this single occasion.

In the meantime, Pemberton, who had met and engaged Grant on his advance as far south as the Yallobosha River, had been afforded ample opportunity to return his forces to Vicksburg. Here, it will be seen, he severely repulsed Sherman's assault against his impregnable position at Chickasaw Bluffs just north of the city. Whereupon, Sherman, like Grant, drew in his horns and retired. In his *Memoirs,* Grant notes: "Up to this time it had been regarded as an axiom that large bodies of troops must operate from a base of supplies which they always covered and guarded in all forward movements." Fifteen years earlier, Lee had acquired a far more confident view of the relation of communications and supply to strategy: he had seen Winfield Scott at Puebla boldly abandon his line of supply from the sea and live off the country. Then Lee had seen Scott batter his way to Mexico City within the incredible space of thirty-seven days, while he "pursued, found, and destroyed" Santa Anna. However, Scott's experience did not embolden Grant in 1862 to ignore the wreckage of his base by Forrest and Van Dorn.

In addition to checking Grant on the Yallobosha, Pemberton was alert to the danger in his rear caused by the presence of Hovey's and Washburn's troops of Grant's command.[8] The idea had presented itself to Grant of holding Pemberton in his front while Sherman should get in the defenders' rear, and possibly into denuded Vicksburg: "The farther north the enemy could be held the better." But, with his lieutenants' defeat, and the destruction of his stores, Grant had had enough, writing: "... at the time I speak of it had not been demonstrated that an army could operate in an enemy's territory, depending upon the country for supplies." Then he added: "Had I known...that Central Mississippi abounded so in all army supplies, I would have been in pursuit of Pemberton while his cavalry was destroying the roads in my rear....I was amazed at the quantity of supplies the country afforded. ...This taught me a lesson...."

During the campaign here described, Grant wrote that the losses in casualties and in prisoners were about equal on both sides.

Pemberton was fully entitled to consider that he had successfully met the first test of threatened invasion, as far as the conditions and means at hand permitted. Grant had been more than blocked; his superior numbers had even turned back, far back, empty handed and disconsolate.

Pemberton had fashioned the strategy calling for Van Dorn's destruction of Grant's essential base, essential at least from Grant's point of view. He had selected and particularly designated Van Dorn for this duty and, thereafter, had issued all orders received by Van Dorn in the course of executing his daring mission. It was Pemberton's military judgment that dictated this decisive blow; his was the conception and responsibility; his would have been the blame for any failure.[9]

Now to turn in greater detail to Sherman's abortive efforts to aid Grant in his first descent upon Vicksburg and upon Pemberton's army.

There were two parallel lines of approach to Vicksburg from the North and from Grant's base at Memphis, some two hundred miles away. One way was down the railroad, which Grant took and turned back from after the disaster to his base at Holly Springs. The other way was down the river: this was easily the simplest and quickest and the means of approach most favorably viewed by Sherman. "This is my hobby," he wrote to Grant, "and I know you pardon me when I say that I am daily more and more convinced that we should hold the river absolutely and leave the interior alone. Detachments inland can always be overcome or are at great hazard, and they do not convert the people ... with the Mississippi safe we could land troops at any point, and by a quick march break the railroad, when we could make ourselves so busy that our descent would be dreaded the whole length of the river."[10]

As a result of vigilance and energy, Sherman was able to report to Grant his belief that almost the entire force under Pemberton had been moved north of Vicksburg. He then urged Grant to move towards and behind Pemberton—so that the Confederate troops could not interfere with the attack he (Sherman) contemplated from the river. Manifestly, Sherman's intended move through the back door to Vicksburg (in conjunction with Admiral Porter's gunboat flotilla) collapsed with Grant's inability to hold Pemberton firmly in his front. But not until Sherman had made his bid. Unhappily for the Union, the Confederate cavalry intervened to destroy "the perfect concert of action" intended. Sherman was thereby left painfully unaware that Van Dorn and Forrest (for over a week) had cut Grant off from all communication with the North, constraining him (1) to fall back to his very starting point, (2) to release his fleeting contact with Pemberton's army, and (3) to forego communicating any of this bad news to Sherman, who was in consequence "committed to a forlorn venture." Grant was perhaps a little hurried, yielded perhaps too readily to this constraint, "in view of the consequent danger to Sherman." Instead of hamstringing Pemberton, "it was a sorry turn of fortune that...the enemy should have hamstrung Grant."[11]

By Grant's retirement Pemberton had been able to fall back to Vicksburg and there quickly concentrate 12,000 men to deal with Sherman's unsupported effort.[12] It was shortly after this that General Magruder wrote Richmond that Pemberton should have 50,000 more men at once or the Mississippi Valley would be lost and the cause ruined. He was insistent that there should be a concentration of troops there immediately, no matter how much other places might suffer. The enemy there should be beaten and the Mississippi secured at all hazards. If not, Mobile was lost, and perhaps Montgomery, as well as Vicksburg.[13] But there would be no 50,000 extra troops, though during the next month President Davis himself would come west to inspect the armies of Bragg, Johnston, and Pemberton. In the end, this visit would result in a presidential order, over Johnston's objection, to transfer Stevenson's division of 8,000 men from Bragg to Pemberton. This scanty addition satisfied no one.

On Christmas Day, 1862, Sherman, with Porter's armada, reached Milliken's Bend on the Mississippi. Sherman thus describes the impression their advance left on him some ten years later: "In proceeding down the river, one or more of Admiral Porter's gunboats took the lead; others were distributed throughout the column, and some brought up the rear. We manoeuvred by divisions and brigades when in motion, and it was a magnificent sight as we thus steamed down the river .... some few guerrilla-parties infested the banks, but did not dare to molest so strong a force as I then commanded."

On the day after Christmas the Union fleet steamed up the Yazoo and disembarked on a "broad flat shelf beneath the steep clay cliffs, two hundred feet high, of the Walnut Hills, on which the town of Vicksburg stood." But the gunboats were too far away to cover Sherman's attack on the bluffs—and Grant was not there!

The troops pushed forward on December 27 and 28, skirmishing with Pemberton's pickets, until they reached a last and broad bayou almost at the foot of Chickasaw Bluffs. "Beyond this a strip of firm ground was lined with rifle pits and batteries, which also crowned the bluffs behind." But the natural obstacles proved impassable. "Thus Sherman had to draw in ... and trust to a narrow frontal assault in the centre. ...

"Eagerly and vainly Sherman waited for some news or sound of Grant—but only heard enemy troop trains steaming into Vicksburg. Delay would have forfeited the bare chance that remained, and so on the morning of the 29th Sherman decided to launch the assault."[14] He ordered the first attack to begin on the flanks and later gave orders for the main assault. One of the assaulting brigades crossed the bayou at the foot of Chickasaw Bluffs and found shelter under the bank; another regiment soon crossed lower down at the one other practicable crossing; but the movement was not well supported and the disheartened men in blue held on in scooped-out caves in the bank only until such time as darkness enabled them to withdraw.

On the day following (an hour's rise in the river would have drowned his whole force), Sherman got together a fresh detachment to make one further landing effort at a greater distance from Vicksburg and secured the help of Admiral Porter to protect the hazardous venture. Naval opinion had previously opposed landing at the now designated point on account of torpedoes which Pemberton was known to have placed in the river. However, the sailors were finally won over and co-operated loyally, contriving a prow to ram and explode these underwater obstructions to their passage. Accordingly, on December 31, and in the night, Sherman assembled 10,000 men and prepared to attack Chickasaw Bluffs at dawn. The attack never took place. On New Year's morning, around daylight, Porter reported that a dense fog on the river would prevent the movement of his flotilla. Next day, increasing numbers of Pemberton's men were plainly visible on the heights; rain was falling heavily; the cover of Porter's cannon was lacking; the element of surprise had long since passed. So Sherman "took his decision swiftly" and sailed away, not far, but safely distant, nonetheless. Perhaps it was as well for Porter, too, since in fog or sunshine Vicksburg sat too high for the Federal gunboats to hit effectively, while the fort's own plunging fire could shatter them.

Writing with his habitual frankness to Mrs. Sherman, the invader was humble in admission of defeat: "Well, we have been to Vicksburg and it was too much for us and we have backed out." Then Grant's "right hand" made his official report to Halleck, General in Chief of all the Union armies, the same Halleck whom Pemberton had known at West Point. It was Sherman's briefest report in all the war: "I reached Vicksburg at the time appointed, landed, assaulted and failed, re-embarked my command unopposed and turned it over to my successor."[15]

Controversy has long raged around, by, and about Pemberton's ultimate surrender of Vicksburg. There can be none about this first campaign.

After Sherman's complete failure, the Union armada noisily departed without loss of time. They steamed up the Mississippi, then quickly veered off and up the Arkansas River—to pounce on the Confederate post there. This post in particular threatened the communications of any Union forces at Vicksburg. Meanwhile, Pemberton observed with merited pride the withdrawal of Sherman, his 40,000 men, his large fleet of steamboats, and Porter's strung-out gunboat flotilla.

In time they would all return and try again, Grant, Sherman, and Porter with his gunboats. But as he saw them round the river's bend and pass from view, Pemberton, less reticent on paper than in speech, addressed his men with unconcealed emotion and frank gratitude:

"The Lieutenant-General commanding the Department desires to express to the troops of his command his high appreciation of their recent gallant defense of this important position. All praise is due them, not alone for so bravely repulsing the renewed assaults of an enemy vastly superior in numbers, but equally for the cheerful and patient endurance with which they have submitted to the hardships and exposure incident to ten successive days and nights of watchfulness in the trenches, rendered imperatively necessary by the close proximity of the opposed armies. While all have performed their duties with benefit to their country and honor to themselves, still, as must ever be the case in war, fortune has bestowed her opportunities unequally—to those who, by Her favor, held the posts of honor, and by their own resolute courage availed themselves of their opportunities, especial thanks are due; and it will be the pride and agreeable duty of the Lieutenant-General commanding to claim for them from their country the distinction and honor they have so justly deserved.

J. C. PEMBERTON,
Lieutenant-General Commanding"[16]

Return they did, within the month, Grant, Sherman, Mc-Pherson, Porter, Farragut, and Sherman's erstwhile successor, Major General John A. McClernand. (McClernand was a former congressman from Lincoln's home town; he was not a West Pointer.)

And now from his wife Sherman carefully concealed his bitterness at being supplanted: "McClernand has arrived to supersede me by order of the President himself. Of course I submit gracefully.... The President...has a perfect right to choose his agents." In this spirit of resignation did he write his wife, while to his brother, Senator Sherman, he revealed his true feelings, confiding some days later: "Mr. Lincoln intended to insult me and the military profession by putting McClernand over me.... I never dreamed of so severe a test of my patriotism as being superseded by McClernand...."[17] But before the end of the month, Grant, confirmed in *his* position as commander of all the Union forces operating on the Mississippi, promptly came on from Memphis. He traveled by steamboat to the region of former hostilities, took charge, and at once claimed loyalty from the shaken Sherman. Then the forces were once more put to the main task of finding the way to capture Vicksburg. Instead of doing so, they lay confronting the fortress ineffectively for six months, not inactive, but ineffective. It is now clear that Grant's original plan of

GRANT'S FIRST ATTEMPT 71

maneuvering overland against Jackson and the rear of Vicksburg, distracting Pemberton's forces from the river threat, was the best strategic approach. Sherman always claimed that had Grant (or Banks from New Orleans) been within sixty miles of him, the line of bluffs manned by Pemberton's forces at Chickasaw Bayou could have been broken.

It has been asserted that historical estimate of Sherman "is much furthered by his own self exposure in his Memoirs—written by himself." In any view, his detailed allusions to the first movement on Vicksburg furnish irrefutable testimony of Pemberton's achievement in defeating his opponents' soundly fathered strategy. As Sherman writes: "...the bluffs of Vicksburg...were found to be strong by nature and by art, and seemingly well defended.... Our loss had been pretty heavy, and we had accomplished nothing, and had inflicted little loss on our enemy.... The rebels held high, commanding ground, and could see every movement of our men and boats, so that the only possible hope of success consisted in celerity and surprise, and in General Grant's holding all of Pemberton's army hard pressed meantime...." Then Sherman continues: "Still, my relief, on the heels of a failure, raised the usual cry, at the North, of 'repulse, failure, and bungling.' There was no bungling on my part,...and General Grant, long after,...described the almost impregnable nature of the ground.... But, had we succeeded, we might have found ourselves in a worse trap, when General Pemberton was at full liberty to turn his whole force against us."[18] This force, then strung from Vicksburg to Haines's Bluff, Sherman estimated at fifteen thousand men.

Perhaps Sherman was right in suspecting a worse trap. For Stephen D. Lee's guns were there to greet him. And Colonel Lee's artillery was somehow uniformly in the right place: "You are just where I wanted you," R. E. Lee said to the alert young Colonel at the Second Battle of Manassas, "stay there."[19] At Sharpsburg as well, D. H. Hill had reported this artillerist as fighting magnificently.

Nonetheless there is serious doubt as to how much even Colonel Stephen Lee could have accomplished with the few heavy guns lining the front. The batteries from Snyder's Mills to Vicksburg, a distance of nearly ten miles, mounted not more than thirty-five heavy-type cannon. Those directly fronting the city mounted but twenty-eight.[20]

At bottom, the first movement against Vicksburg was blocked largely by the Confederate cavalry's destruction of railroads in Grant's rear. For this caused him to give up the direct overland approach to Vicksburg and to "change to the immensely more difficult and complicated amphibious operation along the river."

A commander who balks two enemy forces each exceeding seventy-five per cent of his one army is not to be charged with failure. Viewed from this distance the unsuccessful outcome of Grant's and Sherman's first operations appears to have hinged upon the reckless daring and effectiveness of the Confederate cavalry. With the horsemen's hearty co-operation, Pemberton's first campaign was near faultless in his full employment of a small force for a defensive battle on the inner line. It must have given him new confidence.

CHAPTER VIII

Grant's Second Failure

IN THE WINTER and early spring of 1863 Grant faced his task anew. How could the river goal be had and held: Vicksburg, that quiet Southern town, call-station and landing depot for Mississippi side-wheelers, first settled by the Spanish and later an outpost of the French.

Vicksburg was founded in the same year its Civil War defender was born. In that year, 1814, the Reverend Newitt Vick, Methodist minister and planter, "came from Virginia and established one of the first missions in Mississippi in the open woods. It was then a frontier clearing, six miles east of the present city of Vicksburg....A few years later, the people named their sprawling village in Vick's honor."[1] Unhappily, the city's founder died before the little community had grown to any size. At the time of the siege it was counted near to five thousand inhabitants.

Two hundred feet above sea level stands the range of hills upon whose sides, summit, and valleys Vicksburg was builded, its once busy levees laved only by the Mississippi's waters. All know the city itself clings to bluffs. To the northeast, east, and south there was ample dry ground, though northward along the river dry footing was nowhere to afford standing space for large numbers. And northward was the way

Grant must come. Directly, it was impossible to advance down the main river and so at the fortress. At the same time, Sherman's earlier and conclusive frustration disclosed the obstacles preventing passage of the bottoms and marshes found northeast of the town, patrolled and strongly guarded as they were by Southern snipers.

When Grant, in general command of the invading armies, returned from Memphis on January 18, 1863, he found there were many alternative plans of attack to canvass. The plan, or plans, decided upon sickened Sherman. He summed up his sharp disapproval in a sentence: "Here we are at Vicksburg again, on the wrong side of the river trying to turn the Mississippi by a ditch, a pure waste of human labor." Sherman favored going back up the river and advancing overland to the rear of Vicksburg, but as Grant put it, "to make a backward movement ... would be interpreted by many ... as a defeat. ... There was nothing left to be done but to go forward to a decisive victory." For a time Sherman spoke of resignation, though not unexpectedly this mood quickly vanished in hearty collaboration with Grant's determination to "dig ditches." Despite later and long months of discouragement, there grew gradually an expanding bond of sympathy between these two; rarely did they see other than eye to eye.

Sherman was set by Grant to widen and deepen the canal across the peninsula in front of Vicksburg, a distance of a little more than a mile. The canal had been started the year before by General Williams and, if successfully completed, the Union forces could slip by Vicksburg, running the enemy batteries for a shorter distance, thus arriving safely below the city. Without an hour's interruption the digging went on; meantime heavy rains gobbled up land that had earlier been found dry enough for the soldiers' camps. Sherman's corps was finally forced to seek the safety of their transports, while

McClernand's command was soon moved up the river from Young's Point to Milliken's Bend.

Even Grant had little faith in the project: the Confederates plainly observed their operations and were quick to place and range their batteries accordingly. The "ditch" work was pushed, however, until early in March. Then a sudden rise in the river swept away the dam protecting the workmen. Even then dredgers held to their task until the fire of the Vicksburg defenders stopped all operations at this point.

In the interval other projects were afoot. McPherson was to cut the levee at Lake Providence and thus attempt to find a route by way of the lake, several rivers, and bayous—into the Mississippi again—four hundred miles below Vicksburg. Grant says in his *Memoirs* that he didn't feel the projected route was possible, but he "let the work go on, believing employment was better than idleness for the men. Then, too, it served as a cover for other efforts which gave a better prospect of success."

Two like "efforts" were undertaken by way of the Yazoo River, which is one river with three names—Yallobusha, Tallahatchie, and Coldwater—whose combined length is over five hundred miles. At that time there was no passage from the Mississippi into the tributaries of the Yazoo, and Grant endeavored to revive a passageway of former years, directing his diggers to cut the levee at the Yazoo Pass (a winding bayou, ten miles long, eighty feet wide, and thirty deep). Thus he hoped to inundate the inlet, letting light-draft gunboats as well as transports pass through into the Yazoo and so down to the first of the Vicksburg defenses.

Accordingly, on February 2 the levee was cut and the waters of "Ole Man River" tore through in a rushing torrent. As a result, no boats could pass through the gap. But the water finally subsiding, a detachment under Brigadier General L. F.

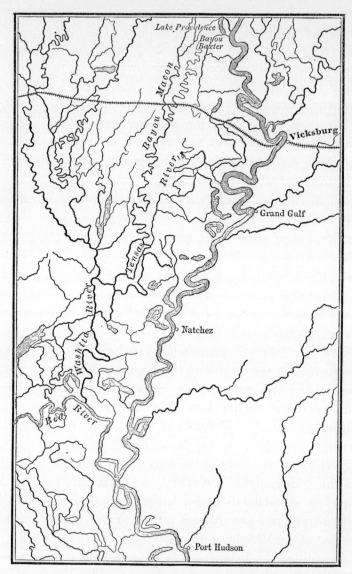

The Lake Providence experiment. From Fiske, The Mississippi Valley in the Civil War.

Ross passed through into the Coldwater and the Tallahatchie sections of the Yazoo, only to find their progress impeded by trees chopped down so as to fall into and across the narrow swampy channels of the Yazoo proper. In one case eighty fallen trees interlaced for more than a mile. These difficulties eventually surmounted, the Union forces found themselves, on March 11, confronting Fort Pemberton, "a little work hastily built of cotton bales and earth, mounting but three guns and manned only by Loring's brigade of fifteen hundred men." The attacking troops were then disheartened to discover they could not land on the flooded bottom, particularly in the face of the determined fire of Loring's men. "Old Blizzards" himself paced the parapet of cotton bales, calling on his men to "give them blizzards, boys!"[2] For the bluecoats there was nothing to do but turn around. On the way back Ross, with his forty-five hundred men, passed fresh troops coming forward under Brigadier General I. F. Quinby (March 22). Quinby was persuaded to push on down the river to see the fort for himself; on doing so, he likewise counseled retreat, though the course over these winding streams had been seven hundred miles long. Subsequently John Fiske called it "perhaps the most gigantic flanking movement ever attempted in military history."

In checkmating the Union forces at Fort Pemberton, Loring deserves high praise. But Pemberton had not such later cause to value "Old Blizzard's" services at Champion's Hill the following May. A native of South Carolina, Brigadier General Loring had since boyhood resided in Florida. Not a West Pointer, he was a rugged Indian fighter and had seen more field service than most of his superiors. Four years Pemberton's junior, and far below him in rank, Loring clearly felt he needed no supervision. "Had not Loring been brevetted colonel for gallantry in Mexico? ... Did he not have a good record as commander in New Mexico, where he had whipped Indians more elusive than the raw Federal troops, and in a country more difficult?"[3]

While Ross and Quinby were having their troubles with Fort Pemberton, Grant became concerned for the safety of Ross, not knowing that Quinby had joined him. Accordingly, Grant devised a fantastic rescue scheme, one that, if successful, would also serve as a "back door" to Vicksburg, by penetration of the forest labyrinth through employment of the Yazoo's tributary, the Big Sunflower River.

Hence it was that on March 15 Grant and Admiral Porter started out on a reconnaissance up Steele's Bayou with five gunboats, and they decided there was a navigable route over swampy land across to the Yazoo through a network of creeks and bayous. Grant at once returned for reinforcements, ordering Sherman to "proceed as early as practicable up Steele's Bayou, and through Black Bayou to Deer Creek, and thence with the gunboats now there by any route they may take to get into the Yazoo River. . . ." This "cross-country" route would be shorter than going up the Mississippi and coming back down the Yazoo, and it would get the troops into the Yazoo above Haines's Bluff and the Confederate defenses.

Progress was painfully slow through the narrow sluggish streams, obstructed as they were by logs beneath, and above by the branches of overhanging trees. The gunboats led the way, clearing the course somewhat for Sherman and his men in the wooden troop transports lagging behind.

In the meantime, Admiral Porter had about reached the Big Sunflower River. There the way would have been unobstructed had the gunboats not been blocked by newly felled trees: the defenders were ahead of the Admiral. That very day Pemberton's forces had raced one of their brigades up the Big Sunflower by boat—twenty-four hours ahead of the main

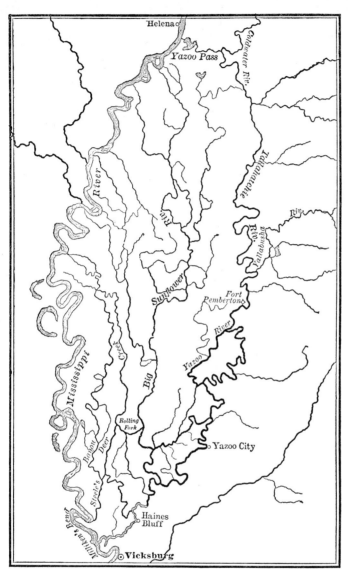

The rivers and bayous above Vicksburg, illustrating the
Yazoo Pass and Steele's Bayou experiments. From Fiske,
The Mississippi Valley in the Civil War.

Union force—hoping to capture any advance parties before the attacking troops could arrive in effective numbers. Now besides the natural difficulties of the tortuous channels, Porter had to contend with Pemberton's deadly sharpshooters. These natives picked off all men trying to fend the boats away from the banks or attempting to remove debris from their path. Porter was indeed in a tight spot, and Sherman, who had stayed behind to clear out the passage for the rest of the troops, now heard the navy guns "booming more frequently than seemed consistent with mere guerilla operations."

On the night of the nineteenth Sherman, thirty miles in the rear, received a message from Porter, "written on tissue paper, brought through the swamp by a negro, who had it concealed in a piece of tobacco." The Admiral begged him to "come to his rescue as quickly as possible," says Sherman. Porter was in fact critically endangered with every hour's delay.

Luckily for the Admiral, Sherman himself had been exploring the country ahead of his own forces; he was in a tugboat without an escort. Sending on what forces were at hand, Sherman set out in a canoe, paddling along until he came up with a shallow-draft transport loaded with fresh troops. Preceded by a tug with a coal barge in tow, the troop-ship went "crashing through the trees, carrying away pilot house, smoke-stacks, and everything above-deck." As soon as they reached the first strip of ground above water, "Sherman disembarked the troops, sent back for fresh boat-loads, and led the men through the dense canebrake—an eerie procession as they picked their steps by the flickering light of candles held aloft."[4]

At daylight Sherman's rescue party again took up their forced march. They had had but a few hours' rest in the open cotton fields next the banks of Deer Creek. The gunfire sounding in their ears, the rescuers finally performed the incredible—marching twenty-one full miles by noon. Sherman so describes the dramatic ending: Major Kirby "galloped down the road on a horse he had picked up the night before, and met me. He explained the situation of affairs and offered me his horse. I got on *bareback,* and rode up the levee, the sailors coming out of their iron-clads and cheering most vociferously as I rode by, and as our men swept forward across the cotton field in full view. I soon found Admiral Porter, who was on the deck of one of his iron-clads, with a shield made of the section of a smoke-stack, and I doubt if he was ever more glad to meet a friend than he was to see me."

An hour later Sherman's arrival would have been too late. A Confederate force had made its way behind the Union fleet and Porter's plans were already laid to blow up his gunboats and try escape on foot through the swamps.

There was no room for the ironclads to turn around; three days were therefore taken in backing the fleet out of the bayous and creeks, with Sherman covering the retreat. On March 27 fleet and men were back at their camps on the Mississippi, "after an eleven-day excursion into futility."

Pemberton had won again. But Grant, whether he knew it or not, had seriously embarrassed Pemberton's labors to keep his troops supplied. As the winter season closed in, the army defending had grown to some 40,000 effectives. By then sufficient time had elapsed for the effect of Pemberton's organization to be felt, for the completion of contracts with local citizens and farmers, and for supplies to begin to come in.

The sources from which Vicksburg could be supplied were as follows: from the country west of the Mississippi, from the Yazoo River, and from the interior of the state. In the latter contingency, provisions, etc., had to be transported over long lines of creaking unprotected railroads. As for Port Hudson, three hundred miles away (with whose defense and that of

Jackson, Pemberton was additionally charged), supplies were limited to the Mississippi River, since it was distant more than sixty miles from the nearest railway depot.[5]

Regarding the problem of how to draw a steady flow of food and other necessaries from the interior of Mississippi: all exportation of provender, rations, and other stores from this Department was promptly prohibited by Pemberton;[6] depots were widely established, and agents for the army dispatched in all directions to find, purchase, and gather up stock, fodder, ordnance. Transportation was time and again held up or denied altogether, such was the shifting of troops throughout the Department's thinly protected area, threatened now here, now there, by Grant's increasing reinforcements.

During this feverish season of effort to provision Vicksburg, Jackson, Port Hudson, Fort Pemberton and Port Gibson, local railroads in effect collapsed. Lacking replacements, repairs, or even the rudest substitutes, the rolling stock proved pitifully inadequate. Worse were engines, more often the cause of costly accidents than the tracks along which they crawled. That section of the Southern Railroad connecting Vicksburg and Jackson was in so miserable a state of repair as to be for all practical purposes impassable. But as soon as the wet season set in and navigation became practicable in the small tributaries, supplies of beef, cattle, bacon, corn, and salt—loudly called for by Pemberton—were rushed by the government from the West. Then, in the very midst of these activities, came Grant's gunboats in early February, putting an end to safe navigation of all rivers plied by the tiny carriers of the Confederate commissary. Thus ended hope of drawing provisions from the country west of the Mississippi via the Red and Big Black rivers.*

---

* Although most of the Union fleets under Porter and Farragut were above Vicksburg and below Port Hudson, enough ships got by the batteries to play havoc with Confederate shipping. See the following chapter, pp. 85 ff.

Reduced to one last watercourse, Pemberton had looked to the subsistence of his large standing garrisons from the Yazoo River, from the neighborhood of Haines's Bluff, and from the country on Sunflower River and Deer Creek. These streams, however, were not navigable until far into the winter season, and then only light-draft boats could be put into use. For the most part, corn was all the bordering country offered, and even this presented a difficulty when it came to arranging for actual delivery to the army on the river banks. Being without all transport, the most patriotic planters pleaded their inability to deliver. So it was that only a small portion of the rich grain from those fertile fields ever reached the Confederate army.

Porter's raids through the numerous bayous of this district were a further hindrance; and after Grant's descent upon Fort Pemberton, it was no longer practicable to siphon into Vicksburg water-borne additions to Pemberton's commissaries.[7]

Forced off the rivers, Pemberton looked hopefully to haulage by wagons. But here again man and nature conspired against the Confederates. So churned and mired were the wretched roadbeds, the shortest hauls bogged down for days. "Against these odds, no man could have contended more energetically, more resourcefully than Pemberton"; such was the judgment of his equally active chief of staff, Major R. W. Memminger. In the Richmond *Sentinel* that year of 1863, Memminger wrote: "In passing judgment upon Lieutenant-General Pemberton, the people seem to have considered, not what he *has* done, but what he has *not* done. They say, 'why did he not provision Vicksburg,' and not, 'Did he do everything that could be done for that object?' ... It [Vicksburg] was not provisioned for an *indefinite* siege nor could be. ... Notwithstanding all these difficulties, Vicksburg was sufficiently provisioned to hold out for forty-seven days, and Port Hudson sustained a siege of seven weeks."[8]

In spite of the fact that Grant had kept Pemberton fully occupied all winter, very little had actually been accomplished toward Vicksburg's capture. What should Grant do next? The system of canals, three times undertaken—at Young's Plantation opposite Vicksburg, at Lake Providence sixty miles up the river, and at the Yazoo Pass—surely had been given full and fruitless trial.

Grant "had confidently promised the Washington authorities that he would be in Vicksburg before the end of March, and now his credit had fallen. With 130,000 men at his disposal, and over 50,000 immediately at hand, he seemed to be, and geographically was, further from Vicksburg than Sherman's 30,000 had been at Christmas. Lincoln and Halleck began to show signs of impatience.... The despondency induced by the multiple checks was not lessened for Grant by the suspicion that his subordinate, McClernand, was again at work to oust him. Sickness, too, of a malarial type, was rampant among the troops after the wet and trying winter in this flooded country. And Grant, in consequence, was now being energetically chased by press and public as a scapegoat for prospective sacrifice."[9]

On the other hand, Pemberton's staunch and successful series of defenses repelling Grant's ingenious, if narrow, maneuvers had created a feeling of genuine confidence in the minds of Pemberton's fellow officers, the defending troops, and the now grateful Mississippians.

CHAPTER IX

Grant Tries Again

PORTER FELL INTO Grant's newest plan at once: "The co-operation of the navy was absolutely essential to the success (even to the contemplation) of such an enterprise," writes Grant in describing his new-born designs. The experiment now to be tried called for the passage of the Vicksburg batteries by the Union navy, so that, if the Federal troops could somehow be got below Vicksburg, at least part of the fleet would be there to protect their crossing to the river's other side.

So it was while Grant's land forces had been vainly trying to change and channel the river's course, the navy determined to attempt the running of the river as it was. The *Queen of the West,* under Charles R. Ellet, had already succeeded; down and past the Vicksburg batteries on February 2, she found herself free to roam the river's length as far as Port Hudson— the important Confederate work on the same side of the river as Vicksburg, that is, the east. This portion of the river was a near three-hundred-mile stretch of clear water, vastly important since it included the outlet of the Red River—by which provisions from Louisiana and Texas came through the trans-Mississippi country.

Unmatched in audacity, hard and sharp as a diamond, young Ellet pounced upon three Confederate supply ships and then started on a second raid without meeting serious opposition. But on the fourteenth of that month of February, the *Queen of the West* was captured in the Red River by the Southerners. (Ellet, with some of the crew, drifted safely downstream on cotton bales.) Now under Confederate command, Ellet's Federal ironclad, together with the *Webb* and two cotton-clad steamers, returned to the Mississippi, bent on retaliation against the invading Union craft. First to be attacked and captured was the Union's *Indianola*. For a brief interval thereafter control of the Mississippi's three hundred miles between Vicksburg and Port Hudson was once again in Southern hands.

Up to this time Grant had never met Lincoln.[1] Not yet the hero of Vicksburg or Pemberton's captor, Grant was to all appearances hopelessly entangled in the defender's toils. Now, his failures in mind, visitors to the Union camps went home with dismal stories to relate to the anxious Lincoln, asserting, Grant tells in his *Memoirs,* that the Union Commander was "idle, incompetent and unfit to command men in an emergency." Press and public clamored with equal insistence for Grant's removal, suggesting as his successor, McClellan (the Philadelphian), Frémont, Hunter, and others. With all the pressure brought to bear upon him, Lincoln stood by Grant to the end. This was the time of Lincoln's apocryphal retort as to the magical effect of certain brands of whiskey. If he indulged in the repartee so widely attributed to him, Lincoln's *bon mot* lacked originality in any aspect. Over a hundred years earlier, "King George II of England had been so far converted by young Wolfe's merits and the disasters which had befallen earlier commanders, that when Lord Newcastle declared that General Wolfe was mad and ill-qualified to enter the lists against Montcalm (secure in Quebec), the King retorted: 'Mad is he? Then all I can say is, I hope he will bite some of my other Generals.' "[2]

The following month (on the fourteenth of March) Farragut finally ran the Port Hudson batteries, commanded for
the Confederates by Major Frank Gardner of Pemberton's
Department.   Only Farragut on his flagship, the *Hartford,*
and one other ship from his fleet at the Gulf of Mexico got
by.   But they soon were joined by one of Ellet's rams which,
in turn, had run the Vicksburg batteries, and the control of
the Red River then passed into Union hands.

At the near approach of "the seaman who achieved most
for the Union," a man of Southern birth and married to a
Southern woman, the paradox of Farragut's and Pemberton's
swapping sides appeared the more extraordinary.   "Born in
Tennessee, of a Tennessee mother and a Minorquin father, he
[Farragut] had passed nearly half of his short early life ashore
in New Orleans.   Adopted almost as a son by the famous
Captain David Porter, he had sailed away from that port at
the age of nine—to return more than half a century later, with
a fleet organized at the suggestion of David Porter's son, and
to the command of which he had been appointed upon his
urging. . . . his conception of duty called him to stay with the
Union.   He left Norfolk and retired to New York, whence he
reported himself as ready for duty.   And there he stayed, for
the better part of a year.   There was, in some circles, a reluctance to put officers of southern birth and connections in
command in those days.   It was at the urging of the younger
Porter that Farragut was brought from his semi-retirement
and sent to the Gulf, there to become the most famous of
American sailors."[3]

On the other hand, Pemberton's conception of duty caused
him to go South, though neither he, nor any member of his
family, ever owned a slave or aspired to!   But what of that?
Had not President Lincoln on taking his oath of office sol-
emnly proclaimed: ". . . I declare that I have no purpose,

directly or indirectly, to interfere with the institution of slavery where it exists. I believe I have no lawful right to do so; I have no inclination to do so."

Although Ellet of the Union navy had earlier run the Vicksburg batteries on board the *Queen of the West,* her sister ship in the successful dash, the *Indianola,* was soon a hulk and the *Queen* was in Confederate hands. Up to this time, therefore, Grant's long campaign, despite the Union navy's support, had indisputably been a failure. By elimination, then, ultimate conquest of Vicksburg and its unwavering defender beckoned down the river. But how? It was a brief last period of success for Southern arms in Mississippi; and for Pemberton these were the supreme hours of his life as a soldier.

With the prompt addition of promised guns and cavalry, Pemberton felt he could hold his ground, at least until the arrival of essential reinforcements, even if all were not brought up at once.

Telegraphing from his headquarters at Jackson, Mississippi, Pemberton advised the President on March 11: "I have fully 20,000 effectives for defense of Vicksburg and over 15,000 at Port Hudson.... If enemy increases his fleet you will have to increase my *guns.*"[4] Manifestly, the first and primary cause if Vicksburg fell would be the shortage of heavy guns on the river front; the trifling aggregate, it so transpired, *did* render it utterly impossible to prevent the passage of the Union gunboats for long. The batteries from Snyder's Mills to Vicksburg, a distance of nearly ten miles, mounted not more than thirty-five guns, and those directly fronting the city mounted but twenty-eight, of which there were two smooth-bore thirty-two pounders, two twenty-four pounders, one thirty pounder Parrott, one Whitworth, and one ten-inch mortar. To further handicap the defense, two of the firing pieces burst during the siege.[5] Every possible exertion was made to procure accessions to the ordnance, even guns indispensable to the pitifully few Confederate watercraft being diverted to the army's use.

But "the Confederate powder mills, armories and arsenals were inadequate to the enormous demands on them.... They were created from nothing and worked with improvised equipment and substitute materials.... In charge was General Josiah Gorgas, of Alabama, father of the surgeon who, half a century later, led the United States Army in the conquest of tropical diseases and so made possible the Panama Canal." It must not be lost sight of that "the South had to provide from her seven millions of white population, an army larger than that of Imperial France";[6] and from a nation of agriculturists, countless strange instruments of war to enable her soldiers to keep the field. There were few answers to Pemberton's requisitions for Vicksburg.

Meanwhile, the Valley of the Mississippi was beset by Union armies so that it was difficult to find a safe passage across the river for the supplies furnished by the prairies of Texas and Louisiana. Moreover, communication with Arkansas likewise was slow—and uncertain. Notwithstanding these burdening conditions, to maintain possession of the great waterway seemed more and more important. As the sea power of the Union grew day by day, from Cairo to New Orleans, nearly every mile of the great river was patrolled by Federal gunboats; "and in deep water, from the ports of the Atlantic to the road-steads of the Gulf of Mexico, Union frigates held to their vigilant blockade."

Between December 24, 1862, and January 5, 1863, Pemberton's Department was strengthened by the addition of approximately 13,000 infantry and field artillery. The Department was weakened during the same period by the withdrawal under General Joseph E. Johnston's orders of at least three-quarters of all cavalry.[7] This force, 6,000 horsemen under command of Van Dorn, was transferred to Tennessee—to make a diversion in favor of General Bragg.

And there in Tennessee Van Dorn and cavalry remained, while Mississippi was overrun by the mounted forces of the North. Meantime, Pemberton—like Lee at Gettysburg in Stuart's absence—deprived of his eyes, became a blinded leader dangerously in the dark. From the day of Van Dorn's depart-ure, the positions, numbers, and movements of Grant's various corps reached Pemberton only after long delay, often too late. Without cavalry, he had no way of knowing what disaster might result from movement in any direction; or what oppor-tunity he might lose completely at any time by failure to con-centrate or disperse his forces.

Before the emergency became acute, Pemberton protested only mildly. From Jackson on March 21 he telegraphed to General Johnston in Tullahoma, Tennessee: "Have you sep-arated the Cavalry with Gen'l Van Dorn from my command entirely? If so, it very much diminishes my ability to defend the Northern portion of the State as the planting season comes on."[8] Three days later, in reply to General Buckner in Mobile, Alabama, Pemberton telegraphed: "I cannot spare an infantry soldier from this command, but want your cavalry regiment for our mutual good for northeastern counties, to enable planters to sow crops. The enemy press me on all sides."[9]

Major General Simon Bolivar Buckner, whose cavalry Pem-berton so badly needed, was a West Point graduate. At the war's start he had been commander of Kentucky's forces, and later on had surrendered to Grant the Confederate garrison at Fort Donelson.

Other appeals were made by Pemberton to Buckner, but all failed of results. On April 27 the hard-pressed Vicksburg defender turned again to his superior, Johnston: "However necessary cavalry may be to Army of Tennessee, it is indispensable to me to keep my communications. The enemy are to-day at Hazlehurst, on New Orleans and Jackson Railroad. *I cannot defend every station on the road with infantry.* Am compelled to bring down cavalry from Northern Mississippi here, and the whole of that section is consequently left open. Further, these raids endanger my vital positions."[10]

Fully aware that Grant was making heavy cavalry raids into the northern part of the state, Pemberton necessarily used large numbers of his infantry to hold important and widely separated points against these cavalry incursions. But these make-shift attempts to fight cavalry with infantry were soon thrown out of gear by the government's sudden and ill-timed policy of gingerly increasing forces elsewhere.

On April 7 (1863) Pemberton received a telegram from the President, inquiring as to the practicability of his sending reinforcements to General Bragg in Middle Tennessee. The telegram directed immediate compliance if existing circumstances in the Department would admit of it. Less than two weeks before, Pemberton had been forced to deny General Loring's similar request. To Loring he had replied: "It is utterly impossible to give you 5,000 more men.... Neither can I ... send you any more heavy guns.... Have already sent more [ammunition] than can be spared from other places.... I have many other calls upon me."[11] In informing the President that he needed every man in his command, Pemberton added: "Enemy is constantly in motion in all directions.... My operations west of Mississippi must greatly depend on movements of the enemy's gunboats."[12]

According to the *Official Records,* the North, at the beginning of this month of April, had more than 900,000 soldiers under arms; the South, so far as can be ascertained, not more than 600,000. Slowly but surely, before the pressure of greater

numbers the Confederacy's frontiers were contracting. Nor
did uncertainty of reinforcement and wide dispersion point
to success in the forthcoming Vicksburg campaign—with Pemberton fatally and additionally hampered by the desire of the
President to hold Vicksburg at all cost. Yet did the government forget the value of time, "and the grand principle of
concentration at the decisive point."

As spring advanced, and the dirt roads became practicable
for the enemy's artillery and wagons, Pemberton hastened to
so advise Colonel B. S. Ewell, chief of General Johnston's staff.
The advice to Ewell detailed many signs indicating Grant's
intention to establish a base of operations higher up the river
by means of his boats and by repairing and connecting the
railroads at Memphis. Pemberton went on to point out to
Ewell that not only could Grant thus draw supplies from
northwest Mississippi, but, what was of more import, that
his activity "also affords him a means of rapidly concentrating
his troops from Middle and West Tennessee for operations
against Vicksburg.... Should he continue his threatening attitude against Vicksburg and Port Hudson by the Mississippi
River, and move a heavy force by land from the base supposed,
unless greatly re-enforced in infantry I shall need all the cavalry force withdrawn from this department, under General
Van Dorn, to cut his [Grant's] communications. The enemy
is now using every effort to get possession of Vicksburg."[13]

During all this period of fencing and constant movement
between the belligerents, all reports received by Pemberton
seem to have been transmitted by him to Johnston in the words
of the Confederate scouts; hence Johnston would appear to
have been as fully informed as Pemberton, and equally able
to judge whether the reports were reliable. If they were, Grant
had never deviated from Vicksburg as his target—feints, raids,
and movement elsewhere being no more than camouflage.

Nonetheless, the camouflage partially succeeded, since on April 11 Pemberton wired Johnston: "I think most of Grant's forces are being withdrawn to Memphis." However, almost immediately a revealing letter of Lincoln's to Grant appeared in the papers. This letter's contents, plus the arrival in Memphis of Inspector General Lorenzo Thomas of the United States army and a further report from scout Eastham, together indicated that a new stab at Vicksburg was imminent.

While all this swirling activity went forward in Pemberton's Department, the gunboat flotilla of Admiral Porter lay in snug anchorage along the Mississippi's banks. The boats faced towards Vicksburg, waiting for Grant's signal to make the dash below the city's batteries.

Just above the mouth of the Yazoo dense forests came down to the river's edge and shrouded the restless fleet. Moreover, the swamps were a further obstacle to scouts' prying movements from the land side, and on the closely patrolled river there was little likelihood of Confederate reconnaissance. But one day a small skiff was detected, quietly and mysteriously moving upstream towards the fleet. When overhauled, a tiny white flag was run up. This, it soon developed, covered the presence of Brigadier General Jacob Thompson. Thompson had been secretary of the interior during Buchanan's presidency, now was inspector general of Pemberton's army. After some conversation with Grant, the "Rebel" was allowed to return downstream on his skiff "no wiser than he had come, as to the Union fleet's place of concealment."[14]

After Thompson's perplexed departure, Admiral Porter went ahead with the interrupted buttressing of the Federal gunboats and transports. Bales of hay and cotton, bolstered by sacks of grain, were stacked around the vessels' boilers for protection and to conceal the ships' fires. Furthermore, the hay and grain would be useful below. Finally all was ready.

And so, at ten o'clock on the night of April 16, Porter's
flagship in the lead, the stealthy procession got under way.
There were seven gunboats and three transports, the latter
towing barges. Grant's six months' hunt for a dry place to
stand and attack was about to be rewarded: the way to Vicksburg was about to be found.

It will be recalled that the Union leader's search had commenced in November, 1862. Convinced, says Liddell Hart, that
his past months' hammer-and-tongs warfare would be repulsed for an indefinite span, Grant had now changed to a
more difficult and complicated operation along the river. This
new strategy distinctly marked the navy's assumption of the
leading role. Vicksburg and Pemberton's army from this
time on were to be subjected to warfare of a different pattern:
encirclement, preceded by widely scattered cavalry infiltra-
tions. Unopposed, the cavalry kept going—even to the sea.

Two days before, and the day of the Union fleet's passage
of his thin cluster of waterfront batteries, Pemberton notified
Johnston that, according to reports of scouts, Grant had ordered two hundred wagons sent down from Helena and that
all of the Vicksburg army was coming up. The enemy spoke
of mounting two thousand men, in addition to eight hundred
cavalry, to scout around Corinth. "Reports reach me from
the front, that enemy are sending more troops down to assault
Vicksburg soon."[15]

Of the accuracy of his deductions, Pemberton was not long
in doubt, and he shortly followed this report with a fuller
letter. His record in interpreting the enemy's moves is, like
that of Lee, remarkable when we recall that his Department's intelligence service at this time had no help from the
cavalry on any sector. To Johnston he had said, on the thirteenth, that he was establishing depots at Macon, Meridian,
Enterprise, and Columbia. He felt that, without a cavalry

force much larger than any available within his Department, it was not safe to locate depots above Macon—beyond any possibility of protection from enemy raids.[16]

Upon his first convincing intimation of the enemy's intentions, Pemberton promptly notified Johnston that the plans of the enemy apparently had been changed or that "his movement up the river was a ruse. I ought to have back Buford's Brigade; certainly no more troops should leave this Department. . . . 'Sixty-four steamers left Memphis since Thursday, loaded with soldiers and negroes, ostensibly to assault Vicksburg.' The raft in Yazoo, at Snyder's Mill, has given way and gone entirely. Am therefore forced to strengthen batteries there, at the expense of Vicksburg."[17]

Barren of results as were Pemberton's urgent and renewed applications for some helpful measure of reinforcement, more particularly the return of his so sorely needed cavalry; unheeded as went his sober, timely warnings as to the probable theatre and manner of the enemy's next assaults—candor here calls for acknowledgment that in March, Johnston's praise was warm indeed in recognition of Pemberton's foresight and exertions. Congratulating him in handsome fashion, Johnston wrote: "Your activity and vigor in the defence of Mississippi must have secured for you the confidence of the people of the State—that of the Government you had previously won. . . . I have no apprehension for Port Hudson from Banks. The only fear is, that the Canal may enable Grant to unite their forces. I believe your arrangements at Vicksburg make it perfectly safe, unless that union should be effected. Van Dorn's cavalry is absolutely necessary to enable General Bragg to hold the best part of the country from which he draws supplies."[18]

Johnston was still commanding from Tennessee when this letter was written. From Chattanooga, his sphere of authority stretched out over a vast territory and included sections of the country of more value to the North than any other—with the exception of Richmond only. His position was not an easy one; with both his Mississippi and Tennessee armies in danger, he didn't feel that he should weaken one for the other. To increase Johnston's difficulties, he had no authority over the Confederate forces in Arkansas, which, it so happened, he considered to be the only area from which reinforcements could be spared for Pemberton. Over Johnston's objection, Pemberton finally got from Bragg the division of Major General C. L. Stevenson; but Bragg was permitted to retain Pemberton's cavalry under Van Dorn. Splendid fighter that Stevenson was, Pemberton continued destitute of cavalry!

Thus matters stood in Pemberton's Department on the night of April 16 when Admiral Porter's fleet started down the river. First signs of the approach of Porter reached Pemberton's ears through hurried messages relayed from pickets in small Confederate river boats. These vigilant water folk had to their consternation "found bearing down on them from above a darkened and muffled fleet. They gave the alarm and then, instead of making for Vicksburg and safety, they paddled for the Louisiana shore, held by Federal forces, where they fired houses in the village of De Soto, to light up the river for the Confederate gunners on the opposite bluffs. So doing, the courageous pickets not only ran the risk of capture, but put themselves in the direct line of fire from the Confederate batteries booming away at the moving fleet as it passed between the guns and the light of the burning houses."[19] The blazing cotton was all afire on one of the transports—the *Henry Clay*— disabled by the shore batteries; and the bonfires on the bluffs further lighted up the fleet's passage. The scene soon became pyrotechnical in the extreme.

In expectation of a heavy loss, Sherman had four yawl-boats hauled across the swamps until they got below Vicksburg.

This done, he manned these awkward craft with soldiers ready to pick up wrecks which were expected to float by. Sherman himself was watching in the stream as the fleet lurched past, a vivid account of this action appearing in his *Memoirs*.

Porter's was truly a naval feat, though Pemberton's batteries were nothing like as formidable as anticipated. Still, the Vicksburg gauntlet was run with surprisingly little loss, and so provided Grant with an adequate reserve of food, ready for his army when in time it should get below.

On the night of April 16 no less than ten vessels got by, the only casualty of consequence having been the burning of one lone transport, although some of the barges lashed alongside were likewise lost. Soon half a dozen more transports started and—with one exception—ran through successfully some six days later. Now Grant had all the boats he needed to lift his army to the eastern bank. There his troops would be dangerously on Pemberton's left flank.

President Davis was immediately advised of these portentous developments, Pemberton reporting to him: "The passage of batteries at Vicksburg by a large number of enemy's vessels, on the night of [16th], shows conclusively that we have an insufficient number of guns. There are so many points to be defended at this time—Vicksburg, Grand Gulf, Port Hudson, Snyder's Mill, and Fort Pemberton—that I have only twenty-eight guns at Vicksburg. Of these, two are smooth-bore 32s, two 24s, one 30-pounder Parrott, one Whitworth, and one 10-inch mortar. Vicksburg and Port Hudson, and if possible Grand Gulf, ought to be greatly strengthened in guns. I have also sent 4,000 men from Port Hudson to General Johnston. The enemy has eleven armed vessels between Vicksburg and Port Hudson. A large supply of ammunition and projectiles should be constantly forwarded."[20]

Of the twenty-eight guns at this time in position at Vicksburg, five, when "set off," had proved incapable of carrying shot a sufficient distance to reach the passing vessels—much less do them the slightest damage.[21]

Johnston likewise received prompt notification from Pemberton of Porter's successful passage. He was further advised: "Enemy has now nine boats between Vicksburg and Port Hudson. He has land-forces at New Carthage from Grant's army, and can re-enforce them to any extent. He can use his nine boats to cross his troops to this [the east] side."[22]

Pemberton's army still held the lines it had occupied for the past six months; yet, as a profound British soldier has well said, "The strength of a position is measured not by the impregnability of the front, but by the security of the flanks."[23]

When the Union fleet weathered and passed Pemberton's batteries, his left flank was no longer secure—and he knew it. Had he not notified General Johnston on April 17 that it was practicable for Grant to cross his army to the east side of the river, since from then on Grant had sufficient boats below Vicksburg to do so?

Months earlier, Johnston had formed a very definite opinion of the proper strategy that should be employed by Pemberton "for driving Grant off." To Pemberton he had said in a letter from Jackson, dated December 31, 1862: "It seems to me that in Vicksburg we should have just the force necessary to its defence: the remaining infantry, to constitute an active army, which, if you should be invested, might attack the enemy in rear. This seems to me the only chance for driving him off. Should he invest the force you have ordered to the place, the remaining force, only 11,000, could not attack with decided hope of success. At the same time, your auxiliary positions, Chickasaw Bayou and Snyder's Mills, depend for connection with the place upon the difficulty of the ground along the

Yazoo. I fear that the Federals may causeway the swamp, as
well as bridge the Lake. In which event, upon reaching the
firm ground, the garrisons of the outposts would either be
captured or driven off. I regret that so difficult a system was
undertaken. By holding Vicksburg alone, with the other
troops in observation, I think we would have been safer."[24]

There can be no sort of doubt that Johnston underestimated
the defensive strength of "the difficult system" undertaken by
Pemberton; for Pemberton—though Johnston in Tennessee
had not yet received the intelligence—had written but a day
before telling of his sharp repulse of Sherman's and Admiral
Porter's joint attack at Chickasaw Bayou, December 28 and
29. Johnston's apprehension that the garrisons of Pemberton's outposts "would either be captured or driven off" had
been dispelled; instead, it was Sherman and Porter who had
been driven off by Pemberton.

And now, though Grant was below and accessible to Pemberton's left flank, "Johnston held back directing the abandonment of Port Hudson, of Vicksburg and its dependencies,"
should it be necessary to do so in order to beat Grant or hold
him in his tracks. "Instead," says Pemberton, "I received
neither instructions nor suggestions. Strangely I was not then
ordered, when it was practicable, to concentrate and to attack
Grant immediately on his landing! I would not then have
been in doubt as to Johnston's intentions; and I would at least
have had the time to concentrate and provide transportation
and supplies in part. But all such orders were withheld by
Johnston until near two weeks hence. Up to the 2nd of May
at best, Johnston gave me no intimation that under *any* circumstances I should abandon Vicksburg and its outposts to
repel Grant. By May 2nd, Grant had made his crossing and
fought a winning battle at Port Gibson.[25]

"With the President's and my estimate of Vicksburg's importance to the success of the Confederate cause, I would have been in heart a traitor to that cause had I weakened the place and its flank defences—while still in doubt where Grant might attempt a landing. To have concentrated an army of sufficient strength to warrant a reasonable hope of successfully encountering Grant's very superior forces at Grand Gulf, Bruinsburg, Rodney or elsewhere, would have meant stripping Vicksburg and its outposts of even the slimmest protection. Then, indeed, would Vicksburg have fallen an easy prize."

Then Pemberton continues: "Was not Sherman's large force—two thirds of my entire strength—still at Haines' Bluff on the City's very rim, prepared to march in if I marched out."[26] On turning to the Federal leader's *Memoirs,* it will be seen this was precisely the movement planned for Sherman's troops. Grant has thus outlined the course he then proposed for his lieutenant: "Since Sherman had not yet left his position above Vicksburg, on the morning of the 27th I ordered him to create a diversion by moving his corps up the Yazoo and threatening an attack on Haines' Bluff. My object was to compel Pemberton to keep as much force about Vicksburg as I could, until I could secure a good footing on high land east of the river." Then Grant adds, "The move was eminently successful...." Could it have been otherwise, with Pemberton so clearly, to purloin the South's expressive phrase, "between Hell and Harper's Ferry"?

Pemberton had now to contend with the devastating raid of the Union cavalry—some seventeen hundred horsemen under the command of Colonel B. H. Grierson. At least one highly reputed military authority holds this to be "the most successful cavalry raid during the war, or during any other war."[27] No doubt it was, since of opposition there was none at all.

Pemberton's plight at this time is vividly mirrored in an

importunate telegram he addressed some days later to Lieutenant General Edmund Kirby Smith, across the river at
Shreveport, Louisiana. General Smith was informed: "...the
country from the Mississippi River towards Jackson [is] open
to the approaches of the enemy. My cavalry is weak and
wholly inadequate, either to cut the lines of communication
of the enemy with the Mississippi River, or to guard and protect my own. Vicksburg (consequently the navigation of the
Mississippi River) is the vital point indispensable to be held.
Nothing can be done which might jeopardize it. My force is
insufficient for offensive operations. I must stand on the defensive, at all events, until re-enforcements reach me. You
can contribute materially to the defence of Vicksburg, and the
navigation of the Mississippi River, by a movement upon the
line of communication of the enemy on the western side of the
River. He derives his supplies and his re-enforcements, for
the most part, by a route which leads from Milliken's Bend
to New Carthage, La., a distance of some thirty-five or forty
miles. To break this would render a most important service.
I trust you will be able, as I know you desire, to co-operate
with me in this vital undertaking. I hope you will let me
hear from you."[28]

Colonel Grierson's raid was under way on the very morning
Porter got his fleet below Vicksburg. A few miles out from
Memphis, at La Grange on the Memphis and Charleston Railroad, the two-weeks' raid of Union cavalry started out, wrecking railroads and causing panic from one end of Mississippi
to the other. To meet the threat, Pemberton unceasingly
strove against farmers' opposition to impress private horses,
with which he subsequently mounted his *infantry*. Always
was the scant total of animals gathered up "relinquished with
the piteous lamentations of the local inhabitants, whose lands
were thereby stripped of the means of plowing, and cultivating

their meager produce." But horses were a grave necessity.

Stations, bridges, and railroad trackage were effectively destroyed by Grierson's raiders, and Pemberton's transportation of supplies was much embarrassed. Beyond this, Grierson had caused a heavy diversion of the forces under Pemberton, who thus summarized the raid's cost to him: "About the 16th or 17th of April simultaneously with the passage of the Vicksburg batteries by the enemy's gunboats, I learned that several columns of Federal cavalry starting from different points were making inroads into the northern part of Mississippi and that one of them under Colonel Grierson was apparently strong enough and bold enough to push on perhaps to the southern limits of the Department. Strong enough to defy any cavalry that I could oppose to it, and to destroy my depots with their large accumulation of subsistence and quartermaster's supplies, the workshops of the Department as well as railroads, and to break up or interrupt to my serious detriment the communications of the latter, unless protected by a sufficient force of infantry.... Purposes of plunder had nothing to do with the preparation or execution of Grierson's movement, but I did fear, and not without reason, that it was part and parcel of the formidable invasion preparing under my eyes. It had indeed so effective a share in Grant's combined operations, that it compelled me to divert Loring's entire Division to the line of the Mobile & Ohio, and other railroads, when I most needed the presence of this Division nearer Vicksburg."[29]

So great, indeed, was the consternation created by Grierson's expedition that it was impossible for Pemberton to obtain any reliable information of the enemy's movements, rumor placing him in various places at the same time.[30] In consequence of his great deficiency in cavalry, the force of that arm in his command being scarcely adequate for the necessary picketing, Pemberton was powerless to acquaint himself with the raiders' rapid and changing movements, but only knew in the most general way of their ravages.

General Johnston having informed Pemberton about the middle of April that he had ordered a cavalry brigade to him, but it never having *entered* the limits of Pemberton's department, the latter on April 20 addressed the following communication to his superior at Tullahoma: "Heavy raids are making from Tennessee deep into this State. One is reported now at Starkville, 30 miles west of Columbus. Cavalry is indispensable to meet these expeditions. The little that I have is on the field there, but totally inadequate. Could you not make a demonstration with a cavalry force on their rear.... I have literally no cavalry from Grand Gulf to Yazoo City, while the enemy is threatening to pass the river between Vicksburg and Grand Gulf, having now twelve vessels below the former place."[31] Nor, for the want of necessary water transportation, could Pemberton operate effectively on the *west* bank of the river, where Grant's corps were speedily gathering in force.

Placing Major General Loring in command of all available Confederate troops to meet these Federal raids as far as possible, Pemberton was constrained to limit that General's operations with the following instructions: "... Not to leave the line of the road [Mobile and Ohio Railroad] for any great distance, to keep in telegraphic communication with me, and constantly to advise me of his position, and that, operations upon that line being minor in importance to those upon the Mississippi River, his troops must be so disposed as to enable him to move them in that direction at a moment's notice."[32] Then, hoping that Richmond might be able to prod Johnston into returning some of his cavalry, Pemberton urged Adjutant and Inspector General Cooper to lend his aid: "I have so little cavalry in this department that I am compelled to divert a portion of my infantry to meet raids in Northern Mississippi.

If any troops can possibly be spared from other departments, I think they should be sent here."[33]

In the impressment of horses and their necessary equipments, Pemberton's officers were loyally aided by the Governor of Mississippi, who also mounted by the same process a portion of the state troops in northern Mississippi. All the cavalry that was thus variously collected was eventually placed under the command of the energetic and highly capable Colonel Wirt Adams. But outside of "a smart skirmish near Union Church, Colonel Adams' force was too weak to effect anything important."[34] And so it continued till the end, Johnston replying to Pemberton's requests with this unchanged ultimatum: "In the present aspect of affairs, General Van Dorn's cavalry is much more needed in this department [Tennessee] than in that of Mississippi and Eastern Louisiana, and cannot be sent back as long as this state of things exists. You have now in your department five brigades of the troops you most require, viz., infantry belonging to the Army of Tennessee. This is more than a compensation for the absence of General Van Dorn's cavalry command."[35]

Lee without cavalry at Gettysburg, Hooker without cavalry at Chancellorsville, Pemberton without cavalry at Vicksburg—all point the answer.

In Colonel G. F. R. Henderson's *Stonewall Jackson* the author concludes: "Stoneman's absence proved the ruin of the Federal army [at Chancellorsville]....Jackson...was asked what he thought of Hooker's plan of campaign. His reply was: 'It was in the main a good conception, an excellent plan. But he should not have sent away his cavalry; that was his great blunder....Had he kept his cavalry with him, his plan would have been a very good one.'"[36]

As to the effect of Lee's fighting without cavalry the first few days at Gettysburg, his biographer has written: "Once

in Pennsylvania, Lee's operations were handicapped not only
because he lacked sufficient cavalry, but also because he did
not have Stuart at hand.... in Stuart's absence, he had no
satisfactory form of military intelligence.... Had 'Jeb' Stuart
been at hand, Lee would have had early information of the
advance of the Federals and either would have outfooted them
to Gettysburg or would have known enough about their great
strength to refrain from attacking as he did...." After the
battle, Lee told Captain Ross, the Austrian observer, "that his
lack of accurate knowledge of the enemy's concentration was
due to the absence of Stuart's cavalry." Several years after
the war, Lee, on April 15, 1868, wrote to one William M.
McDonald: "As to the battle of Gettysburg, I must again
refer you to my official accounts. Its loss was occasioned by
a combination of circumstances. It was commenced in the
absence of correct intelligence."[37]

Once before, in August, 1862, Lee had suffered from his
cavalry's absence. Then he nearly reached Bull Run too late
to unite with Stonewall Jackson; he was near to not being
at Second Manassas at all. On the morning of August 27,
Lee and his staff were suddenly confronted, on the road near
Salem, with a detachment of Federal cavalry. "Who were
the Federals, and what did their presence signify? Lee had
no cavalry to whom he could look for an answer.... time was
lost, valuable time, in trying to ascertain what a regiment of
cavalry could have established in half an hour. So much for
the mistake in detaching the whole of the cavalry to help
Jackson."[38]

Nor had Pemberton, after Van Dorn was detached under
Johnston's orders, cavalry to whom he could look for answer
to his questions and intelligence of Grant's and Sherman's
movements. And consequently, as with Lee at Gettysburg,
Pemberton's actions were of necessity often commenced and

continued entirely "in the absence of correct intelligence."

About March 11, fearing that Grant might succeed in opening a canal practicable for the passage of gunboats and transports across the peninsula opposite Vicksburg (in which enterprise his failure has been remarked), Pemberton considered
it prudent to occupy and fortify Grand Gulf, at the mouth of
the Big Black River. Furthermore, Grand Gulf was also on
the eastern shore of the Mississippi River, about twenty-five
miles below Vicksburg in direct line, and nearly fifty as the
river winds. Brigadier General John S. Bowen, with his Missouri Brigade, was accordingly assigned to that point. His instructions were to construct batteries for the protection of the
mouth of the Big Black and as a secondary obstacle to the
navigation of the Mississippi River. Shortly after his arrival
Bowen saw to it that Pemberton's orders were promptly executed, viz., that the approaches by the Bayou Pierre were prepared for defense on both sides. Within ten days Bowen had
mounted five heavy guns and made them ready for service.
It being impracticable to obtain them elsewhere, Pemberton
reluctantly removed two guns from his Vicksburg batteries,
while three more intended for gunboats in the trans-Mississippi Department were detained by his order.[39] In no other
way could Grand Gulf have been fortified, even so slenderly.

On April 17, 1863, Bowen was hurriedly notified of the passage of the Vicksburg batteries by Admiral Porter's flotilla.
He was also immediately reinforced by the Sixth Mississippi
Regiment, the First Confederate battalion, and a field battery.[40]
Insufficient as Pemberton knew Grand Gulf's batteries to be,
they were the very heaviest he could place there. It should be
recalled here that the position had not been selected for land
defense, but for the protection of the mouth of the Big Black
and as a precautionary measure against the passage of transports. Nevertheless, the batteries, such as they were, had been

constructed by Bowen so as to be capable of defense against an assault from the river front as well as against a direct attack from or across the Big Black.[41]   In consequence, when Porter's flotilla and Grant's transports succeeded in passing down sufficient vessels to cross the Federal troops—from the west to the east bank of the river—the position of Grand Gulf, *above,* lost most of its obstructive strength.   Nevertheless, it still held some threat, so that from Vicksburg, distant forty miles by dirt road, and from Jackson, over forty-five (in addition to a considerable run by rail), Pemberton's hard task of reinforcement went ahead without let-up.   Handicapped by a serious dearth of guns, ammunition, and wagons,[42] a substantial portion of the reinforcements would arrive too late.

In the midst of all these scattered exertions, General Bowen telegraphed Pemberton on April 28 that "transports and barges loaded down with troops are landing at Hard Times, on the west bank."   To this, Pemberton immediately replied: "Have you now force enough to hold your position.   If not, give me the smallest additional number with which you can.   My small cavalry force necessitates the use of infantry to protect important points."[43]

How had Grant's troops gotten to Hard Times?   Though Porter's exploits in running past the feeble Vicksburg batteries had shown that empty transports could be carried past them, some other way to move the troops needed to be found. "Milliken's Bend, on the right bank, is twenty miles upstream from Vicksburg.   Landing from the upper transports there, Grant's men marched by devious ways seventy miles through the wide Louisiana bottoms, to strike the main river again at Hard Times...."[44]

Just below Hard Times—over on the Mississippi side—stood Grand Gulf.   Suddenly, upon its newly-set-up batteries of five guns, Admiral Porter let fire from his encircling gunboats.

At the moment of their closing-in, it was just after daylight on April 29. Surprisingly, Porter's fleet met with no success; Bowen held out stubbornly. So that night the Union Admiral ran farther downriver—past Bowen and his trifling cannon. Meantime, Grant marched his troops from Hard Times to a landing below. "There, on April thirtieth, the army and the fleet met, and the crossing of the river began. By night of the thirtieth, the same night on which Hooker completed his concentration at Chancellorsville, Grant was across the Mississippi, at Bruinsburg, with twenty thousand men."[45]

CHAPTER X

Could Grant's Crossing Have Been Prevented?

"GRANT'S MOVEMENT should not have been unknown to Pemberton," concludes one of the more recent students of the campaign.[1] Historians generally have confirmed this judgment. Nonetheless, as Douglas Freeman has said in connection with criticisms of Lee's strategy in Maryland, the reader himself "must be the judge of the fairness of these criticisms." A biographer can only set down the facts; "the reader, at the same time, must examine all the circumstances in their relation to the desperate leadership of a desperate cause."[2] If this be done, it is necessary to inquire to what extent Pemberton was responsible for the dispersal of force in his Department— and for failure to concentrate against Grant on his first crossing to the east bank of the river.

In harping on the principle of concentration, critics generally have failed to bear in mind that its successful application in this instance depended upon the extent to which Pemberton could risk uncovering the rest of his unprotected Department (including, of course, Vicksburg) and the extent to which Grant's concentration could be prevented by distraction. For Grant's concentration could always overmatch Pemberton's since, except for Sherman's corps (at Haines's Bluff), there was no reason whatsoever for any dispersal of Union forces.

The only commanders with available forces to distract Grant on his march to concentrate on Pemberton's left flank were appealed to in vain: Generals Kirby Smith and Richard Taylor had been advised in detail that to break Grant's route of supplies, reinforcements, and communications on the western side of the river would render a most important service.[3] Johnston had been asked (April 20 and 22), "Can you not make a heavy demonstration with cavalry, etc."[4]

Grant's base of operations higher up on the river—on the western side—afforded him a means of rapidly concentrating his troops for operations against Vicksburg. Should he (Grant) move a heavy force by land from the base supposed (on the western side), unless greatly reinforced in infantry, Pemberton needed all the cavalry force withdrawn from his Department, under General Van Dorn, to cut Grant's communications. Grant had now land forces at New Carthage and could reinforce them to any extent; he could use his boats to cross his troops to the east side at will. Such was the heart and substance of Pemberton's reiterated contemporary advices.[5]

Certainly, Pemberton from the east bank was powerless to hinder Grant's march on the western side—with the Union gunboats between them "patrolling nearly every mile of the great river from Cairo to New Orleans." Moreover, even in the absence of such naval vigilance, Pemberton had no means of getting over to the western bank. This lack of any agency to bridge the river gap is clearly pictured in Pemberton's telegram of April 17 (1863) to Generals E. K. Smith and Richard Taylor. To them he said: "For the want of the necessary transportation, I cannot operate effectually on the west bank of the river; the enemy is now in force at New Carthage and Richmond. I beg your attention to this."[6]

Further along in the quoted critique of the Vicksburg campaign, astonishment is registered at Grant's landing having been unopposed: "To the amazement of all—no Confederates had appeared to dispute the landing of Grant's troops." This is not an uncommon point made against the Southern commander; it therefore deserves attention.

"Weighing necessity, advantage, and risk in the scales of his judgment," Pemberton virtually decided that it was demonstrably impossible to protect every foot of the river against Grant's landing. The distance from Vicksburg to Grand Gulf was "nearly fifty miles as the river winds," and there were no indications that a landing lower down the river might not (with equal probability) be chosen in preference to that selected in the end. To have concentrated an army of sufficient strength to repel Grant at Bruinsburg, Rodney, Grand Gulf, or elsewhere, would inevitably have meant turning over Vicksburg to Sherman. For Sherman with his large force, two-thirds of Pemberton's entire strength, was ceaselessly waiting and watching at Haines's Bluff near-by.

In his official report Pemberton thus graphically describes how Grant's landing came to be unopposed. "When, on April 28, General Bowen informed me by telegraph that 'transports and barges loaded down with troops were landing at Hard Times, on the west bank,' I made the best arrangements I could, if it became necessary to forward to his assistance as rapidly as possible all the troops not, in my opinion, absolutely indispensable to prevent a *coup de main,* should it be attempted against Vicksburg. It was indispensable to maintain a sufficient force to hold Snyder's Mill, Chickasaw Bayou, the Vicksburg city front, and Warrenton, a line of over 20 miles in length.

"In addition to his troops at Young's Point (whose strength I had no means of ascertaining), which constantly threatened my upper positions, the enemy had, as has already been shown, a large force at Hard Times and afloat on transports between Vicksburg and Grand Gulf....

"To concentrate my whole force south and east of Big Black for the support of General Bowen against a landing at Grand Gulf, or any point south of it not yet apparently even threatened, would, I think, have been unwise, to say the least of it. To show that I was not alone in my opinion, I add a telegram from General Stevenson, then commanding the troops in and about Vicksburg:

" 'The men will be ready to move promptly. To cross the Mississippi, both gunboats and transports must pass the batteries at Grand Gulf. An army large enough to defend itself on this side would consume much time in crossing. As it is not known what force has been withdrawn from this [the Vicksburg] front, it is not improbable that the force opposite Grand Gulf is there to lay waste the country on that side and a feint to withdraw troops from a main attack here. I [Stevenson] venture to express the hope that the troops will not be removed far until further developments below render it certain that they will cross in force.' "[7]

It was still black night on this same April 28 "when the sporadic fire of the Federal skirmish lines far off on the Confederate left, and across the river, broke into the steady rattle of an approaching general engagement." Bowen's night dispatch had no sooner been received than Pemberton hurried the news along to Johnston and to Davis—repeating his hope of aid from each. To Johnston in Tullahoma went this word: "The enemy is at Hard Times, Louisiana, in large force, with barges and transports, indicating an attack on Grand Gulf, with a view to Vicksburg. I must look to the Army of Tennessee to protect the approaches through Northern Mississippi."[8] Then followed quick notification to the President:

"A demonstration is now being made in large force at Hard Times. It is indispensable that I have more cavalry—The approaches to North Mississippi are almost unprotected and it is impossible to prevent these raids with Infantry."[9]

His superiors promptly apprised of the latest developments, Pemberton next directed Major General Stevenson at Vicksburg to hold 5,000 men in readiness to move to Grand Gulf on the requisition of General Bowen.[10]

To the gallant Bowen himself, Pemberton at the same time sent the following message of reassurance: "I have directed General Stevenson to have 5,000 men ready to move on your requisition, but do not make requisition unless absolutely necessary for the safety of your position. I am also making arrangements for sending you 2,000 or 3,000 men from this [Jackson] direction in case of necessity. You cannot communicate with me too frequently."[11]

In the darkest uncertainty as to what might be Grant's next move, to maintain that Pemberton, under all the circumstances recited, should have anticipated his opponent's specific point of debarkment is to argue that Pemberton should have been possessed of considerably more than mortal prescience in relation to the crafty and unhurried enemy across the river and, hence, still quite beyond his reach. Criticism of this character has been rejected by Jackson's famed biographer. In his view, "... it is too often overlooked, by those who study the history of campaigns, that war is the province of uncertainty. The reader has the whole theatre of war displayed before him. He notes the exact disposition of the opposing forces at each hour of the campaign, and with this in his mind's eye he condemns or approves the action of the commanders. In the action of the defeated general he usually often sees much to blame; in the action of the successful general but little to admire. But his judgment is not based on a true foundation. He has ignored the fact that the information at his disposal was not at the disposal of those he criticises. . . ."[12]

To quote but one other, Captain B. H. Liddell Hart, apropos of Pemberton's neglect to greet Grant's landing party: "Historically and practically, it is far more important to discover what information [opposing commanders] had, and the times at which it reached them, than to know the actual situation. . . . Those who believe that exactness is possible can never have known war, or must have forgotten it. And even if by supernatural means we could recreate the action . . . it would be historically valueless."[13]

Apart from his inability to divine Grant's exact crossing locale and, after that, to have on hand just the force necessary to check it without endangering the safety of Vicksburg and other points with whose safety he was likewise charged, Pemberton had looked to something more. He had hoped that his cohorts across the river would be able to break up Grant's immensely difficult sixty-mile trek, encumbered as were the Federals with long columns of wagon trains and all the other paraphernalia of an invading army.

The tedious march of the twenty thousand invaders who first reached the crossing goal on April 30 had started a month before. It had been not only a slow process; it had been a long nightmare. "Although the winter floods were beginning to recede, the wagon road to New Carthage was as yet barely above the water—and beneath it for a couple of miles at the further end, owing to a break in the levee. Across the submerged interval the troops had to be ferried in boats collected locally, and thus the leading division only reached New Carthage on April 6, and the others were still strung out far behind. And although the land route was drying too slowly, the water route was drying too fast. For, as a further complication, the shrinking level in the bayous soon nullified the original hope of ferrying the troops and supplies in barges by the inland waterways to New Carthage."[14]

Sherman had wisely been entrusted with the further task of improving and protecting the invaders' hazardously slender line of communication and supply.

In the end, a month was "spent in switching the Union forces sixty miles south of their camps above Vicksburg, and the time thus forfeited to nature's troublesome claims would probably have been fatal" had the Confederate forces on the western bank not suffered Grant to make this toilsome march wholly undisturbed. Yet Pemberton (from April 17 on) had kept pounding at Taylor, Smith, and Johnston for some movement upon Grant's western line of communication and supply. His final plea—four days after Sherman's corps, crossing, had been united to the other two—points to the heart of his unanswered entreaties: "You [Kirby Smith] can contribute materially to the defense of Vicksburg, and the navigation of the Mississippi River, by a movement upon the line of communication of the enemy on the western side of the River."[15]

It is an interesting commentary upon this strangely unmolested Union march to note that Sherman did his best to dissuade Grant therefrom, "representing how grossly he was overriding the fundamental axiom of strategy in exposure of his army...."[16]

Pemberton's great difficulties up to this point, before Grant crossed the river to his left flank, might be summarized as follows: He was charged with the defense of Vicksburg, Port Hudson, Jackson, Fort Pemberton, Grand Gulf, Snyder's Mills and Bruinsburg. These were all widely separated points on the Mississippi, and it was essential to the Confederacy that they be maintained.[17] The roads and communications between them were poor. Pemberton, thus restricted to the defensive, was anchored to various points and hence lost entire liberty of action. He had no cavalry to act as the eyes and ears of his army; he had no troops to hinder, delay, or obstruct the march of Grant's army on the western bank to the crossing at Hard Times and Bruinsburg. He had no means of determining where Grant's crossing might be undertaken and achieved.

In the dimness of this confusion, there took place a perilous change in Vicksburg's previous impregnability. Clearly, its further defense became a matter of greater and increasing difficulty, since to be besieged would cast a drastic limitation upon Pemberton's future checkmate of Grant's maneuvers. A blind man could foresee the consequences, unless relief arrived. To impose the hypnotic thought that west of the Mississippi would be for long territory of the Confederacy if Vicksburg fell was a phantasy in contempt of reason and possibility. Truly the South would be cut in two.

In the clear perspective of following years, Grant's grand strategy against Vicksburg boiled down, in those last despairing weeks, to snuffing out the army of Pemberton by starvation and stagnation. In Washington it seemed a tedious process.

The crossing of the Mississippi below Grand Gulf truly ranked as an event of capital importance. Yet, unless it could be assumed that Grant would be permitted—by the combined Confederate armies—to actually whittle away the defensive impregnability of Vicksburg, "the crossing" was still only preliminary to the real test of strength.

CHAPTER XI

Across the River: Port Gibson

VERILY HAD the spring of 1863 opened a third year of inde-
cisive battles. "By this time Jefferson Davis at Richmond saw
his worst forebodings fall short of the paralyzing facts, for the
Confederacy was strangled by a cordon of warships that
choked its ports.

"His government couldn't sell cotton to buy munitions, or
even to secure medical supplies so desperately begged for by
overflowing hospitals. Southern women brought out their
long-discarded spinning wheels and made rough cloth on hand
looms. Planters produced little or no cotton but more and
more corn to feed half-rationed troops.

"The commonest food brought such excessive prices that
even a [commanding general] had scarcely enough to eat. The
families of private soldiers suffered most because their pay in
depreciated currency would not keep the babes at home from
going hungry. Thousands of farm wives wrote their husbands, 'Me an' the chillun is starvin',' so that thousands of
husbands sneaked away from the front, went home and
planted some corn, then returned to duty. Officers had to
wink at their absence and nothing could be done to punish
these 'crop deserters' who kept the gray ranks thinned. . . .
New Orleans had fallen and the river below Vicksburg lay

open to Union warships.... Grant ... was moving southward
along the west bank of the Mississippi ... , his slow march
impeded by rising waters in the bayous and marshes of Louisiana.... Hurricane would lie directly in [the path of the fleet],
so the brother of the Confederate President must abandon his
property.... this place that represented the toil of a lifetime."[1]

As Porter, with his force of eight gunboats, assaulted Bowen
at Grand Gulf on the twenty-ninth of April, General Grant
seated himself comfortably in a chair lashed to the deck rail.
He was on board a small, fast tug, which, however, was without armament. "All this time McClernand's 10,000 men were
huddled together on the transports in the stream ready to
attempt a landing if signalled." Then Grant's *Memoirs* continue—as if he felt a personal pride in the stout-heartedness
of Bowen, his former friend: "For nearly five and a half hours
Porter's attack was kept up without silencing a single gun of
the enemy." Although Bowen had only five guns, Porter's
fleet—seeing their efforts were entirely unavailing—withdrew
about half past one.[2] Later, as night came on, the whole Union
fleet ran past Grand Gulf, while Grant's men marched still
further south: they continued down the Louisiana side, still
untroubled by Confederate opposition along that shore. Next
day, and until nightfall, close to two-thirds of the invading
forces crossed over from De Shroon's, Louisiana (three miles
below Grand Gulf) to Bruinsburg, six miles farther down on
the eastern side of the river.[3]

After the war, Grant confided that when his troops climbed
into their boats the evening of the twenty-ninth, he had expected it would be necessary to drift down and across as far
as Rodney, a point about nine miles below, before dry landing
space could be found. But that night, a colored man came
into the Union lines, ingratiatingly informing the Federal
leader that good footing was to be had at Bruinsburg, a few

miles above Rodney; and from Bruinsburg there was an excellent road leading to Fort Gibson some twelve miles in the
interior. The Negro's information was correct, and Grant's
men stepped ashore without meeting opposition for hours.[4]

On April 30 Pemberton received his first information of
his enemy's landing on the east bank of the Mississippi.[5] This
disaster tripled his task, for now the city of Jackson had plainly
become an additional and immediate objective of the invaders.[6]

General Bowen unavoidably lost some time in reporting the
vital news of the successful crossing. His first message was
sent by telegraph on April 30 and advised Pemberton that
3,000 Federal troops had been at Bethel Church (ten miles
from Port Gibson) since 3:00 P.M. of the twenty-ninth.[7]

Before this first definite advice of Grant's having reached
the east bank, Pemberton, the day before, notified Johnston
from Jackson: "Very heavy firing at Grand Gulf. Enemy
shelling our batteries above and below. The wires are down.
Do not know whether the enemy has made a landing this
side of the Mississippi River."[8] Simultaneously, Pemberton
sent General Stevenson the following, in quick succession:
"Is anything going on at Vicksburg or Grand Gulf. If *General Bowen* is *attacked,* send on the *column I directed*. As soon
as possible I will send on more troops to Vicksburg." Then,
again to Stevenson: "Hurry forward re-enforcements to Bowen
tonight. Endeavor to send him ammunition for heavy guns.
Troops on the way from here [Jackson] to replace those sent
away." This done, Bowen was heartened with the information that "General Stevenson has re-enforcements on the way
to assist you. Can I [Pemberton] do anything to assist you
from Jackson?"[9]

In a word, Pemberton made every effort to shuttle his com-
pulsorily dispersed forces from the points least threatened to
those in greatest danger—on the basis of developments as re-

ported to him. The succeeding quotation, from Pemberton's official report, further shows his concern for Bowen's safety at this time, as well as for Jackson and Vicksburg, all within his charge and Department: "I believe that I fully estimated the importance of preventing an advance upon Jackson, if it could be done without sacrificing Vicksburg; but if the latter was lost, the former was comparatively of little value. Vicksburg might still be held with Jackson in possession of the enemy, but it was the hope of being able to hold the position on Bayou Pierre [Grand Gulf], upon which the safety of Jackson depends, that made me most anxious to re-enforce General Bowen, or failing in that, at least to have a sufficient force at hand to secure his retreat across the Big Black."[10]

On the other hand, Grant's most critical worry, as Pemberton strained to race reinforcements to Bowen, was to make good his footing on the bluffs above Bruinsburg and to capture the bridge across Bayou Pierre, both near Grand Gulf and Port Gibson, from which roads diverged to Vicksburg and to Jackson. For a time the *invaders* must needs have a river base.[11]

As the Union troops landed, they were at once supplied with ammunition and quickly pushed forward toward Port Gibson.

For a day, Bowen's little garrison near-by stood their ground with great courage, fending off the strong attacking columns plus fresh additions ferried from the western shore.

The first of Bowen's couriers to reach Pemberton returned with the commanding general's richly deserved congratulations: "In the name of the Army, I desire to thank you and your troops for your gallant conduct to-day. Keep up the good work, by every effort to repair damages to-night. Yesterday I warmly recommended you for a Major-Generalcy. I shall renew it."[12]

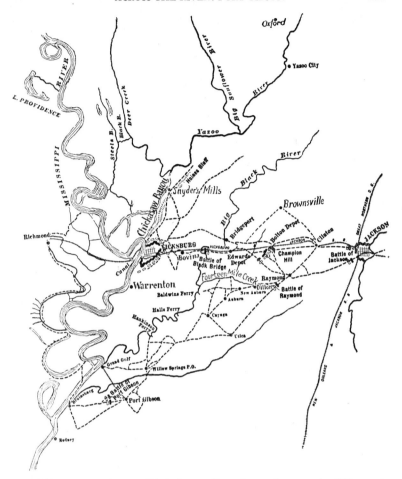

The approaches to Vicksburg. Based on the map in Vilas,
The Vicksburg Campaign.

In the interval, despite every exertion, neither General Loring, with two regiments of infantry and a battery of artillery
from Jackson,[13] nor Colonel A. W. Reynolds' brigade of Stevenson's division from Vicksburg[14] was able to reach Bowen
before he had been compelled to fall back from Port Gibson.
In so doing, he took the direction of Grand Gulf, reporting

that with about 8,000, he had been outnumbered trebly.[15]

In communicating news of this battle to the President and to Johnston, Pemberton said: "Enemy can cross all his army from Hard Times to Bruinsburg, below Bayou Pierre. Large re-enforcements should be sent me from other departments. Enemy's movement threatens Jackson, and, if successful, cuts off Vicksburg and Port Hudson from the east. Am hurrying all re-enforcements I possibly can to Bowen."[16]

Port Gibson must have been a stirring battle: reinforcements, marching much of the time in double quick,[17] found the ground when they arrived at the battlefield so much intersected by hollows, woods, and deep ravines that companies were compelled to act independently. "From opening daylight till after dark on the first of May, though he posted his forces with advantage and skill, [Bowen] was assailed and driven from hill to hill in what was virtually a succession of battles, over ground of great difficulty; being a series of ridges, seventy-five to a hundred feet high, with deep and narrow intervening ravines filled with timber, canes, vines, and thorns."[18]

Captain Watts of Baldwin's staff (on the Southern side) had three horses shot under him and was himself severely wounded. By the time Baldwin's command had retired from the battlefield and returned to Vicksburg, they had "in less than five days, marched over 100 miles, besides being engaged with the enemy more than ten successive hours."[19]

About noon (May 1) Bowen had attempted to turn Grant's right flank, and nearly succeeded. The Federal troops, he wrote, "formed three brigades in front of a battery to receive our charge. The first was routed, the second wavered, but the third stood firm, and, after a long and desperate contest, we had to give up the attempt."[20]

For some time it appeared as if no notice was to be taken by Johnston of word from Pemberton that "a furious battle has been going on since daylight just below Port Gibson 40 miles distant from Vicksburg and its dependencies, and from 50 to 100 miles from other points occupied by my troops."[21] But twenty-four hours after Bowen had been defeated at Port Gibson, four days after General Johnston had been informed of Grant's landing at Hard Times, and two weeks after Johnston had been informed that Grant had the means of crossing at his disposal, Johnston belatedly advised Vicksburg's commander: "If Grant's army lands on this side of the river, the safety of Mississippi depends on beating it. For that object you should unite your whole force." Then followed this renewal of the previous day's suggestion (or instruction?): "If Grant crosses, unite all your troops to beat him. Success will give back what was abandoned to win it."[22] Both these dispatches came from General Johnston in far-off Tullahoma (Tennessee), and when received found Pemberton's army under Bowen and Loring retreating from their positions near Grand Gulf and Port Gibson, and in the act of recrossing the Big Black River.[23]

In describing the impossibility of immediate compliance with these tardy injunctions, Pemberton later wrote: "General Johnston's adherents consider his order to 'unite all my troops,' meant that I should evacuate Vicksburg and Port Hudson to 'beat' Grant. It may be so; but if he did intend that construction to be given his despatches, there was a time when such orders might possibly have been capable of execution; that time was immediately after I had notified him (April 17th) that it was *practicable* for Grant to cross his army: when he did direct it (if he really meant it) the order was simply absurd. He had deprived me of my cavalry; Loring's division was guarding the railroad communications and important depots; Fort Pemberton was still occupied; Port Hudson was near one hundred miles distant; Bowen had just been discomfited; the railroad had been destroyed in several places between Meridian and Jackson; also on the I. & N. O. R. R. by Grierson's cavalry; and finally, *Grant had already crossed,* and could re-enforce to any extent. With Vicksburg for his base, he would at once have had the game in his own hands."[24]

Though hard pressed to meet the Union's multiplying threats after the encounter at Port Gibson, Pemberton and his forces continued full of fight and were determined to make the best of matters. Writing of the "Rebel" spirit after the crossing of his men, and of the battles that so shortly ensued, Grant notes: "When the crossing was effected I felt a degree of relief scarcely ever equalled since. Vicksburg was not yet taken, it is true, nor were its defenders demoralized by any of our previous moves. . . . But I was on dry ground on the same side of the river with the enemy."[25]

Grant was right. Not demoralization, but high hopes still rode with the Confederate command in Mississippi. In spite of the appalling military difficulties, the uncertain prospect of reinforcement, they did not sense the story's end. With the altered position of the Federal forces now across the river, the underlying advantage shifted so decisively that, for long days to come, there were a series of unbroken Union successes, to which Pemberton, unsupported, could find no means to reply.

And still, that spring along the Vicksburg front each side fancied itself superior in the stuff of war—steel and blood and bullets. "With re-enforcements and cavalry promised in North Mississippi, think we will be all right," wrote Pemberton to Davis on May 3, 1863.[26]

CHAPTER XII

After Port Gibson

THE DAY following the battle of Port Gibson, Grant's forces constructed a home-made pontoon bridge which they were able to throw across the Bayou Pierre. Near 2,000 cavalry gleaned the country of everything movable, gathered up some 2,500 Negroes and all the wagons, oxen, and mules they could lay their hands on. An ammunition train was made up of every sort of vehicle, drawn by every sort of animal, and loaded to the breaking point. "The campaign was based on speed—speed, and light rations foraged off the country, and no baggage, nothing at the front but men and guns and ammunition, and no rear; no slackening of effort, no respite for the enemy."[1] In the meantime, Pemberton—Vicksburg now being occupied by but one brigade—concentrated and started moving his troops between Grant and the stronghold. He had considered the advisability of an advance towards Jackson, in case Grant moved upon the capital, but would not do so blindly and in the absence of any information as to what was afoot in the Federal camps.[2]

Grant's plan to cut loose from his river base and line of supplies at Grand Gulf, and to make for Vicksburg via Jackson to the east, had now crystallized. The operation would be favored by the topography and lie of the land, which went far toward keeping Pemberton in constant doubt whether Jackson was Grant's actual objective or "whether he might not at any moment swerve due north against Vicksburg." In order to further becloud his movements and strengthen the illusion of a direct advance on Vicksburg, patrols were sent out by the Federal leader towards the Big Black River, and Hankinson's Ferry was seized.[3]

Before Grant got started, Pemberton had undertaken to have the railroads furnish him, "even at a moment's warning, with the greatest possible amount of transportation at their united command," so that he might "be enabled to throw to any point on either road the greatest possible number of troops."[4] To this end the transportation of private freight was suspended, and orders were issued that the cars of one road be permitted to pass on to the other without the delay of transfer of freight or troops. Incredible as it may now seem, much resentment and noisy protest followed. But the order stuck, despite its wide unpopularity.

On the basis of scout reports, Pemberton telegraphed the President on May 2: "I think the enemy has landed nearly his whole force on this side. . . . You know the country about Port Gibson and approaches to Vicksburg and Jackson. . . . Enemy is evidently re-enforcing heavily. I shall concentrate all the troops I can, but distances are great. Unless very large re-enforcements are sent here, I think Port Hudson and Grand Gulf should be evacuated, and the whole force concentrated for defense of Vicksburg and Jackson. It will require at least 6,000 cavalry to prevent heavy raids and to keep railroad communications, on which our supplies depend."[5] Pending the President's reply, Pemberton immediately moved all his available forces at Grenada, Columbus, and Jackson so as to parry any attack that might be made in the rear of Vicksburg by Grant's army.[6]

But Grant, figuring that a quick advance before the Confederate forces could be concentrated against him would more than compensate for any lack of supplies that might come later, was off! Sherman stayed behind to guard Grant's exposed flank, while McClernand's corps on the left, and McPherson's corps on the right, moved off with three days' rations in their haversacks. That proved quite sufficient when coupled with provisions the advancing columns gathered off the country. Soon, though, "too much chicken and turkey and corn-bread palled before they got back to their regular diet of bacon and hardtack."[7]

McPherson, who had started off at an early hour (May 7) took the road to Jackson, via Rocky Springs, Utica, and Raymond. That night he and McClernand (who had gone by the Rocky Springs-Edwards road) met ten miles from Hankinson's Ferry, at Rocky Springs. Counting Sherman's corps, in the rear and center, Grant's forces approximated 41,000 men, plus some cavalry.[8] Pemberton's movable army "might reach 18,500. I give this number as the maximum," he said in his official report.[9]

What steps did Pemberton take to halt this formidable invasion, now that it was actually under way, with "the incalculable direction of the enemy's advance helping to paralyze his counter-offensive and to tire out his troops in marching and counter-marching."

On May the sixth Johnston had telegraphed Pemberton, making substantially this same inquiry: what had Pemberton done by way of preparation. Johnston asked, "Let me know the location of your troops, number, and places, in cipher."[10] Then followed Pemberton's reply:

"VICKSBURG, May 7, 1863
"GENERAL JOSEPH E. JOHNSTON, *Tullahoma:*
"General Loring's and Stevenson's divisions, and one

brigade of Smith's and one of Forney's, between Warrenton and Baldwin's Ferry. General Bowen's division
at Big Black bridge, one brigade on either side of river.
General Hébert's brigade between Snyder's Mill and
Chickasaw Bayou. General Vaughn's north of city, to
support Hébert or Bowen. General Lee's, including heavy
artillery, in the city. One brigade, about 5,000 infantry,
cavalry, and artillery, at Port Hudson; two *en route* from
there to this place. Chalmers', about 1,100, yesterday at
Oxford, awaiting to co-operate with Forrest. Ruggles at
Columbus; small force of cavalry and State troops.
    "General Bowen ... had to leave his position. . . .
                                J. C. PEMBERTON."

Answering at once, Johnston gave his approval:

                        "TULLAHOMA, May 8, 1863
"LIEUTENANT-GENERAL PEMBERTON:
    "Your dispatch in cipher received. Cannot decipher
about Port Hudson. Make entirely new cipher of that
part. Disposition of troops, as far as understood, judicious;
Can be readily concentrated against Grant's army.
                            J. E. JOHNSTON"[11]

Midway in the course of this exchange between Pemberton
and Johnston, Davis had notified Pemberton on May 7: "To
hold both Vicksburg and Port Hudson is necessary to a connection with Trans-Mississippi."[12] This was in answer to
Pemberton's recommendation of May 2 that Port Hudson be
evacuated and his whole force concentrated for defense of
Vicksburg and Jackson. His opinion thus overruled by the
President, Pemberton at once sent the following telegram:
                        "VICKSBURG, May 8, 1863
"GENERAL GARDNER, *Osyka:*
    "Return with two thousand troops to Port Hudson, and
hold it to the last. President says both places must be held.
                                J. C. PEMBERTON"[13]

For Pemberton's army, then, the center of gravity was hence-forth definitely to be Vicksburg and Port Hudson—"President says both places must be held." Anchored to these positions, Pemberton was thus restricted to the defensive and lost entire liberty of action. He therefore determined "to concentrate all my troops, not in Vicksburg, but between that fortified posi-tion and the enemy—a policy unchanged, so far as my judg-ment guided me, until the results brought about by the orders of my superior [Johnston] compelled me to withdraw into the defences of Vicksburg itself....

"My matured plans were, to keep constantly between Vicks-burg and the enemy by conforming my movements to his; if possible, to hold the line of the Big Black (where the de-fensive positions allowed it to be done); or if compelled to cross that stream, not to advance beyond Edwards' Depot, where I was fortifying, and where my flanks virtually rested on the Big Black; whilst my communications with the western bank were perfect, and supplies were brought by rail directly to my army from my principal depot (Vicksburg), and where, from facility of communication, I could have employed almost my entire force in the field, and yet have secured the safety of the vital position, Vicksburg.

"As long as I could pursue this system, I was accumulating supplies from the Yazoo. My great object was to prevent Grant from establishing a base on the Mississippi River, above Vicksburg. The farther north he advanced, towards my left, from his then base below, the weaker he became; the more exposed became his rear and flanks; the more difficult it be-came to subsist his army, and obtain reinforcements. I had been promised a large force of cavalry, and troops of the other armies, and was daily expecting their arrival. If Grant, dis-regarding my army, in position at Edward's Depot, should attempt to advance upon Snyder's Mill by the rear, my whole army on either side of the river (Big Black) would have been upon his flank and rear. True, he might destroy Jackson and ravage the country, but that was comparatively a small matter. To take Vicksburg, to control the valley of the Mississippi, to sever the Confederacy, and to ruin our cause, a base upon the eastern bank immediately above was absolutely necessary."[14] Such was Pemberton's realistic view of the problem he faced after the battle of Port Gibson.

In the view of one eminent authority the real test of capacity "consists of judging men by their conception rather than by their execution, by the vision and realism of their ideas rather than by results.... in a man's own explanation of the reasons which prompted his acts, one can often find the fairest measure of his calibre."[15]

As for Pemberton's opponents, there can be little question that there were no others so able throughout the Federal armies. Grant was indeed fortunate in having two such lieutenants as Sherman and McPherson. Of Grant, the biographer of Jackson has remarked, "The Federal Commander-in-Chief was unquestionably a great soldier, greater than those who overlook his difficulties in the '64 campaign are disposed to admit. As a strategist he ranks high.... [But] it may be questioned whether on the field of battle his ability was equal to that of Sherman."[16]

While Pemberton was resolved to hold his army between Grant and Vicksburg, watching an opportunity for attack upon his rear and moving columns, Grant concluded: "It would not be possible for Pemberton to attack me with all his troops at one place, and I determined to throw my army between his and fight him in detail.... Vicksburg [after the river crossing] could have been approached and besieged by the south side. It is not probable, however, that Pemberton would have permitted a close besiegement." Then Grant adds,

"The broken nature of the ground would have enabled him [Pemberton] to hold a strong defensible line from the river south of the city to the Big Black, retaining possession of the railroad back to that point." All of which would seem to accord with Pemberton's identical conception of what the terrain and conditions offered and invited. So Grant wisely planned to get to the railroad east of Vicksburg and approach from that (Jackson) direction.

Had Pemberton hurriedly pushed forward his movable army of 18,000 to catch and concentrate against Grant's force of some 41,000 on its march to the east, McClernand's corps, upon the Confederate right, could have interposed between Pemberton and Vicksburg or have moved at once upon Pemberton's rear.[17]

Both before and after the war, Pemberton's close study of famous campaigns was unusually wide. Whenever he was taxed with his failure to follow up Grant more quickly in his march to the east, he was wont to ask the questioner, "Do you recall what happened when Napoleon uncovered Paris? Marshall Blucher and Alexander's Cossacks marched in; the city was surrendered by Napoleon's brother Prince Joseph; while the Emperor could only lament, 'If I had come four hours sooner, all would have been saved'."[18]

The recent Memoirs of General de Caulaincourt afford confirmation of Pemberton's conclusion as to what, under the circumstances pictured, would have been Vicksburg's fate had it, too, been uncovered. Writes the Duke of Vicenza: "... Tettenborn's Cossacks had seized a letter from Napoleon to Marie Louise, wherein the Emperor was sending word that he had crossed the Marne so as to draw the enemy wide of Paris.... The Emperor had no doubt but that the enemy's main army was following him.... 'What Alexander wants is to parade my capital with his Guards.'... 'The enemy will not dare to go in there so long as I am at their rear.'....Nothing could convince him [Napoleon] that the enemy were threatening Paris, regardless of their rear.... Berthier and I begged him to cross the Marne at once and move by forced marches upon Paris—but all in vain. He could not believe that the enemy would let him from sight and leave him at their rear, across their lines of communication.... [The capitulation of Paris was signed by Marmont and the Allied representatives on March 31.] Prince Joseph had ordered the surrender, in the belief that to hold out any longer would be a vain risk for the troops and Paris both."[19]

During the days that Grant was marching to the east—May 7 on—Johnston, still in Tennessee, rose from a sick-bed in Chattanooga and on telegraphic orders from Richmond started on May 10 for Jackson, Mississippi, to take personal command of the Vicksburg campaign. Because of invading armies on the direct route, he had to travel a roundabout way through Atlanta, Montgomery, and Mobile to Meridian and Jackson, over war-racked railroads. It was night of May 13 when he arrived in Jackson to take up the work of defense.[20]

The President and Secretary of War in Richmond both agreed with Pemberton, who had telegraphed on May 6, "The stake is a great one. I can see nothing so important."[21] But would Johnston share their view? And if not, what measure of co-operation, or opposition, would he supply to the President's insistence "that the river posts be held to the last."[22]

On the very day of Johnston's arrival in Mississippi, General Longstreet, who had become a lieutenant general in the autumn of 1862 together with Pemberton and five others, stopped in Richmond on his way back to Lee's army at Fredericksburg. He had been asked by Secretary of War James Seddon for "his advice on the unpromising situation at Vicksburg. Longstreet had proposed that he take two divisions of his corps, reinforce the army under Bragg, etc." The War Department favored the dispatch of two such divisions to the Mississippi; but *"Lee explained that, in his opinion, the Confederacy had to choose between maintaining the line of the Mississippi and that of Virginia."* Vicksburg was a bit without the Virginia sphere of interest or, in any aspect, was at most secondary. Since Lee planned to relax the tightening grip of Grant on Vicksburg by invading Pennsylvania, an invasion which, he said, "gave promise of success and would either end the war or allow the army rest for some time to come,"[23] the Confederate government at a Cabinet meeting deferred to his opinion.

Meanwhile the last Confederate segment of the great river wedged between those determined confreres, Grant and Sherman, was nearing isolation: "For Grant and Sherman were bent on using the river's broad sweep to enrich the Union cause, and to cut off the western territory still in Confederate hands."

Unopposed for the most part, Grant's three corps pushed eastward under their respective major generals—McClernand, McPherson, and Sherman.

It was the second week of May, and Pemberton maintained, as earlier, his screen between Vicksburg and the enemy. For this task he had a movable force of 18,000—all that remained to him after leaving sufficient troops to defend the river front of Vicksburg, the approaches by Chickasaw Bayou, Snyder's Mill, and Warrenton.[24] Of the might-have-beens, Pemberton later wrote in his official report: "With a moderate cavalry force at my disposal, I am firmly convinced that the Federal Army under General Grant would have been unable to maintain its communications with the Mississippi River, and that the attempt to reach Jackson and Vicksburg from that base would have been as signally defeated in May, 1863, as a like

attempt from another base [Holly Springs] had by the employment of cavalry been defeated in December, 1862."[25]   In
a later account of the campaign, Pemberton wrote: "Without
cavalry I was entirely unable to make a reconnaissance in
force, and to prevent the enemy from obtaining from the
adjacent country those supplies without which he could not
have reached Jackson, fought the battle of Baker's Creek or
sat down before Vicksburg. These are not after thoughts on
my part, as my correspondence at the time will sufficiently
show."[26]   An infantry colonel with Grant's army confides,
"[Our] route of supplies was so long as both to be inadequate
and perilous."[27]

Even against the negligible opposition pictured, the advance
of Grant's three corps towards Jackson was not fast. Sherman's troops were an exception: pushing up into the center
of the others, his forces were aligned along Fourteen Mile
Creek when McPherson, on May 12, gained Raymond. Raymond was eighteen miles west of Jackson. Yet on the night
of the thirteenth Sherman, too, was at Raymond; "and despite torrential rain all night and roads sometimes a foot deep
in water," he caught up with the corps in advance, within
three miles of Jackson. There "the old burner pillaged and
set fire to the town."[28]   Said the London *Times:* "Sherman
is indeed the modern Attilla."

To explain fully the eastern march of Sherman and the
others (to Raymond and to Jackson), it is necessary to turn
back for a moment. When Grant had first established himself at Grand Gulf (May 3), news reached him that General
Banks, away up the Red River toward Alexandria (Louisiana),
could not get to Port Hudson when expected. So Grant, who
did not want to wait so long for only 15,000 reinforcements,
disobeyed orders from Halleck, who was far away in Wash-

ington. These orders were to effect a junction with Banks and join with him in the capture of Port Hudson. Instead, Grant boldly marched for Vicksburg by way of Jackson.[29]

Grant's own explanation of his disobedience is amazingly frank. He says, "The news from Banks forced upon me a different plan of campaign from the one intended. . . . Grand Gulf was accordingly given up as a base, and the authorities at Washington were notified. I knew well that Halleck's caution would lead him to disapprove of this course; but it was the only one that gave any chance of success. The time it would take to communicate with Washington and get a reply would be so great that I could not be interfered with until it was demonstrated whether my plan was practicable."[30] The plan was practicable, so, not only was there a total absence of censure or criticism, the act of disobedience was widely hailed as a happy one for the country and Grant's fame. Halleck was in the forefront of all who approved Grant's independence of orders, and recognized his achievement by rushing reinforcements from all the Union armies. Hence it was that Grant soon had one hundred thousand men under his command.[31] True, the President and General in Chief had expected him to move south and join Banks against Port Hudson, but "long before his own daring plan could be known and countermanded, it was tried to conclusion."

It has long been acknowledged there are many occasions in war when even the private must use his wits and prove his self-reliance. But if the act of independence (or disobedience) is to pass unpunished or uncensured, it must *not* have failed. This, Pemberton was to learn—as an object of selective indignation.

Satisfied that, if successful, even the President would approve his following "a different plan of campaign from the one he was ordered to take in conjunction with Banks," Grant proved a good judge of human nature. Two months later the President was to write:

"EXECUTIVE MANSION,
Washington, July 13th, 1863
"MAJOR-GENERAL GRANT.
"My Dear General:—I do not remember that you and I ever met personally. I write this now as a grateful acknowledgment for the almost inestimable service you have done the country. I wish to say a word further. When you first reached the vicinity of Vicksburg I thought you should do what you finally did—march the troops across the neck, run the batteries with the transports, and thus go below; and I never had any faith, except a general hope that you knew better than I, that the Yazoo Pass expedition and the like could succeed. When you got below and took Port Gibson, Grand Gulf, and vicinity, I thought you should go down the river and join Gen. Banks; and when you turned northward, east of the Big Black, I feared it was a mistake. I now wish to make the personal acknowledgment that you were right and I was wrong.

A. LINCOLN."[32]

When Lincoln's letter was published in the Northern papers, the Rebel War Clerk (Jones), in Richmond, noted in his diary: "If Pemberton had acted differently, if the movement northward had been followed by disaster, then what would Mr. Lincoln have written to Grant? Success is the only standard of merit in a general."

In the hour of fulfillment, Sherman also would be quick with congratulations to Grant. "Thus when a party of official visitors came soon after to Vicksburg Grant was surprised to hear Sherman declaiming, 'Grant is entitled to every bit of the credit for the campaign. I opposed it. I wrote him a letter about it'."[33]

CHAPTER XIII

The Battle of Raymond, the Fall of Jackson

ABOUT TWO MILES out of Raymond, McPherson's corps of Grant's command encountered a brigade of General Gregg's sent up from Port Hudson, and of Walker's just arrived from the Department of South Carolina and Georgia. The Southern army opposing Grant was now in three separate detachments and in open country. Pemberton, with some 18,000, was on the way to Edward's Depot; Johnston was at Jackson with near 6,000; Gregg's 5,000 were at Raymond.[1]

In Pemberton's view the Battle of Raymond should never have been fought; for "General Gregg, gallant and noble gentleman that he was, did not conform to my [Pemberton's] repeated and positive orders, 'If the enemy advance upon you in too strong force, fall back upon Jackson'."[2]

Brigadier General John Gregg with his brigade from Port Hudson, having arrived at a point near Jackson, but being without his wagon transportation, was ordered by Pemberton to take position at Raymond. That seemed an advantageous point for the collection of Gregg's troops either to move on the flank of the enemy advancing on Edward's Depot or to retire on Jackson. There, on being joined by the reinforcements, which were expected, and daily arriving at Jackson (including, as Pemberton hoped, a force of cavalry), Gregg was to move on the flank and rear of the enemy—should he attack at Edward's Depot. The day before the Battle of Raymond, Gregg and Walker (commanding a brigade in Jackson) were in turn notified by Pemberton:

"RAYMOND, VIA CLINTON, May 11th, 1863
"GENERAL GREGG:
"I directed a telegram to you from General Loring's headquarters. If the enemy advance on you too strong, fall back on Jackson. All the South Carolina troops will be ordered to Raymond to support you, or cover your retreat, as the case may be. If, however, the enemy approaches Big Black bridge, hold your command in readiness to attack him in rear or flank. If you should be superseded, communicate this to commanding officer. Employ the cavalry actively in scouting and harassing his movements.   J. C. PEMBERTON"[3]

"VICKSBURG, May 11, 1863
"BRIGADIER-GENERAL WALKER, Jackson:
"Move immediately with your command to Raymond. General Gregg has been ordered, if the enemy advance on him in too strong force, to fall back on Jackson. You will do likewise in conjunction with him. If the enemy advance on you in not too strong force, you will meet them. If, instead of advancing on Jackson, he should advance on Big Black Bridge, the command, under direction of the senior officer, will attack him in rear and flank.   J. C. PEMBERTON,
          Lieutenant-General, Commanding"[4]

"VICKSBURG, May 11, 1863
"BRIGADIER-GENERAL WALKER, Jackson:
"Enemy is reported advancing in heavy force on Jackson. Hold your command in readiness, and move toward Raymond,

either to support General Gregg at that place or to cover his retreat. Telegraph to hurry up re-enforcements.

J. C. PEMBERTON,
Lieutenant-General, Commanding"[5]

In consequence of this prolonged uncertainty, Gregg was again admonished to be particularly cautious not to allow himself to be flanked or taken in the rear.

We do not know by whom the engagement was brought on; but the Battle of Raymond was fought by Gregg with McPherson's entire corps. The Union General Logan came on in advance and commenced assaulting. Then, before Crocker's Federal division got up, Gregg's forces retired.

Southern sources report: "... the stout resistance of Gregg at Raymond led Grant to believe that a large Confederate force was being concentrated at Jackson."[6] ... "Gregg and his small command ... behaved with great gallantry and steadiness, but after an obstinate conflict of several hours they were finally overwhelmed by superior numbers and compelled to retire. The command was withdrawn in good order, and retired to Jackson."[7] Northern reports paint a somewhat different picture of the affair, a Wisconsin colonel writing: "On the 12th, McPherson suddenly extended to the right and threw Logan with his division upon Gregg, and sent him flying in rout to Jackson, with a loss of over 800."[8]

Turning to the Raymond reports given out by Grant's corps commanders, we find the details boiled down to two short and sizzling paragraphs: "McPherson encountered the enemy, five thousand strong with two batteries under General Gregg, about two miles out of Raymond. This was about two P.M. Logan was in advance with one of his brigades. He deployed and moved up to engage the enemy. McPherson ordered the road in rear to be cleared of wagons, and the balance of Logan's division, and Crocker's, which was still farther in rear, to come forward with all dispatch. The order was obeyed with alacrity. Logan got his division in position for assault before Crocker could get up, and attacked with vigor, carrying the enemy's position easily, sending Gregg flying from the field not to appear against our front again until we met at Jackson.

"In this battle McPherson lost 66 killed, 339 wounded, and 37 missing—nearly or quite all from Logan's division. The enemy's loss was 100 killed, 305 wounded, besides 415 taken prisoners."[9]

The day after the Battle of Raymond Johnston arrived in Jackson to command in person. He found but two brigades to withstand two Union army corps, although Pemberton had ordered all his outlying forces in Mississippi, including that at Grenada, to concentrate at Jackson. As a result, Johnston felt that there was nothing for him to do but leave Jackson, which he did; but before he could get out Sherman's corps carried out an outflanking movement, capturing three of Johnston's field batteries and two hundred of his troops. As Johnston made his emergency departure—retiring northwards—the distance was increased between his command and Pemberton's forces who were nearing Edward's Depot.[10]

Although it rained in torrents that day, by 10:00 P.M. Johnston was on the Canton road eighteen or twenty miles distant from Clinton, to which he had directed Pemberton by telegraph, dated May 13: "If practicable, come up in [Sherman's] rear at once. The troops here could co-operate." As matters developed, the movement suggested by Johnston was not practicable—a blessing in disguise: for, at the time and place appointed by Johnston for his and Pemberton's joint attack on Sherman, Johnston's co-operating troops were some twenty miles away from his proposed battlefield.[11]

So quick had been Johnston's withdrawal from Jackson on the fourteenth that Grant and Sherman found the looms of a Confederate factory still turning out tent cloth marked C.S.A. Grant recounts the incident in his *Memoirs*, telling how he and Sherman, unnoticed, for a time watched the operatives, most of whom were girls. Finally, Grant says, "I told Sherman I thought they had done work enough. The operatives were told that they could leave and take with them what cloth they could carry. In a few minutes cotton and factory were in a blaze."

Pemberton's first information that Johnston had actually arrived from Tennessee had been a dispatch dated at Jackson, May 13. The dispatch was received by Pemberton near Bovina (on the west of the Big Black River) on the morning of the fourteenth of May between nine and ten o'clock. It was in these terms: "I have lately arrived, and learn that Major-General Sherman is between us with four divisions at Clinton. It is important to re-establish communication, that you may be re-enforced. If practicable, come up in his rear at once. To beat such a detachment would be of immense value. The troops here could co-operate. All the strength you can quickly assemble should be brought; time is all-important."[12]

Up to the day before this word from Johnston, Pemberton, without cavalry, had been groping his way towards Edward's Depot. General Loring, already there, had received the following instructions:

"BOVINA, May 13th, 1863

"GENERAL LORING, *Edwards' Depot:*

"The Lieutenant-General Commanding directs that you make a reconnoissance, of such a character as you may deem proper, to find out where the main force of the enemy is, and in what direction moving. If on Jackson, he thinks his move will be to fall on their rear, and cut their communications; but he must have accurate information from you, that he can rely on, before making this move, which would leave Vicksburg, by way of Big Black bridge and the ferries, in so critical a position. It is necessary that the Lieutenant-General should be informed, not only what force has moved on, but the strength and position of that which is left.

J. C. TAYLOR, A.D.C."[13]

On the twelfth of May, which was the day before Loring's reconnaissance was ordered in Pemberton's front, and likewise the day before Johnston reached Jackson, the latter and the President were notified by Pemberton: "The enemy is apparently moving his heavy force toward Edwards Depot, on Southern Railroad; with my limited force I will do all I can to meet him. That will be the battle-field if I can carry forward sufficient force, leaving troops enough to secure the safety of this place (Vicksburg). Re-enforcements are arriving very slowly, only 1,500 having arrived as yet. I urgently ask that more be sent; also that 3,000 cavalry be at once sent to operate on this line. I urge this as a positive necessity. The enemy largely outnumber me, and I am obliged to hold back a large force at the ferries on Big Black lest he cross and take this place. I am also compelled to keep considerable force on either flank of Vicksburg out of supporting distance."[14]

Pemberton's plight, as he reached out for the enemy while seeking to maintain the Confederacy's hold on Vicksburg, calls to mind the picture of that other Southern leader as he neared the battlefield at Gettysburg. "Over the hills from Cashtown, along a road he had never travelled before, Lee galloped toward Gettysburg like a blinded giant. He did not know where the Federals were, or how numerous they might be. Ewell—and doubtless Hill also—he had cautioned not to bring on a general engagement with a strong adversary until the rest of the infantry came up, but with no cavalry to inform him, he could not tell what calamity he might invite by advancing at all, or what opportunity he might lose by advancing cautiously. Never had he been so dangerously in the dark."[15]

CHAPTER XIV

Battle of Baker's Creek or Champion's Hill

WHEN PEMBERTON first heard from Johnston on the morning of the fourteenth of May to come up at once on Sherman's rear at Clinton, Grant's intentions still remained wholly hidden from the Confederates; and the direction of the fluid lines of Federals advancing eastwards from the river was still entirely blurred. Did Grant plan a march on Jackson, or on Vicksburg? Was he preparing to march around, or straight at those cities—or at their defenders? Equally in the dark as to the enemy's positions, Pemberton later reported to the Secretary of War, "I . . . only knew that the whole of Grant's army (three corps) had taken the general direction (northeast) toward the railroad. At what point on this they would strike, or the positions of the corps not mentioned nor seemingly regarded by General Johnston, I was not informed, except inasmuch as I had learned from prisoners that Smith's division was at Dillon's and the rest of the corps to which he was attached were near. . . ."[1]

Pemberton's understanding of the movement contemplated by Johnston's dispatch of May 13 "was to move as rapidly as possible to attack Sherman's corps at Clinton, or wherever I might find it, and I believed that his instructions were influenced by his supposing that these were the only troops I should encounter, as no reference is made [by Johnston] to any other force of the enemy."[2]

From Bovina, Pemberton informed Johnston that he would move at once. But on arriving some two hours later (noon) at Edward's Depot, he learned that the "detachment" Johnston spoke of in his communication of May 13 constituted an entire army corps, numerically greater than Pemberton's whole available force in the field. In addition, he soon learned that there was at least an equal force of the enemy to the south. This second force was on his right flank, which would be nearer to Vicksburg than himself, should he make the movement proposed by Johnston.[3]

Johnston's dispatch of May 13 had been sent almost immediately after his arrival in Jackson from Tennessee. He had consulted with no member of Pemberton's staff, was in ignorance of his surroundings, had no knowledge of the enemy's strength, nor of the disposition of the greater part of his troops. Moreover, he had apparently given no consideration whatsoever to the fate of Vicksburg.[4]

It has been repeatedly said of Lee that he was ever anxious to defer to the opinions of the man on the spot.[5] It cannot be said of Johnston. Removed and distant as he was from the scene of action in Pemberton's vicinity, it was indeed fatal that he sought to direct and change the local commander's chosen field of battle.

Prior to his receipt of Johnston's first instructions, it had not been Pemberton's intention to make *any* forward movement from Edward's Depot. There, from facility of communication, he could employ almost his entire force in the field and yet secure the safety of his vital position, Vicksburg. Now, since his arrival at Edward's Depot, in possession of fuller information as to the enemy's dispositions, could he afford to make the movement on Sherman's one corps at Clinton, irrespective and regardless of the major forces of the enemy upon his right flank? Would not the latter force, in this event, either interpose between his troops and Vicksburg— or move at once upon his rear?[6] Pemberton's own views were strongly unfavorable to any advance which would separate him farther from Vicksburg, his base. But a majority of his general officers expressed themselves as being in favor of the movement indicated by Johnston.[7]

So Pemberton called a council of war, the first in his uninterrupted military career of more than thirty years. He was to hold two more. In cold truth, by no other means could the Northern commander of this Southern army gain his subordinates' co-operation. Even the obedience of some was grudging, as this later full and frank report indicates:

"ENTERPRISE, July 21, 1863

"LIEUTENANT GENERAL J. C. PEMBERTON:

"General—Until very lately I was not aware that you expected those members of your staff, who were with you in the military movements in front of Vicksburg, to furnish you a statement of the part they bore in the same. I seize the first opportunity to comply with your request, so far as observations and experience enable me to do so. After the landing of the enemy at Bruinsburg, and the Battle of General Bowen at Port Gibson, and the falling back of our troops to the Big Black at the Rail Road bridge, and across that stream below the bridge, you resisted persistently the desire expressed in various quarters of the army to cross the Big Black River, and to give him battle. For several days it was believed very generally that the enemy would attempt to cross the Big Black River at what are known as the lower ferries, and move upon Vicksburg from the south, with their gunboats, attacking Warrenton on one side, the column moving on Edwards' Depot or the R. R. bridge on the other. The almost total want of cavalry, not only kept you in ignorance of his movements, but deprived you of all means of annoying or retarding him, in his movements. About 11th of May, information was received that at least one corps of the enemy's forces was moving on Raymond, and the probability was (though I do not think it was certainly known) that a division, if not a corps, was moving on Edwards' Depot. On the evening of the 12th you left Vicksburg for Bovina, having previously ordered Major-General Loring and Stevenson to bring all of their divisions to Edwards' Depot.

"I accompanied you to Bovina, and we reached there on the night of the 12th May. The next day, the troops, consisting of Loring's, Stevenson's and Bowen's divisions, were drawn up in line of battle, in front of Edwards' Depot. They remained all the 13th in line, and nothing was seen of the enemy. On the 14th a communication was received from General Johnston, then in Jackson, informing you of the presence of the enemy in Clinton, and indicating a forward movement as desirable. Immediately a council of war was called, consisting of all the general officers. I was present at that council, and heard your views and those of the different officers expressed. You stated at great length, and to my mind with great force, that the leading and great duty of your army was, to defend Vicksburg; the disposition and numbers of the enemy, and your forces; the bad effect of a defeat, and the probability of such result if you moved forward. After canvassing it, *there was not a voice in favor of moving on Clinton.* But inasmuch as the enemy had moved in force on Jackson, leaving as was supposed, only a single division on the Big Black, it was first suggested by General Loring and afterwards acquiesced in by all the other officers, that it would be wise and expedient to move the next day on the Southern or Raymond road to Dillon's, which was on the main leading road by which the enemy carried on his communications, give battle to the division left in the rear, and thus effectually break up the enemy's communications. In this

council it seemed to be taken for granted by all the officers
that the enemy was then engaged in an effort to reduce
Jackson, and was therefore too far removed to participate
in the expected fight. You gave in to the views of the
officers with reluctance, and expressed yourself as doing
so against your convictions. But being present and hearing every thing said, I did not see how you could have
done otherwise, with any expectation of retaining your
hold upon the army. . . .

JACOB THOMPSON
Major and Inspector General"[8]

Many within and out the ranks never forgot Pemberton's
nativity. On that account the Secretary of War on more than
one occasion was earnestly petitioned to remove the Northerner from command. But he had the full confidence of his
superiors at all times, and nothing came of these petitions, no
matter their frequency or source. The President's vexation
on this score has already been noted.

As for Pemberton's action in calling a council of war, it
was unquestionably "a step condemned by the greatest soldier
of all time."[9] Yet, Bonaparte himself rendered but lip service
to this maxim. He may have felt it qualified by another of
his maxims (XLII)—"Nothing is absolute in war." True,
Stonewall Jackson never held but one council; contrariwise,
Lee seldom made an important movement without one.[10]

Two days before Pemberton's first council, the President
had written him, "In your situation . . . it is necessary to add
conciliation to the discharge of duty. Patience in listening to
suggestions . . . is sometimes rewarded. . . ."[11] To this letter
Pemberton replied, "I appreciate all your kindness, I will endeavor to profit by your advice. . . ."[12] And then within twenty-
four hours he had, for the first time, consulted his fellow officers, as to the manner of compliance with Johnston's dispatch
of the thirteenth—to move on Sherman's rear at Clinton.

What if the event *was* to suggest that it might have been better had he stood his generals before him and bluntly reminded them that he, not they, commanded the army charged
with Vicksburg's defense? "A general is not necessarily incapable because he makes a false move; both Napoleon and
Wellington, in the long course of their campaigns, gave many
openings to a resolute foe, and both missed opportunities.
Under ordinary circumstances mistakes may easily escape
notice altogether, or at all events pass unpunished, and the
reputation of the leader who commits them will remain un-
tarnished. But if he is pitted against a master of war a single
false step may lead to irretrievable ruin; and he will be classed
as beneath contempt for a fault which his successful antagonist
may have committed with impunity a hundred times over."[13]

A century earlier Napoleon called a council of war at Jaffa.
"Bonaparte wavers," recounts Ludwig, "thinks matters over
for three days, and finally agrees [with the others]." Another
time he holds a council of war—in Italy—much to the astonishment of his generals. "In this critical situation, he proposes
to retreat across the Po, but the mad Augereau thumps the
table, shouting: 'For the sake of your own fame, I insist that
we attack.' . . . The counsels of the others are divided. . . . He
decides to fight. Next day, he is victorious at Castiglione. . . ."
In Moscow, Bonaparte once more calls a council, "although
he knows that only one way lies open to him."[14]

The decision Pemberton took (under the pressure of his
first council of war) after reaching Edward's Depot on May
14, where he learned for the first time of the enemy's corps
on his right flank, was to move on the fifteenth of May with
a column of 17,000 men to Dillon's. This little settlement
was situated on the main road leading from Raymond to Port
Gibson. It was seven and a half miles below Raymond and
nine and a half miles from Edward's Depot. "The object,"

he informed Johnston, "is to cut the enemy's communications and to force him to attack me, as I do not consider my force sufficient to justify an attack on the enemy in position or to attempt to cut my way to Jackson."[15] This was Pemberton's second note of May 14 to Johnston. Dated 5:40 P.M., it was written after he dismissed the council of war at Edward's Depot. It plainly shows that his purpose in the movement there indicated was, by coming up on the enemy's rear, to draw him from Jackson and from the line of the Southern railroad and, by threatening the enemy's communications, to reopen those of the Confederates, thus uniting Johnston's troops and his by a co-operative movement.[16] The new decision not to move directly on Sherman's rear was the result of the component factors cited.

And now it seemed that a great opportunity was presented for a convergence of force in an attack on a moving enemy encumbered with a long wagon train. Moreover, while Grant had provided in some measure against this contingency ("the most important consideration in my mind was to have a force confronting Pemberton if he should come out to attack my rear"), he (Grant) would nonetheless have found it difficult, with the small force left behind, to take care of Blair, who had with him "200 wagons loaded with rations, the only commissary supplies received [by the Federals] during the entire campaign."[17]

No advance by Pemberton was possible until the fifteenth. In order that the army in position at Edward's Depot could move, it was necessary that additional rations should be forwarded from Vicksburg; large supplies had not been held at any other point upon the line of operations—the enemy's movements constantly compelling a change of position by the Southern troops. Furthermore, on the fourteenth a heavy rain fell and raised the waters of Baker's Creek (over which Pemberton's forces had to pass in going to Dillon's), so that it could not be crossed without swimming. This necessitated a delay for the construction of a bridge. About ten o'clock the night of the fifteenth, all the troops having crossed over and the march resumed, they bivouacked on the road connecting the two Raymond roads.[18]

Before Johnston received advice of Pemberton's movement against Grant's line of supplies and rear, he telegraphed Pemberton on May 14, suggesting the very movement which Pemberton was making, and for the very purpose the latter had indicated. In making the suggestion, Johnston said, "Can [Grant] supply himself from the Mississippi? Can you not cut him off from it; and, above all, should he be compelled to fall back for want of supplies, beat him?"[19] A week earlier, the President had seen Pemberton's proper strategy in the same light, telegraphing him on May 7 from Richmond: "... want of transportation of supplies must compel the enemy to seek a junction with their fleet after a few days' absence from it. To hold both Vicksburg and Port Hudson is necessary to a connection with Trans-Mississippi. You may expect whatever is in my power to do."[20] However, it so happened that Johnston's dispatch of the fourteenth, approving, in effect, Pemberton's second note of that date and the movement in course of execution across Grant's rear, did not reach Pemberton until eleven hours after Johnston's following and later "countermanding" instructions under date of May 15:

"CANTON ROAD, TEN MILES FROM JACKSON,

May 15, 1863—8.30 a.m.

"Our being compelled to leave Jackson makes your plan impracticable. The only mode by which we can unite is by your moving directly to Clinton, informing me, that we may move to that point with about 6,000 troops. I have no means of estimating enemy's force at Jackson.

The principal officers here differ very widely, and I fear he will fortify if time is left him. Let me hear from you immediately. General Maxey was ordered back to Brook-haven. You probably have time to make him join you. Do so before he has time to move away."[21]

This revocation by Johnston of his earlier order of the four-teenth (suggesting Pemberton's march to Grant's rear, a march then going ahead in accordance with the determination of Pemberton's council of war) was handed to Pemberton at about 7:00 A.M. on the morning of the sixteenth of May. An excited courier had brought it from General Johnston's head-quarters, ten miles from Jackson, on the Canton Road. In other words, Johnston was marching away from, rather than towards, the point—Clinton—he had proposed for the uniting of his forces with Pemberton's.

Though Pemberton in a double sense was the commander on the spot, he was at no time invited to submit his plans to General Johnston for consideration.[22] Hence it was that when Pemberton received the countermand of his march from John-ston's courier (7:00 A.M., May 16), he immediately executed an enforced about-face. Then began a reverse movement in the only mode possible, viz., at half the speed Pemberton had been headed for Grant's rear and for his train of two hundred wagons. The return march was so hobbled because the head of the column was now become the rear. This meant that Pemberton's wagon trains, which on the advance had been at the end, were now at the head of the column. Moreover, the field artillery and the ordnance wagons of the other divisions were unable to move forward in the new direction until the road became wide enough to open a passage between, or on the flanks of, the train. The narrow country roads were in bad condition from recent and unusually heavy rains; the stalling of a single wagon would block the way for all other wagons, as well as hold up the troops seeking to press through from behind them.[23]

Doubtless when Johnston, on May 13, notified Pemberton that Sherman was at Clinton, he had in mind that Pemberton should assail Sherman promptly "while separate and beyond support." But as a matter of actual fact, Sherman was at that moment in the act of advancing on Jackson, which he entered at twelve o'clock on the next day, May 14. He was closely followed by two other corps—McPherson's, at Raymond, and McClernand's, near-by at Dillon.[24] "If Grant's force, by these new dispositions, became a loose-linked chain it was not insecurely linked. For although it stretched over some forty-five miles the intervals were not excessive, while the lie of the rivers and the nature of the country increased its capacity for resistance."[25]

Under these circumstances, not then known to Johnston or to Pemberton, an immediate attack by Pemberton on Sherman at Clinton, in compliance with Johnston's first note of May 13, would have resulted in the destruction of Pemberton's entire army. For, by the fourteenth, Johnston himself had moved with his small force (6,000) from Jackson, some seven miles towards Canton. Thus he had placed himself not less than fifteen miles by the nearest practicable route from Clinton. On the following day he marched ten and a half miles *farther* from Clinton.[26]

Truth to tell, Grant was praying (at least to himself) that the projected Clinton attack on Sherman would be attempted by Pemberton. In his *Memoirs* he relates: "The concentration of my troops was easy, considering the character of the country.... I naturally expected that Pemberton would endeavor to obey the orders of his superior, which I have shown were to attack us at Clinton. This, indeed, I knew he could not do; but I felt sure he would make the attempt to reach

that point."[27]   Why Grant was so supremely confident that
Pemberton could not reach Clinton is a tale of one of those
accidents of war. It was akin to Pope's capture of Lee's orders
to J. E. B. Stuart near Clark's Mountain, and to McClellan's
stroke of good fortune in getting hold of a lost copy of Lee's
orders, which brought on the Battle of Sharpsburg.

Moltke avers that "the junction of two armies on the field
of battle is the highest achievement of military genius."[28] The
junction between Pemberton and Johnston, as the former put
his divisions' march in reverse, was to be balked by one of
those accidents "which play so large a part in war."

Now, on the morning of May 16, as Pemberton's forces returned to Edward's Depot to take the Brownsville Road and
thence to proceed toward Clinton by a route north of the railroad, now, as never before, Pemberton needed full and instant
information of his enemy. For twenty-four hours more he
was ignorant that Johnston had been driven so far from Jackson and that he (Pemberton) was marching upon Grant's
whole army.[29]

Chance had presented Grant with an opportunity as deter-
minative as any that thereafter befell him, even to the war's
end: one of Johnston's couriers had betrayed his "Clinton"
dispatches to the Union forces. "Did not the very gods of
war seem to wear blue?" Shortly, Grant stood squarely between the Southern armies. As a result, the Union commander was soon in position to repel Pemberton irrespective
of the route he took, or might have taken;[30] for Johnston's
plan to unite near Clinton was in Grant's hands as soon as
it was in Pemberton's. With nothing to delay him, Grant
moved first on Jackson and that night (May 14) slept in the
room occupied the night before by Johnston. Next day Grant
would turn west and head back for the Mississippi River to
get between Pemberton and Johnston.

Of Johnston's orders having been betrayed to Grant, Pemberton would know nothing for a decade. Then, from the White House in Washington his former opponent, as chief magistrate, would write him in confirmation.[31] Here is Grant's own version of the affair: "One of the messengers happened to be a loyal man who had been expelled from Memphis some months before by Hurlbut for uttering disloyal and threatening sentiments. There was a good deal of parade about his expulsion, ostensibly as a warning to those who entertained the sentiments he expressed; but Hurlbut and the expelled man understood each other. He delivered his copy of Johnston's dispatch to McPherson who forwarded it to me. Receiving this dispatch on the 14th I ordered McPherson to move promptly...."[32] With this account, Sherman's *Memoirs* are in reasonable accord, though he with more delicacy speaks of "intercepted dispatches." Sherman notes the occurrence in this wise: "Generals Grant, McPherson, and I, met in the large hotel facing the State-House [in Jackson], where the former explained to us that he had intercepted dispatches from Pemberton to Johnston, which made it important for us to work smart to prevent a junction of their respective forces. McPherson was ordered to march back early the next day on the Clinton road to make junction with McClernand, and I was ordered to remain one day to break up railroads, to destroy the arsenal, a foundery, the cotton-factory of the Messrs. Green, etc., etc., and then to follow McPherson."[33] According to Grant, "Sherman was to remain in Jackson until he destroyed that place as a railroad center and manufacturing city of military supplies."

As the reverse movement of Pemberton's army commenced in the early morning of May 16, the cavalry pickets of Colonel Wirt Adams in the lead were almost immediately fired upon and soon were driven in. Thereafter but a slight interval elapsed before the enemy opened on the head of Pemberton's column—with artillery at long range—on the Raymond Road.[34]

At the hour of Pemberton's march Grant, asleep at Clinton, was awakened to receive two men, employees of the Jackson and Vicksburg Railroad, who had passed through Pemberton's army the night before. They reported Pemberton as still marching east. On hearing this, Grant relates, "I had expected to leave Sherman at Jackson another day to complete his work; but getting the above information, I sent him orders to move with all dispatch to Bolton... and to march with all possible speed until he came up to our rear."[35] Again, it seemed the very gods of war were garbed in blue!

The fire first encountered by the head of Pemberton's column on the way to Clinton (still on the Raymond Road) came from the advance guard of McClernand's and McPherson's corps; but having had no opportunity for extended or adequate reconnaissance, Pemberton did not know whether this was an attack in force or simply a strong group of skirmishers. He had not long to wait for answer to his doubts. "The demonstrations of the enemy," he remarks, "soon becoming more serious, orders were sent to division commanders to form in line of battle on the cross-road from the Clinton to the Raymond road, Loring on the right, Bowen in the center, and Stevenson on the left. The line of battle was quickly formed, without any interference on the part of the enemy."[36]

The position selected (Champion's Hill) appeared strong by nature and proved strong by test. Of its selection, Grant came near to being complimentary, noting, "Champion's Hill, where Pemberton had chosen his position to receive us, whether taken by accident or design, was well selected." Then he adds, "It is one of the highest points in that section, and commanded all the ground in range. On the east side of the ridge, which is quite precipitous, is a ravine running first north, then westerly, terminating at Baker's Creek. It was grown up thickly with large trees and undergrowth, making it difficult to penetrate with troops, even when not defended. The ridge occupied by the enemy [Pemberton] terminated abruptly where the ravine turns westerly. The left of the enemy occupied the north end of this ridge. The Bolton and Edward's Station wagon-road turns almost due south at this point and ascends the ridge, which it follows for about a mile; then, turning west, descends by a gentle declivity to Baker's Creek, nearly a mile away. On the west side the slope of the ridge is gradual and is cultivated from near the summit to the creek. There was, when we were there, a narrow belt of timber near the summit west of the road. From Raymond there is a direct road to Edward's station, some three miles west of Champion's Hill. There is one also to Bolton. From this latter road there is still another, leaving it about three and a half miles before reaching Bolton and leads direct to the same station.... Pemberton's lines covered all these roads, and faced east."[37]

First contact between the invading and defending forces took place at about 6.30 A.M., but for several hours it was doubtful whether the main attack would be in the middle Raymond Road, on which Pemberton's left (Stevenson's division) rested, or on his right, held by Loring's division.

Pemberton's headquarters had been selected to the left of the center of the line, so that ready access could be had to the whole line. In view of the continued uncertainty as to the point of Grant's main attack, one of Pemberton's aides, Lieutenant J. C. Taylor, was sent forward to ascertain on what point the enemy was moving his heaviest forces. He found the skirmishing was equally severe on the right and left, and no definite conclusion could be formed as to which was the advance of the bulk of the Union force. A second time he went forward, conveying on this occasion an order to Colonel Adams, "When forced to retire, fall back with your whole command in front of the strongest column of the enemy." About 9:00 A.M. Colonel Adams with all his cavalry retired on a by-road just to the left of the Raymond Road.[38] Soon, it became evident that the main attack was to be on the left; and the fighting had not continued long before word came from Stevenson, saying that he "was hard pressed."[39]

The enemy continued strenuously trying to turn Stevenson's left flank. This necessarily compelled Stevenson to make a similar movement toward the left, thus extending his own line and causing a gap to occur between his and Bowen's division next him on the right. It was now Bowen's turn. Ordered to close the widening gap, rapidly increasing (as Stevenson extended with his left now in the air), Bowen came into action promptly. But would it be possible to hold the left of the line against such terrific fire and such heavy assaults as Stevenson reported were being delivered in that direction by the Union troops? Pemberton had merited faith in the superb infantry of Bowen, who were now plainly seen to be moving into the gap or, clinging unshaken, to dominate either side of it. Still, with the disparity of force so heavy, help must be had, and at once. From where could it come? Obviously only from the right. Of course an equally heavy attack might be made there at any time, "but in war, all risks are relative." It was far better to take the chance of having the right assailed than of having the left enveloped, then broken. So word was sent to Loring on the right, he having already been ordered "to keep the interval closed between his and General Bowen's division."[40]

Meanwhile, Stevenson had informed Pemberton that unless

reinforced at once he could no longer resist "the heavy and repeated attacks now along his whole line." At this, one of Bowen's two brigades, under Colonel F. M. Cockrell, and within a quarter hour his second brigade, under Brigadier General Martin E. Green, came up at a double quick, charging in fine style and driving back the enemy for more than half a mile.[41]

Field-Marshal Wolseley has accurately remarked, "the position of a brigade, the strength of a company, the command of a detachment, may affect and decide the whole outcome of a battle."

Where was Loring? For a time, the splendid charge of Bowen's brigades "turned the tide of battle in favor of the Confederates"; these are the words of the Federal General McPherson in making his official report. "Just at this juncture," writes Grant, "a messenger came from Hovey, asking for more reinforcements." Then Grant adds, "There were none to spare." Nevertheless, Grant pushed over one of McPherson's brigades even further beyond and almost around Stevenson's extended left flank, thus increasing the greatly superior Federal weight in that sector. To offset this maneuver, and feeling assured that there was no longer an important force in Loring's front, Pemberton despatched "several staff officers in rapid succession" to Loring; again ordering him to Stevenson's immediate assistance—where he was already overdue (having been momentarily expected to put two of his brigades into the fight on that front).[42] In a word, both sides had sought to stem the tide alternatingly running against them by moving into action all available reserves they had. Even so, there was no assurance either had sufficient. As Freeman sums up another crisis, "To state these facts is to measure the emergency." The description fits the tug of war at Champion's Hill as well as Sharpsburg. Much earlier than either of these battles, the greatest soldier of all time observed, "everything depends upon the individual man at his post, since the failure of any one individual may give the totality of circumstances a new trend." Champion's Hill stitched out this ancient pattern.

As victory beckoned after hours of doubtful outcome, Loring debated following orders, twice delivered, or adopting what he deemed to be a wiser course. Ere long he decided—and marched! But where? Had he bent his energies to prompt compliance, his mere obedience would have won the day for Pemberton.

About 4:00 P.M. a part of Stevenson's division broke badly and fell back in great disorder. They were partially rallied by the strenuous exertions of Pemberton and his staff, who quickly got the men back into the fight under their own officers.[43] Once again, to quote the immortal Frenchman, "In every battle a moment comes when the bravest of soldiers would like to turn tail. It needs but a trifle to put heart into him again." This done, Pemberton himself then went in search of Loring, supposedly no more than a mile distant at the most. But Loring had fallen away to the south, finally, after a wandering journey, making his way to Canton and to Johnston—inert, irresolute, and ill.[44]

A vivid picture of the efforts made by Pemberton's staff to speed Loring to Stevenson's hard-pressed left sector of the Confederates has been preserved in Pemberton's papers and in the Dorsey memoir of General (later Governor) Allen. The report that follows here comes from Pemberton's inspector general, Major Jacob Thompson, who wrote (shortly after the surrender) July 21, 1863: General Bowen was first ordered "to fall on the left with all his force. At the same time orders were sent to General Loring to follow up the movement of General Bowen." When there was some delay at Loring's coming, Thompson continues in his report to Pemberton, "you directed me to carry a renewal of the order, which I did, at the full speed of my horse. The order I delivered was, that 'General Pemberton desires you to come immediately, and with all despatch, to the left, to the support of General Stevenson, whatever may be in your front.' General Loring replied by asking me 'if General Pemberton knew that the enemy was in great force in his front.' I replied I did not know whether General Pemberton knew the fact or not, but I knew I repeated the order correctly; and if he did not comply with it, the responsibility was his, not mine. I returned to your headquarters, and repeated the conversation. Soon after, it was discovered that some two regiments had broken, and I went to endeavor to rally them. You soon came up, and by a few appropriate words addressed to them, closing by proposing to lead them back yourself, if their officers did not, the regiments rallied, and the officers petitioned you to let them lead them, which they did.

"We then moved along in their rear, far into the front, and on finding the enemy was making a flank movement to our left, the inquiry was made again, 'Where is Loring?' and some of the staff were sent to hunt him. On returning to headquarters, General Buford with his brigade was met; and after you had pointed out to him the position he was to take, you again directed me, if possible, to find General Loring. General T. H. Taylor and myself undertook to do so. We were gone for some time before we ascertained where he was; but finding he had gone on a road we did not know, to the left, we returned to report the fact to you. Upon our return we met with General Stevenson, who informed us, you had gone in the direction of the late headquarters of General Loring....

"Being near your person throughout three several days of

trial, I was struck with admiration at the prompt manner in which you discharged every duty devolved upon you, in your responsible position. I am, with great respect, your obedient servant.—J. Thompson, A. I. G."[45]

Some months after Champion's Hill, in October of 1863, the Confederate Secretary of War, James A. Seddon, in commenting on Pemberton's official report, stated that the President suggested it would be gratifying to have elucidated or explained "the extraordinary failure of General Loring to comply with your reiterated orders to attack, and do you feel assured your orders were received by him." Continuing, the Secretary of War added, "[Loring's] conduct, unless explained by some misapprehension, is incomprehensible to me."[46] It was, and remained, equally incomprehensible to Pemberton, who replied: "General Loring had been ordered to attack before General Cumming's brigade gave way, and the order had been again and again repeated; and in my opinion had Stevenson's division been promptly sustained, his troops would have deported themselves gallantly and creditably. I have received no explanation of the extraordinary failure of General Loring to comply with my reiterated orders to attack, and I do feel assured that my orders were received by him."[47] Had Seddon and Pemberton been more familiar with Loring's history under Stonewall Jackson their mystification would probably have been somewhat less. Of Loring, Jackson's biographer has written in part: "Loring's division . . . was so discontented as to be untrustworthy. It was useless with such troops to dream of further movements among the unhospitable hills. . . . and, more than all, the commander [Loring] had been disloyal to his superior [Jackson]. Although a regular officer of long service, he had permitted himself a license of speech which was absolutely unjustifiable, and throughout the [Valley] operations had shown his unfitness for his position.

Placed under the command of an officer who had been his junior in the Army of the United States, his sense of discipline was overborne by the slight to his vanity; and not for the first time nor the last the resentment of a petty mind ruined an enterprise which would have profited a nation."[48] To no less a degree had Loring ruined the day for Pemberton at Champion's Hill.

The Southern and Northern commanders are in substantial agreement as to the duration of the battle, Grant stating, "The battle of Champion's Hill lasted about four hours, hard fighting, preceded by two or three of skirmishing, some of which almost rose to the dignity of battle.... Osterhaus's and A. J. Smith's divisions had encountered the rebel advanced pickets as early as half-past seven."[49] On the other hand, Colonel Adams of Pemberton's command reported his pickets were skirmishing with the enemy on the Raymond Road at about six-thirty,[50] an hour ahead of Grant's recollection of the first contact.

As to the forces engaged: nearly all historians have greatly overestimated the numbers on both sides. "We had in this battle about 15,000 men absolutely engaged," Grant relates, and adds, "This excludes those that did not get up, all of McClernand's command except Hovey."[51] For his part, Pemberton has written: "General Loring's division of three brigades with an aggregate of 6,500 effective, according to his report of the 10th of May, took no active part in the battle." Champion's Hill was accordingly fought on the Confederate side by less than 11,000 men, viz., three brigades of Stevenson's division, aggregate 6,600, and by the two brigades composing Bowen's division, aggregate 4,300. "There were no other troops on the field, nor near it, except Loring's, who was not seriously engaged. Including Loring's three brigades there *could* have been available for action, 17,400 men."[52]

The withdrawal and retreat of the Confederates from "Sid" Champion's Hill commenced about 5:00 P.M. General Bowen had personally informed Pemberton that his division in the center "could no longer hold its position"; Stevenson's division on the left had given way around 4:30; "and the enemy were slowly pressing all Pemberton's forces engaged steadily back into old fields, where all advantages of position would be in favor of the attackers." Pemberton now felt it to be too late to save the day even should some part of Loring's division "come up immediately."[53]

The main body of the Confederate troops retired in good order to the intrenched line covering the wagon and railroad bridges over the Big Black. By nightfall the entire train of the Southern army had been crossed without loss.

The return of Confederate casualties, killed, wounded, and missing, came to 3,624.[54] Grant reported his total loss to be 2,441;[55] although this was some 1,000 less than Pemberton's casualties, one of Grant's divisions under Hovey lost more than one-third of its numbers. With energy and spirit, pursuit by the Federals had continued as long as it was light enough to see the roads.

At an early hour on the day of the Battle of Champion's Hill, Sherman in Jackson had received an urgent summons from Grant to come out to Edward's Depot as soon as he had completed his "work of destruction." Sherman, thus congenially occupied, took no part in the Battle of Champion's Hill. In his report to Grant he stated, "We have made fine progress today in the work of destruction. Jackson will no longer be a point of danger. The land is devastated for thirty miles around." On the day following the battle he reached the vicinity of Bolton, of which he writes as follows in his *Memoirs*. "Just beyond Bolton there was a small hewn-log house, standing back in a yard, in which was a well; at this

some of our soldiers were drawing water. I rode in to get a
drink, and, seeing a book on the ground, asked some soldier
to hand it to me. It was a volume of the Constitution of the
United States, and on the title-page was written the name of
Jefferson Davis. On inquiry of a negro, I learned that the
place belonged to the then President of the Southern Confed-
eration. His brother Joe Davis's plantation was not far off;
one of my staff-officers went there, with a few soldiers, and
took a pair of carriage horses, without my knowledge at the
time. He found Joe Davis at home, an old man, attended
by a young and affectionate niece; but they were overwhelmed
with grief to see their country overrun and swarming with
Federal troops."[56]

CHAPTER XV

Battle of Big Black River and Retirement to Vicksburg

DEPRIVED OF his last hope of holding the hill and battlefield on "Sid" Champion's land, Pemberton withdrew to, and placed his army in position on, the east bank of the Big Black River.

The Big Black River where it is crossed by the railroad bridge makes a bend somewhat in the shape of a horseshoe. Across this horseshoe, at its narrowest part, a line of rifle-pits had been constructed, making an excellent cover for infantry. Here at proper intervals dispositions were likewise made for field artillery. The line of pits, nearly north and south, was about one mile in length. North of, and for a considerable distance south of, the railroad (and of the dirt road to Edward's Depot, nearly parallel with it) extended a bayou. This in itself opposed a serious obstacle to an assault upon the pits. Furthermore, the bayou abutted north on the river and south upon a cypress brake, spreading itself nearly to the bank of the river.

In addition to the railroad bridge, which Pemberton had caused to be floored for the passage of artillery and wagons, the steamer *Dot,* from which the machinery had been taken, was converted into a bridge. This was managed by placing her fore and aft across the river.

Between the works and the bridge, about three-quarters of a mile, the country was open, being either old or cultivated fields. It afforded no cover should the troops be driven from the trenches. Finally, east and south of the railroad the topographical features of the country over which the enemy must necessarily pass were similar to those above described. But north of the railroad and about three hundred yards in front of the rifle-pits a copse of wood extended from the road to the river.[1]

At this point we come to Grant's single criticism of Pemberton throughout the entire campaign. He says: "We were now assured of our position between Johnston and Pemberton, without a possibility of a junction of their forces. Pemberton might have made a night march to the Big Black, crossed the bridge there and, by moving north on the west side, have eluded us and finally returned to Johnston. *But this would have given us Vicksburg.* It would have been his proper move, however, and the one Johnston would have made had he been in Pemberton's place. In fact it would have been in conformity with Johnston's orders to Pemberton."[2]

Apparently, Grant considered Pemberton's disobedience of Johnston's orders more to be condemned than Pemberton's disobedience of President Davis's admonition: "To hold both Vicksburg and Port Hudson is necessary to a connection with Trans-Mississippi." Clearly, Grant regarded Pemberton's independence of action in an entirely different light from his own disobedience of Halleck's orders. These had just reached him from Washington. "While the troops were standing as here described," says Grant, "an officer from Banks' staff came up and presented me with a letter from General Halleck, dated the 11th of May. It had been sent by the way of New Orleans to Banks to be forwarded to me. It ordered me to return to Grand Gulf and to co-operate from there with Banks against Port Hudson, and then to return with our combined forces to besiege Vicksburg. I told the officer that the order came too late, and that Halleck would not give it now if he knew our position. The bearer of the dispatch insisted that I ought to obey the order."[3]

Of two things we can be sure. Pemberton would have been happier had Grant acted in conformity with Halleck's order; Grant would have been better satisfied to see Pemberton conform to Johnston's order—and thus abandon Vicksburg. As it was, Grant must wait near two months for the Vicksburg prize, suffer heavy casualties in two fruitless assaults on the fort's entrenchments, come close to the shattering of his entire career. For determined efforts were afoot before the fateful siege was ended to have Grant superseded and removed from his command.[4]

When Sherman's corps reached the Big Black River in the early morning of May 17, it was reported that there was no bridge across the river and that it was swimming-deep. Captain Charles Ewing, of the Thirteenth United States Regulars, had been ordered to strip some artillery horses, mount his men, and swim the river. However, Sherman did not approve of this risky attempt. So he crept close to the brink of the river-bank (behind a corn-crib belonging to a plantation house near by) in order that he might make an examination of Pemberton's entrenchments on the opposite bank. A pontoon-bridge was then begun, and the Federal troops at once began their passage. As described by Sherman, "After dark, the whole scene was lit up with fires of pitch-pine. General Grant joined me there, and we sat on a log, looking at the passage of the troops by the light of those fires; the bridge swayed to and fro under the passing feet, and made a fine war-picture."[5]

Near daylight on the morning of the seventeenth, the enemy opened his artillery at long range on Pemberton's entrench-

ments. Very soon he pressed forward with infantry into the
copse of wood north of the railroad. About the same time
he opened on Colonel Cockrell's position (on Pemberton's
right) with two batteries, advancing a line of skirmishers and
throwing forward a column of infantry. However, this column was quickly driven back by the Confederate batteries.
But presently the enemy, amassing a large force in the woods
immediately north of the railroad, advanced at a run and with
loud cheers.[6] The Confederate troops occupying the center
did not do their duty. Instead, they fled. Major Samuel H.
Lockett, Chief Engineer of Pemberton's Department, has left
this description of the precipitate retreat: "The affair of Big
Black bridge was one which an ex-Confederate participant
naturally dislikes to record.... About 9 o'clock our troops on
the left (Vaughn's brigade) broke from their breastworks and
came pell-mell toward the bridges.... After the stampede at
the bridge [4,000 troops deserted in a solid body to the
enemy[7]] orders were issued for the army to fall back to Vicksburg.... General Pemberton rode himself to Bovina, a small
railroad station about two and a half miles from the river. I
was the only staff-officer with him. He was very much de-
pressed by the events of the last two days, and for some time
after mounting his horse rode in silence. He finally said:
'Just thirty years ago I began my military career ... and to-
day—the same date—that career is ended in disaster and dis-
grace.' I strove to encourage him...."[8] But Pemberton had
for the moment lost confidence in himself and in his men.

At Big Black, Pemberton for the first time in his long army
career had found himself commander of a routed army; for
such it truly was. Under terrific pressure since Grant's crossing of the Mississippi, and weighed down with the continued
impasse between the ideas of Davis and Johnston, Pemberton
had suffered a case of nerves in the company of a trusted con-

fidant. Happily for the Confederacy, leader and men speedily regained their lost morale.

Under strain, at least once in their respective careers, Lee, Grant, and even Napoleon had likewise cracked.

"Night fell on the confused [Wilderness] field. . . . The woods were now on fire in many places. Distant flames cast weird shadows. Choking smoke was everywhere. And from the thickets came the cries of the wounded, frantic lest the flames reach them ere the litter-bearers did. It was war in Inferno." [Grant's losses May 5-7, 1864, in the Battle of the Wilderness were 17,666; Lee's, approximately 7,600.] . . . Grant was overwhelmed at his failure. He 'went into his tent, and throwing himself face down on his cot, gave way to the greatest emotion.' Charles Francis Adams said: 'I never saw a man so agitated in my life'."[9]

As for Lee, on the eve of the evacuation of Petersburg, his "nerves were beginning to feel the strain of a day in purgatory, and when he read the President's message, he tore it into bits."[9a] To his son he wrote [1864]: "If defeated, nothing will be left for us to live for."

In Paris after Waterloo, Napoleon, summoned by the Deputies, refused to leave his palace. "I ought to have gone," he said subsequently, *"but . . . I lacked courage;* I am only a man, after all. My memories . . . terrified me."[10]

Neither side suffered heavy losses at the Battle of Big Black River. Grant reported his as under 300; Pemberton gave his as 1,024.[11]

After seeing that all his retreating troops still subject to command had crossed the river to the west bank, Pemberton ordered the bridges fired. This was effectually accomplished under the personal supervision of Major Lockett. Then, such guns as had not been abandoned to the enemy were placed in battery on the bluff on the west bank. There, with others already established and a sufficient force of infantry, they held Grant's advancing columns for some time in check. However, both Pemberton's flanks were now vulnerable. Hence, Grant might reach Vicksburg simultaneously with the Confederates or interpose a heavy force between Pemberton and the stronghold. In consequence, as Major Lockett's report indicates, nothing remained but to retire the defending army within the defenses of Vicksburg—the continued holding of which Pemberton conceived to be the main purpose of the government in retaining his army in Mississippi.

Orders were accordingly issued by Pemberton about 10:00 A.M. and Major General Stevenson directed to conduct the retreat. It was executed without haste and in good order. Pemberton himself proceeded at once from Bovina to Vicksburg to prepare for its defense—in the firm belief that if invested he would before long receive relief.[12]

Grant for one plainly expected an early attempt to free Vicksburg and Pemberton's army. His *Memoirs* supply the evidence: "Vicksburg [after the Battle of the Big Black] was not yet captured, and there was no telling what might happen before it was taken.... Johnston was in my rear, only fifty miles away, with an army not much inferior in numbers to the one I had with me, and I knew he was being reinforced. There was danger of his coming to the assistance of Pemberton, and after all he might defeat my anticipations of capturing the garrison if, indeed, he did not prevent the capture of the city."[13] But Johnston, strictly observant of the established principles of war, was "without a touch of that aggressive genius which distinguished Lee, Grant, and Jackson."[14] So speaks Jackson's biographer. More recently the view has been expressed that "Vicksburg was hopelessly lost to the Confederacy as soon as Grant crossed the Mississippi" below the town. "I have an idea," says the historian in question, "that

General Pemberton might have saved his army for use as a field force and for attacking Grant on his flank, though I know equally well," he continues, "that if he had evacuated the town and its defences without a siege, he would have been called a traitor by everybody in the South. In other words, he was facing an insoluble dilemma, and I do not believe that General Johnston helped him solve it."[15]

Adding to the difficulties of the retreat, after the stunning shock which came with the panic and defeat at Big Black River, the weather turned stifling. "As Grant's onrushing troops swirled all around, the outlines of the hill city rose slowly through the heated dust—Vicksburg and security. Passing raddled fields, turning colorless from the powdered earth that rose beneath their tramp, the grey soldiers slacked off the turnpikes along the high ground until they came inside the city's breastworks. As word carried down the crooked line of march that the race to Vicksburg had been won, the footsore remnants in the rear flooded down the pike."[16]

There was a mile or more of hilly country in easy view from Vicksburg's eminences; as far as one could see, it was crawling with people in blue. As the retreating army settled in its trenches, the successive waves of men close behind them finished throwing up their makeshift barriers. The sun was setting red; treetops were gilded briefly by its last rays—and then it withdrew. "The sky faded to a cool green and it was dark." For forty-seven days at least a portion of the Confederate South was inviolate.

One of the immediate results of the retreat from Big Black was the necessity of abandoning the Confederate defenses on the Yazoo at Snyder's Mill. That position and the line of Chickasaw Bayou were no longer tenable. All stores that could be transported were ordered to be sent into Vicksburg as rapidly as possible, the rest, including heavy guns, to be destroyed.

There was at this time a large quantity of corn (probably 25,000 or 30,000 bushels) on boats, much of which might have been brought in had it been possible to furnish the necessary wagons, but none were available. Two companies were directed to remain at Snyder's Mill, making a show of force until the approach of the enemy by land should compel them to retire. To them was intrusted the duty of forwarding all stores possible and of destroying the remainder. This detachment rejoined its command in Vicksburg on the morning of the eighteenth. Every precaution was taken to guard the important approaches to the city by Forney's and Smith's divisions, while the troops which had been engaged in the battles of the sixteenth and seventeenth were bivouacked in rear of the intrenchments.[17]

On the morning of the eighteenth the troops were disposed from right to left as follows: Major General Stevenson's division of four brigades occupied the line from the Warrenton Road, including a portion of the river front, to the railroad, a distance of about five miles; Major General Forney, with two brigades, the line between the railroad and the Graveyard Road, about two miles; and Major General Smith, with three brigades (the Mississippi State troops) and a small detachment from Loring's division, the line from the Graveyard Road to the river front on the north, about one and a quarter miles. Brigadier General Bowen's division was held in reserve to strengthen any portion of the line most threatened; and Waul's Texas Legion (about 500) was in reserve, especially to support the right of Moore's or the left of Lee's brigades. On the entire line about one hundred and two pieces of artillery of different caliber, principally field, were placed in position at such points as were deemed most suitable to the character of the gun, changes of location being made when occasion called for it.[18]

"A fortified line seven miles long had been built among the ridges and ravines to the rear or east of Vicksburg, extending from the river above to the river below, and enclosing an area about four miles by two. The fortifications anticipated, in some ways, modern trench systems—detached strong points, connected by more lightly held fire trenches or rifle pits. Unoccupied for a year, the works had washed badly. During the two days before Grant's army completed its investment, and the two months of the siege, there was constant work on the lines—work that was made more difficult by the limited supply of shovels. Bayonets could be used as picks, after a fashion, but the total supply of 'regular' shovels, but five hundred to be distributed along a seven-mile line, had to be supplemented by makeshift affairs of wood improvised by the soldiers."[19]

With all this activity and effort under the orders of the laconic Pemberton, there had been a great coming and going of his West Point associates. To the local diggers they seemed "mighty stuck-up," what with their rigid shoulders, stiff manners, and terse commands. Yet, the siege once in full swing, "most men in the ranks owned to a sour admiration of those same West Pointers."

According to Pemberton's chief of staff, "the engineering skill of the commander and his fertility and expedients were conspicuously displayed. Works which under the ceaseless and concentrated fire of hundreds of guns were demolished, reappeared in improved forms which could be suggested only by consummate ingenuity." These works, constructed to withstand guns used in ordinary warfare, proved wholly incapable of resisting the heavy metal of the Federal forces. Subjected to incessant, galling musketry fire, the Confederate batteries could only be discharged erratically. "Here it was particularly," says Major Memminger, "that the trained intelligence of the Commanding General was exhibited. The position of the pieces was constantly changing; embankments disappeared under the fire of the enemy's guns, but the artillery would still be found in position and stronger than before."[20] Apparently there were situations in which a West Pointer had his uses.

From the very day he assumed command of the Department of Mississippi and Eastern Louisiana, October 14, 1862, Pemberton and his staff officers, as noted, had commenced and continued without let-up their efforts to collect an ample store of supplies for Vicksburg and Port Hudson. But the difficulties of transportation—the wretched condition of the railroads and the scarcity of wagons—had proven insuperable obstacles. In addition, during this time positive prohibition had been issued from the War Department in Richmond against the interference of commanding generals or other officers with railroad transportation.[21] That was a function of the *civil* arm of the Confederacy.

Hence, when the retreat to Vicksburg commenced after the Battle of the Big Black, the stores of subsistence for Vicksburg and Port Hudson, though large, were still not ample. Accordingly, further efforts were made on the retreat to supplement the food supply that the garrison would require. All wagons not assigned to more important purposes were commandeered to collect corn, rice, peas, and sugar. In the hands of private parties it was considered these staples would inevitably fall into the hands of the enemy. In the same manner instructions were then given by Pemberton from Bovina that all cattle, sheep, and hogs along the line of march should be driven into the lines of Vicksburg. In this way a large extra amount of provisions were secured; during the first weeks of the siege fresh meat kept the defending army well and fully fed.[22]

In short, Pemberton could truthfully state in his official report that he had spared no exertions to have Vicksburg and Port Hudson abundantly provisioned, and that whenever the supply fell short of the demand, or of his expectations, it was caused by circumstances wholly beyond his control.

In Vicksburg at the start of siege, still to be engaged against the troops of Grant's three corps, were the fresh divisions of Major Generals John H. Forney and Martin Luther Smith. Meantime the destruction of the crossings of the Big Black (the quick work of the Confederate engineers under Lockett in setting fire to barrels of turpentine alongside) had gained time for the others against their pursuers. This happy delay gave Pemberton needed opportunity to properly place his men in their freshly fortified lines.

During the night of the seventeenth nothing of importance occurred. Most of the artillery was speedily emplaced in effective positions, and immediate measures were taken to arm all men who had either unavoidably lost or thrown away their arms on the retreat.[23]

About noon of May 18, while Pemberton was engaged in an inspection of his entrenchments in company with several of his general officers and his chief engineer, the following communication was received by courier from Johnston:

"Camp, Between Livingston and Brownsville
May 17, 1863
"Lieutenant-General Pemberton:
    "Your dispatch of to-day by Captain [Thomas] Henderson was received. If Haynes' Bluff is untenable, Vicksburg is of no value and cannot be held. If, therefore, you are invested in Vicksburg, you must ultimately surrender.

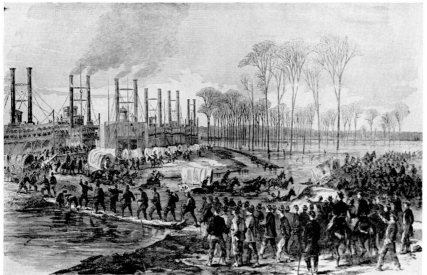

Headquarters of General Grant near Vicksburg. This sketch, by H. Lovie from The Soldier in Our Civil War, *illustrates some of the conditions encountered by the attacking army in the early spring of 1863.*

Admiral Porter's flotilla arriving below Vicksburg on the night of April 16, 1863. General Sherman is in the foreground in a yawl.

Bayou navigation—"crashing through the trees, carrying away pilot house, smoke-stacks, and everything above-deck. . . ."

Union gunboats passing the Vicksburg batteries at night.

Under such circumstances, instead of losing both troops and place, we must, if possible, save the troops. If it is not too late, evacuate Vicksburg and its dependencies, and march to the northeast.

"Most respectfully, your obedient servant,

"J. E. JOHNSTON,

General"[24]

Lee's biographer has lately noted that occurrences affecting some of the major events of the war could not be traced because of missing documents. "This was true," he writes, "of the preliminaries of the Seven Days, of Jackson's Valley Campaign, of Vicksburg, of Gettysburg and of the fearsome months of the winter of 1864-65. One could not be sure, even after searching to the last supplement of the final volume, what Lee had said on some vital subjects, what Jackson had done at certain decisive moments, or how Pemberton had faced the crisis that came when he was forsaken by his comrades in arms."[25]

The documents revealing how Pemberton faced the crisis that came when he was forsaken by his comrades in arms are no longer missing—and the answer follows.

CHAPTER XVI

The Siege

"THE EVACUATION of Vicksburg! It meant the loss of the valuable stores and munitions of war collected for its defense; the fall of Port Hudson; the surrender of the Mississippi River, and the severance of the Confederacy," wrote Pemberton in his official report, August, 1863. "These were mighty interests, which, had I deemed the evacuation practicable in the sense in which I interpreted General Johnston's instructions, might well have made me hesitate to execute them. I believed it to be in my power to hold Vicksburg. I knew and appreciated the earnest desire of the government and of the people that it should be held. I knew, perhaps better than any other individual, under all the circumstances, its capacity for defense. As long ago as February 17 last, in a letter addressed to His Excellency the President, I had suggested the possibility of the investment of Vicksburg by land and water, and for that reason the necessity of ample supplies of ammunition as well as of subsistence to stand a siege. My application met his favorable consideration, and additional ammunition was ordered. With proper economy of subsistence and ordnance stores I knew that I could stand a siege. I had a firm reliance on the desire of the President and of General Johnston to do all that could be done to raise a siege. I felt that every effort would be made, and I believed it would be successful. With these convictions on my own mind, I immediately summoned a council of war composed of all my general officers. I laid before them General Johnston's communication, but desired them to confine the expression of their opinions to the question of practicability. Having obtained their views, the following communication was addressed to General Johnston:

> "HDQRS. DEPARTMENT OF MISSISSIPPI
> AND EASTERN LOUISIANA,
> Vicksburg, *May 18, 1863*.

"GENERAL JOSEPH E. JOHNSTON:

"General: I have the honor to acknowledge the receipt of your communication, in reply to mine by the hands of Captain [Thomas] Henderson. In a subsequent letter of same date as this latter, I informed you that the men had failed to hold the trenches at Big Black Bridge, and that, as a consequence, Snyder's Mill was directed to be abandoned. On the receipt of your communication, I immediately assembled a council of war of the general officers of this command, and having laid your instructions before them, asked the free expression of their opinions as to the practicability of carrying them out. The opinion was unanimously expressed that it was impossible to withdraw the army from this position with such *morale* and material as to be of further service to the Confederacy. While the council of war was assembled, the guns of the enemy opened on the works, and it was at the same time reported that they were crossing the Yazoo River at Brandon's Ferry, above Snyder's Mill. I have decided to hold Vicksburg as long as is possible, with the firm hope that the Government may yet be able to assist me in keeping this obstruction to the enemy's free navigation of the Mississippi River. I still conceive it to be the most important point in the Confederacy.

"Very respectfully, your obedient servant,

> J. C. PEMBERTON,
> *Lieutenant-General, Commanding.*"[1]

First Three Days of Siege, May 18 to May 20

On the morning of the eighteenth of May there was but one brigade in position in the rear of Vicksburg; General Louis Hébert's Louisianians and Mississippians were on the Jackson Road. Along this route the Union troops were fast advancing. But during the course of the day General Martin L. Smith's division marched rapidly to the northeastern corner of the works. By 5:00 P.M. Smith had reached the breastworks in his sector, throwing out skirmishers while forming his front lines, an outer line of defense on the range of hills north of the Fort Hill Road. The precaution was a wise one: within twenty minutes the enemy was up and bickering with Smith's outposts, who shortly withdrew to stronger positions in the inner line of defense. Before long, the whole front occupied by Smith was pelted by infantry, backed up with brisk artillery fire. The siege of Vicksburg had begun.

To man his entire line of close to eight miles, Pemberton was able to bring into the trenches about 18,500 muskets; but it was necessary to keep a reserve ready at all times to reinforce any point heavily threatened. Accordingly, Bowen's division (about 2,400) and Waul's Texas Legion (about 500) were designated for that purpose, thus reducing the force in the trenches to little over 15,500 men.[2]

By the morning of May 19 there was complete contact between the opposing forces. Sherman's corps was closest up; and in front of Grant was an enemy he had had on the run ever since crossing the Mississippi near three weeks before. Victor at Port Gibson, Raymond, Jackson, Champion's Hill and Big Black River, Grant anticipated an easy progression of triumphs before the garrison in Vicksburg had recovered its order and morale. From top to bottom, this feeling ran throughout the invading army. From top to bottom, all were wrong. Once again it was to be acted out in much blood and

many deaths that in defense of a strong position the balance of
endurance and courage inclined neither to the North nor to
the South. Grant in the end—but not yet—"came to see that
it was futile to pursue strategical objects unless tactical success
was possible."

The shelter of stout entrenchments had infused new heart
into Vicksburg's defenders. At 2:00 P.M. on May 19 Grant
made his first assault on Pemberton's lines, advancing in a
straightforward fashion along the main roads, "the natural
avenues of approach."[3] This time, however, as Grant's troops
struck the main line of Pemberton's defense, it was to be no
run-over affair. There were two bloody assaults—and two
bloody repulses. The Union advance had re-acquired the disadvantages of a frontal attack. Until now Grant had benefited from three distinct advantages: from the element of
surprise and uncertainty, from a divided command among the
Confederates, and from the dislocating effect of being on the
Confederates' rear and hence across their communications with
their base at Vicksburg. Now the strategic situation was far
different. As another has so wisely pointed out, "Like snow
which is squeezed into a snowball, direct pressure has always
the tendency to harden and consolidate the resistance of an
opponent, and the more compact it becomes the slower it is
to melt."[4]

The charges of the Federals had come on in four lines.
Mainly they had been directed against Smith's division, but
part of the brunt had been borne by the Sixth Missouri of
Bowen's command. It is true, some of the attackers got so
close that grape and canister were substituted for shell in the
Confederate guns and several Union flags were actually planted
on the face of the works. But the final result was a severe
repulse and the loss of two stand of colors. Grant's account
of these happenings is brief and inadequate: "The enemy had

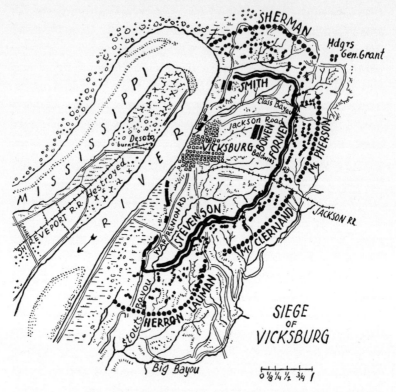

Based on Steele's American Campaigns.

been much demoralized by his defeats at Champion's Hill and the Big Black," he relates, and then explains: "I believed he would not make much effort to hold Vicksburg. Accordingly at two o'clock I ordered an assault. It resulted in securing more advanced positions for all our troops where they were fully covered from the fire of the enemy."[5]   On the other hand, Sherman's statement is franker in admission of rebuff. He states: "Our lines connected, and invested about three-quarters of the land-front of the fortifications of Vicksburg. On the supposition that the garrison of Vicksburg was demoralized by the defeats at Champion Hills and at the rail-

road crossing of the Big Black, General Grant ordered an
assault at our respective fronts on the 19th. My troops reached
the top of the parapet, but could not cross over. The rebel
parapets were strongly manned, and the enemy fought hard
and well. My loss was pretty heavy, falling chiefly on the
Thirteenth Regulars, whose commanding officer, Captain
Washington, was killed, and several other regiments were
pretty badly cut up."[6]

The assaults of the nineteenth finally ended, Pemberton dispatched a courier to the President with this telegram: "We
are occupying the trenches around Vicksburg. The enemy
is investing it, and will probably attempt an assault. Our
men have considerably recovered their *morale,* but unless a
large force is sent at once to relieve it, Vicksburg before long
must fall. I have used every effort to prevent all this, but in
vain."[7]

Twenty days since his crossing of the Mississippi, one hundred and eighty miles of marching done, five battles fought
and won, found Grant "in continuous line from the Walnut
Hills to a considerable distance below the Baldwin's Ferry
Road, communication with the fleet opened on the Yazoo,
and a base of supplies established on its bluffs; a base with
no long line to protect."[8]

"Pemberton was now completely surrounded. Porter's fleet
commanded the Mississippi and Yazoo rivers. The corps of
Sherman, McPherson and McClernand from right to left
closed the avenue of escape to the east and south."[9] But Pemberton did not know it, nor did Davis, Johnston—or Lee. The
Union had forged one more link in a chain of events all point-
ing in the same direction. Johnston held the only key to relief,
if he would but use it.

The day following Grant's first assaults, he commenced,
under cover of heavy cannonading, moving his men from Pem-

berton's right toward the Confederate center and left. At
noon the mortar fleet of Admiral Porter took up its position
on the west side of the peninsula and commenced its bombardment of Vicksburg. Some three hours earlier Pemberton
sent a dispatch by courier to General Johnston: "The enemy
assaulted our intrenched lines yesterday at two points (center
and left), and was repulsed with heavy loss. Our loss small.
I cannot estimate the enemy's force now engaged around
Vicksburg at less than 60,000; it is probably more. At this
hour (8.30 a.m.) he is briskly cannonading with long-range
guns. That we may save ammunition, his fire is rarely returned. At present our main necessity is musket-caps. Can
you send them to me by hands of couriers or citizens? An
army will be necessary to relieve Vicksburg, and that quickly.
Will it not be sent? Please let me hear from you, if possible."[10] Whether or not an army was necessary to relieve
Vicksburg, none was to come: Johnston had already determined in his own mind that all was lost. It was as well for
Pemberton, he did not know this either. Turning to Johnston's report to the Secretary of War, we find his attitude at
this time, plain beyond all doubt: "Convinced of the impossibility of collecting a sufficient force to break the investment
of Vicksburg should it be completed, appreciating the difficulty of extricating the garrison... I [Johnston] ordered the
evacuation of both places [Vicksburg and Port Hudson]....
Vicksburg... was lost when my orders of May 13 and 15 were
disobeyed. To this loss were added the labor, privations, and
certain capture of a gallant army...."[11] When Johnston per-
sisted in this stand, the authorities in Richmond were dumb-
founded. On June 16 the Secretary of War telegraphed him
in protest and in desperation: "Vicksburg must not be lost,
at least without a struggle.... I [Seddon] rely on you still to
avert the loss." Within a few days Grant would be reinforced

to a strength of 71,000 men and 248 guns.[12]   The difficulties
of extricating the garrison and raising the siege were indeed
increasing.

And yet the first siege of Richmond, of Knoxville, and of
Chattanooga were alike raised or abandoned under a sufficient
pressure.   In Napoleon's lifetime and experience, even he
found the way to India barred when forced to abandon his
siege of Acre.   At Mantua, Napoleon's siege was raised by
Wurmser, "who blocked the Great Man's line of retreat upon
Milan, and put the French army in the utmost danger."

Was Grant "a greater than Napoleon"; or Wurmser not to
be compared with Johnston?

FOURTH DAY OF SIEGE, MAY 21

All soldiers confined for trivial offenses were ordered returned
to their commands; chewing tobacco was impressed; skirmishing without special object was forbidden as being a useless
waste of ammunition.   Without intermission Admiral Porter's mortar fleet kept up its bombardment of the city.   In
the afternoon Porter's gunboats steamed up and added their
shell fire to the mortar attack from the river.   Fear being felt
for the safety of the powder magazines, General Stevenson
was directed to organize a protective guard from among the
most reputable of the citizens.   Considering the possibility of
innumerable assaults and the likelihood of having to march
out from his intrenchments to meet and co-operate with an
assisting army expected under Johnston, strict orders were
issued by Pemberton that "ammunition should be hoarded
with the most zealous care."[13]

On the representations of General Stevenson (then charged
with the final responsibility for supplies) that he would not be
able to feed the large number of mules and horses in Vicksburg, orders were at once given to drive them beyond the lines

for pasturage, unless steps could be taken to get these valuable animals to Johnston's army. The effort failed.

Before the day was out, Pemberton by courier reported to General Johnston: "During the past two days the enemy has passed up the river in transports in large force for a point not yet discovered. The enemy has continued a spirited fire all day; also his shelling from mortar-boats. Our men have replied rarely. Two large transports came down loaded with troops. They are evidently re-enforcing their present large force. Am I to expect re-enforcements? From what direction, and how soon? Have you heard anything from General Loring? Can you send me musket-caps by courier? The enemy kept up incessant sharpshooting all yesterday on the left and center, and picked off our officers and men whenever they showed themselves. Their artillery fire was very heavy; plowed up our works considerably, and dismounted two guns on the center. The works were repaired, and the guns replaced last night. The great question is ammunition. The men credit and are encouraged by a report that you are near with a large force. They are fighting in good spirits, and the reorganization is complete."[14]

Meantime, in the Federal camps things were not idle: positions were strengthened; road making in earnest was taken up in the invaders' rear; and the Federal line of supply by river was re-established. Grant in passing around among his men was recognized. "In a moment the cry was taken up all along the line, 'Hard tack! Hard tack!'" Grant told the men nearest to him they would soon have it and the cry was instantly changed to cheers. That night the Union soldiers were relieved of their exclusive diet of poultry and country produce, with corn bread, and were back on the old stand-bys of bacon and hard tack.

Grant had so far profited by a strategy of swift surprises.

What surprise could he now spring that would not demand a fearful sacrifice on the part of his command?

On the twentieth of May Grant's three corps commanders had agreed, on comparing notes, that the assault of May 19 against Pemberton's works had failed (1) by reason of the natural strength of his position and (2) by reason of the attacks having been limited to the strongest parts of Pemberton's line. Sherman remarks, "It was not a council of war, but a mere consultation, resulting in orders from General Grant for us [Sherman, McPherson, and McClernand] to make all possible preparations for a renewed assault on the 22d, simultaneously at 10 A.M.[15]

There would be five stand of Union colors in Confederate hands when the assaults of the twenty-second were ended.

FIFTH DAY OF SIEGE, MAY 22

That day was bright and clear and the Mississippi sun was blistering. In the morning, many indications pointed to a grand assault upon Pemberton's entrenchments: the fire from the Federal artillery and sharpshooters was heavy and incessant until noon. At this time the gunboats also came to life and opened on the city from the river side.

On Stevenson's front (the right of Pemberton's outer lines) at about 1:00 P.M. a heavy force moved out to the assault, making a gallant charge. The Federal troops were allowed to approach unmolested to within good musket range. Then, however, every available gun was opened upon them, and Stevenson's men rising in their trenches fired volley after volley. The effect was so deadly that the ground was literally covered in some places with the Union dead and wounded. This attack had been made by McClernand's corps. Before their retirement, however, the angle of one of Stevenson's redoubts had been breached by the Federal artillery. McClernand's infantry thereupon determined to storm the open ditches. One hundred volunteers were called for, their reward to be a discharge from further service and a bounty of $300. Within no time a hundred "fearless" started on their desperate enterprise for the open hole in the Confederate fortifications. About sixty, under the command of a lieutenant colonel, succeeded in their rush and planted two colors on the parapet. Now there was a call for Confederate volunteers; it was of vital importance to drive the bluecoats out. Response quickly came from Colonel E. W. Pettus, of the Twentieth Alabama Regiment, musket in hand. He came with two companies of Waul's Texas Legion, under Captain L. D. Bradley and Lieutenant James Hogue. Stevenson reported their success, adding, "A more gallant feat than this has not illustrated our annals during the war."[16]

The assaults against General Forney's front—in the center of Pemberton's lines—were carried forward by McPherson's corps. Forney reported several attacks, the first taking place at 11:00 A.M. and the last occurring around 5:00 P.M. To use his exact words: "These assaults were made by larger bodies, and apparently with greater determination, than those of May 19.... The enemy was repulsed in each of his attempts, though he succeeded in getting a few men into our exterior ditches at each point of attack, from which they were, however, driven before night. Hand-grenades were used at each point with good effect.... On this day the casualties in my division were 42 killed and 95 wounded. The loss of the enemy must have reached 2,000."[17]

The third sector to encounter the Union assaults was occupied by the division of General Martin L. Smith. This was the left of Pemberton's line. Here the attacks were to be launched by Sherman's corps. General Smith says in his report: "The 22d passed in the same manner until about 2 p.m., when a column was discovered advancing against the right of Shoup's brigade. It was immediately driven back. Another, then approached on the right of the center. This was dispersed without great effort and with considerable loss. Again the enemy appeared in increased force on my right and Forney's left. He was promptly repulsed with heavy loss. This terminated the day's operations, with the exception of the same heavy fire of musketry and artillery kept up until dark along my entire front. After these several decided repulses, the enemy seemed to have abandoned the idea of taking by assault, and went vigorously at work to thoroughly invest and attack by regular approaches...."[18]

Had Sherman been permitted opportunity for perusal of this drab account, doubtless he would have snorted. His *Memoirs* more vividly picture the cruel repulse that day, and frankly divulge his fruitless casualties: "I reconnoitered my front thoroughly in person, from right to left," his story runs, "and concluded to make my real attack at the right flank of the bastion, where the graveyard road entered the enemy's intrenchments, and at another point in the curtain about a hundred yards to its right (our left); also to make a strong demonstration by Steele's division, about a mile to our right, toward the river. All our field-batteries were put in position, and were covered by good epaulements; the troops were brought forward, in easy support, concealed by the shape of the ground; and to the minute, viz., 10 A.M. of May 22d, the troops sprang to the assault. A small party, that might be called a forlorn hope, provided with plank to cross the ditch, advanced at a run, up to the very ditch; the lines of infantry sprang from cover, and advanced rapidly in line of battle. I took a position within two hundred yards of the rebel parapet, on the off slope of a spur of ground, where by advancing two or three steps I could see every thing. The rebel line, con-

cealed by the parapet, showed no sign of unusual activity, but
as our troops came in fair view, the enemy rose behind their
parapet and poured a furious fire upon our lines; and, for
about two hours, we had a severe and bloody battle, but at
every point we were repulsed....

"After our men had been fairly beaten back from off the
parapet, and had got cover behind the spurs of ground close
up to the rebel works, General Grant came to where I was,
on foot, having left his horse some distance to the rear. I
pointed out to him the rebel works, admitted that my assault
had failed, and he said the result with McPherson and Mc-
Clernand was about the same.... Punctually at 3 P.M., hearing heavy firing down along the line to my left, I ordered the
second assault. It was a repetition of the first, equally unsuccessful and bloody. It also transpired that the same thing had
occurred with General McPherson, who lost in this second
assault some most valuable officers and men, without adequate
result; and that General McClernand, instead of having taken
any single point of the rebel main parapet, had only taken
one or two small outlying lunettes open to the rear, where
his men were at the mercy of the rebels behind their main
parapet, and most of them were actually thus captured....
The two several assaults made May 22d, on the lines of Vicksburg, had failed, by reason of the great strength of the position and the determined fighting of its garrison. I have since
seen the position at Sevastopol, and without hesitation I declare that at Vicksburg to have been the more difficult of the
two."[19]

Grant himself has noted that the attacks of this day "only
served to increase our casualties, without giving any benefits
whatever.... at no place were we able to enter."

The fact that the attacking troops had momentarily planted
their flags on several points along the Confederate parapets

was illusory. "Any other result, would, in the nature of war, have been a fluke."

The Federal losses came to 3,000. What is more—these were the last assaults upon Vicksburg, even to its fall. Grant had determined upon "a regular siege—'to out-camp the enemy' as it were, and to incur no more losses. The experience of the 22d convinced officers and men that this was best, and they went to work on the defenses and approaches with a will."[20]

SIXTH DAY OF SIEGE, MAY 23

With Grant's decision to let the snowball "melt by the force of nature—empty stomachs—with the gentle assistance of harassing fire and mines,"[21] things settled down. Pemberton's diary records the sixth day of siege was unusually quiet, "little artillery firing until late in the afternoon."[22] The enemy's sharpshooters were likewise more cautious; and the impression made was that the besieging force had been genuinely staggered by the severe repulse of the day previous. Many of their dead were still lying unburied in plain sight of the Confederate trenches. Actually, the day's only activity came from the mortar fleet; it kept up an unremitting and heavy fire. At nightfall badly shattered parts of the works were repaired by Pemberton's engineers. After sunset General Stevenson was ordered to collect all ammunition scattered in the defenders front and in the cartridge boxes of the enemy's dead. For the first time, forage was reported as short. In consequence, instructions were issued that the supply for artillery horses should be shared with the animals allotted to ambulance wagons. More grazing was recommended, and horses for the staff were dropped as costly luxuries.

Behind Grant's front all was now ready for the pick and shovel. "Vicksburg was so important to the enemy," he wrote in later years, "that I believed he would make the most strenuous efforts to raise the siege, even at the risk of losing ground elsewhere." As a result, the Federal leader fortified his front and rear. His lines, more than fifteen miles long, ran from Haines's Bluff to Vicksburg, to Warrenton. Before long, his forces were almost within a second Vicksburg. "The ground about Vicksburg," his *Memoirs* attest, "is admirable for defence. On the north it is about two hundred feet above the Mississippi River at the highest point and very much cut up by the washing rains; the ravines were grown up with cane and underbrush, while the sides and tops were covered with a dense forest. Farther south the ground flattens out somewhat, and was in cultivation. But here, too, it was cut up by ravines and small streams. The enemy's lines of defense followed the crest of a ridge from the river north of the city eastward, then southerly around to the Jackson road, full three miles back of the city; thence in a southwesterly direction to the river. Deep ravines of the description given lay in front of these defences. As there is a succession of gullies cut out by rains along the side of the ridge, the line was necessarily very irregular. To follow each of these spurs with intrenchments, so as to command the slopes on either side, would have lengthened their line very much. Generally therefore, or in many places, their line would run from near the head of one gully nearly straight to the head of another, and an outer work triangular in shape, generally open in the rear, was thrown up on the point; with a few men in this outer work they commanded the approaches to the main line completely."[23]

Shut up in such complete and close investment, with a large civil population of men, women, and children to feed (in addition to its combatant force), the fate of Vicksburg was merely a question of time—if Grant could prevent sallies or relief from the outside.

The Siege of Vicksburg, from the painting by Chapelle. The soldiers managed to find a little protection from the burning sun, if not from the fire of the defenders.

Battery Hickenlooper, sketched by Theodore R. Davis for Harper's Weekly *of July 4, 1863. According to the artist, this work was the most thoroughly complete of all the Union approaches. The opposing forces were here within talking distance of each other.*

Vicksburg from the riverbank. Sketched by Theodore R. Davis on the day of surrender. This view of the city appeared in Harper's Weekly *for August 1, 1863. The guns of the river batteries (one is shown on the right), the artist wrote, were "cast rough and mounted, as the technical phrase is, with the skin on, which adds to their strength about 15 per cent."*

Confederate scouts with percussion caps for Vicksburg. The special artist of the London Illustrated News, *in which this appeared, August 29, 1863, sketched the scene on the spot in the moonlight.*

That the outside effort would be made was as fully expected by Sherman as by Grant. Sherman expressed his belief in this wise. "We estimated Pemberton's whole force in Vicksburg at thirty thousand men, and it was well known that the rebel General Joseph E. Johnston was engaged in collecting another strong force near the Big Black, with the intention to attack our rear, and thus to afford Pemberton an opportunity to escape with his men. Even then the ability of General Johnston was recognized, and General Grant told me that he was about the only general on that side whom he feared."[24] In recounting what was apprehended from Johnston at this time, Grant noted: "We were now as strong for defence against the garrison of Vicksburg as they were against us; but I knew that Johnston was in our rear, and was receiving constant reinforcements from the east. He had at this time a larger force than I had had at any time prior to the battle of Champion's Hill."[25]

SEVENTH DAY OF SIEGE, MAY 24

As the rumors of Johnston's accumulating force continued to grow, the Union leaders decided to take stronger measures of defense. From the best information they could gather, Johnston had about thirty or forty thousand men. So the besieging forces constantly reconnoitered the whole country and speedily got their artillery in batteries where they would occupy commanding positions. To supplement the field artillery, Admiral Porter supplied the Union troops with a battery of navy guns of large caliber. When all was completed, Grant's singularly assorted weapons could face towards Pemberton or towards Johnston. His lines nowhere were more than six hundred yards from Pemberton's.[26] All this time, and throughout the siege, the Union troops had an inexhaustible supply of ammunition to draw upon. They used it freely.

In contrast, the need for ammunition within the fortress was so acute that Pemberton renewed his orders "to have the cartridge boxes of the enemy's dead emptied of their contents, it being important to add in any way to our limited supply of ammunition, and of musket-caps especially, of which latter we stood greatly in need, having one million more of cartridges than caps, without which latter, of course, the former could be of no possible value."[27]

Every way was tried to convey caps into the beleaguered city; even hollow logs were filled with them and floated to the shore near the city. Men packed caps round their persons and then tried to get in the town. A few succeeded; the most failed.[28]

All day of the twenty-fourth the fleet kept up its bombardment, while the men on land pressed their mining of Pemberton's works, until driven off by hand grenades.

Meantime, "more than three thousand dead and wounded Union soldiers lay on the ground between the lines—the wounded dying in agonies untellable, the dead rotting in the heat of the early Mississippi summer. Three days they lay, stubborn Grant refusing to ask for a truce for the treatment of his wounded and the burial of his dead, thinking that such a request would be an admission of weakness."[29] There would be one more day of horror. Then, on the afternoon of the twenty-fifth General Pemberton would ask the truce, so that aid might be given his enemy. Later in the war, at the Battle of Spottsylvania in May of 1864, it would be the same. "The wounded lay outside the Confederate lines, untended, while General Grant, as at Vicksburg, would not ask truce to care for them and to bury the dead, and no man could go into the no-man's land between the lines and live. Confederates watched one wounded Union soldier, lying in front of the trenches on the left, try feebly for two days to brain himself

with the butt of his own musket. On the third day he was
dead."[30] In the month that followed Spottsylvania came the
Battle of Cold Harbor: "And then began another of those
three days of horror when stubborn Grant would not ask for
truce to treat his wounded or to bury his dead—three days
of Virginia summer, with Union dead decomposing in the
sun and Union wounded dying in agonies of thirst and
fever."[31]

Eighth Day of Siege, May 25

This day the firing was about as usual until six o'clock.
Then a cessation of hostilities was agreed upon, to permit
Grant to bury his dead, killed in the assault of Friday. The
following is the correspondence on the subject:

> "Hdqs. Department of Mississippi
> and Eastern Louisiana,
> Vicksburg, Miss., *May 25, 1863.*

"Commanding General United States Forces,
  In Front of Vicksburg:

Sir: Two days having elapsed since your dead and wounded
have been lying in our front, and as yet no disposition on your
part of a desire to remove them being exhibited, in the name
of humanity I have the honor to propose a cessation of hostilities for two hours and a half, that you may be enabled to
remove your dead and dying men. If you cannot do this, on
notification from you that hostilities will be suspended on your
part for the time specified, I will endeavor to have the dead
buried and the wounded cared for.

"Very respectfully, your obedient servant,

> J. C. Pemberton,
> *Lieutenant-General, Commanding.*"

To this communication the following reply was received:

"HEADQUARTERS, DEPARTMENT OF THE TENNESSEE,
Near Vicksburg, Miss., *May 25, 1863—3.30 p.m.*

"LIEUT. GEN. J. C. PEMBERTON,
Commanding Confederate Forces, Vicksburg, Miss.:

Sir: Your note of this date, proposing a cessation of hostilities for two hours and a half, for the purpose of giving me an opportunity of collecting the dead and wounded, is just received. As it will take some time to send word to all my forces to avail themselves of the opportunity afforded, and to return this to you, so that notice may be given to your troops of the cessation of hostilities, I will name 6 p. m. to-day as the hour when we will commence collecting any wounded or dead we may have still upon the field. From that hour for two hours and half all hostilities shall cease on our side.

"Very respectfully, your obedient servant,

U. S. GRANT,
Major-General."[32]

It was a relief—though no flag of truce had come from the Federal side asking for permission to remove their wounded and to bury their dead—to have them gone. "Lying in every attitude of agony, on the open fields, in the trenches and the ditches, and among the slashed trees, to see them so had been a hard ordeal even for their Confederate enemies."

Earlier in the day about a hundred prisoners were captured; the largest daily haul since the attacks of May 19 and 22. But as little reliable information could be pumped out of the whole lot, the prize was of doubtful value. It merely meant more mouths to feed and more details from the ranks to guard them; and this, at a time when Pemberton had just confided to the government that if his lines were shortened to provide a further reserve, Grant would take him in flank.[33]

By now, the city proper had been subjected almost without let-up to such a battering from both land and river that many of the civilian population wisely concluded to dig caves. They chose the steep sides of the huge hills on which the famous town is set. Built on (and into) terraces, somewhat similar to an amphitheatre, mounting at regular intervals gradually upwards from the river's banks, many of these subterranean abodes were near to being elegant—what with carpets, pianos, and other such luxuries as the individual proprietors saw fit to install. The denizens of these "burrows" thus found through all the siege complete protection against the Union fire; other sections of the community were literally ploughed with shot, shell, and bombs.

NINTH AND TENTH DAYS OF SIEGE, MAY 26 AND 27

The enemy appeared to be still suffering from the discouragement of their earlier assaults and were concentrating their efforts in attempts to silence Pemberton's upper battery. By the aid of their gunboats the Federals might then effect a lodgment in the trenches immediately above and beyond. On the morning of the twenty-seventh, with this object in mind, four Union gunboats plus the *Cincinnati* (a turreted iron-clad of the largest class, carrying fourteen guns) pushed down the river and rounded the peninsula. The larger craft promptly became hotly engaged at short range with Pemberton's upper battery. "After a spirited engagement of about forty-five minutes, the *Cincinnati* was rendered a complete wreck, and only escaped total destruction by being run aground on the Mississippi shore." This unhappy outcome very definitely discouraged the remainder of the Federal fleet: without exception they lost no time in drawing off to safer distance.[34]

Eleventh Day of Siege, May 28

On this date Pemberton reported: "No circumstance worthy of special note occurred." Yet it so happened, this chanced to be the first of many days when the genius of Grant's disobedience struck Halleck with full force. Truly the Federal field commander had flown in the face of Sherman's earlier warning, "that when any great body of troops moved against an enemy they should do so from a base of supplies." But the successful issue so fired Halleck's mind he proceeded forthwith to tap all the Union armies in order to get reinforcements for the insubordinate one: "Soon he had one hundred thousand men under his command, of whom seventy thousand were in front of Vicksburg...."[35]

Having opened and re-established communication with the Mississippi River, Grant's army was thenceforth provided with an abundance of everything. Pemberton could count only that with which his army had retired into Vicksburg, and that previously accumulated. It was not enough; for the civil authorities as long back as January had been callously indifferent to his forewarning. "If I cannot control the railroads in this department, the business of the department and subsistence of the troops will fail."[36] So they ate what they had in Vicksburg—short rations.

On the evening of the twenty-eighth a courier arrived from Johnston, the first in ten days. He brought 18,000 cartridge caps, but no word of relief.

Twelfth Day of Siege, May 29

That morning the city limits were treated to their worst pommeling. For four hours a storm of shelling was suffered which utterly ruined a large number of buildings besides killing and wounding a great number of citizens and soldiers.[37] There were many sectors along the lines of fortification where the Confederate infantry were almost directly under the muzzles of the Union guns. But as the siege wore on, there was a marked improvement in fortification because of the changed nature of the operations and to the initiative of General Martin L. Smith, whose services Pemberton found especially valuable in this respect.

Major H. M. Matthews, ordnance officer, was instructed to have a substantial lot of the enemy's unexploded Parrott shells (scattered around the front and city) sent back to Paxton's foundry and recapped.[38]

In the afternoon another courier from Johnston came into the lines. This one brought 20,000 cartridge caps and the following dispatch.

"May 25, 1863

"LIEUTENANT-GENERAL PEMBERTON:

"My last note was returned by the bearer. Two hundred thousand caps have been sent. It will be continued as they arrive. Bragg is sending a division. When it comes, I will move to you. Which do you think the best route? How and where is the enemy encamped? What is your force?

J. E. JOHNSTON"[39]

In reply, after first noting that the 200,000 cartridge caps mentioned in Johnston's communication had been captured, Pemberton advised him: "Your dispatch of 25th received this evening with 20,000 caps; Fontaine yesterday with 18,000. No messenger from you since 18th. I have 18,000 men to man the lines and river front; no reserves; I do not think you should move with less than 30,000 or 35,000, and then, if possible, toward Snyder's Mill, giving me notice of the time of your approach. The enemy encompasses my lines from right to left flank, occupying all roads. He has three corps—Sherman on my left, McPherson center, McClernand on my right.

Hurlbut's division from Memphis and Ellet's Marine Brigade, the last afloat. Enemy has made several assaults. My men are in good spirits, awaiting your arrival. Since investment we have lost about 1,000 men—many officers. You may depend on my holding the place as long as possible. On the 27th we sunk one of their best iron-clad gunboats."[40]

THIRTEENTH DAY OF SIEGE, MAY 30

By now the meat ration had been reduced one-half. As a result, rations of sugar, rice, and beans were correspondingly increased. To give further encouragement to the troops, Pemberton issued to them the quantity of chewing tobacco previously impressed under his orders. Although seemingly a little thing, this "chaw" had a beneficial influence all through the command.

Discovery was made of an unpleasant menace: Grant's parallels had reached up to within seventy-five yards of Pemberton's works. The only thing to do was to counter-mine, prepare thunder barrels and petards for the defense of the weakest points.

At the end of the day Pemberton dispatched this additional intelligence to Johnston, "Scouts report the enemy to have withdrawn most of his forces from our right yesterday, leaving Hall's Ferry road open, I apprehend, for a movement against you. I expect this courier to return to me."[41]

Since May 27 the hapless *Cincinnati,* wrecked by Pemberton's upper battery, had lain stranded, temptingly beneath the Southern guns; so a valiant young officer with fifty valiant men sneaked out that night, set fire to the Federal prize and burned it up. Lieutenant Wilkerson, Company B, First Missouri Regiment, did a thorough job.

All officers were not in such high favor as Lieutenant Wilkerson. Complaint having come through to Pemberton that many gentlement of this privileged caste were receiving over-liberal treatment in the matter of allowances for food, soap, and other semi-necessities, the commanding general at once designated Major G. L. Gillespie, acting chief commissary, "to see to it that a report be made every two days covering 'issues' to officers; that they be allowed only one ration per diem and for only one servant."[42] The Major performed this unpopular duty as he did all others, "with energy and good judgment."

FOURTEENTH TO TWENTIETH DAY OF SIEGE, MAY 31-JUNE 6

The bleak entries in Pemberton's diary covering these seven days were unvaried: so many killed, so many wounded, so many captured, ending with the unchanging notation, "our enemy bombard day and night."

Though to the northeast of Vicksburg Johnston "still hovered about," he was getting nowhere. Sherman writes that Johnston "never attempted actually to cross over [the Big Black River], except with some cavalry, just above Bear Creek, which was easily driven back."

As the probability of relief grew dimmer, Pemberton's faith progressively crumbled. While the local press predicted reinforcements "would soon be rolling in," Pemberton's expectations were scaled down drastically. Moreover, the general weariness which had come over all caused him particular concern. Many suffered from jumpy nerves—what with rationing, the difficulty of getting even the little necessities of life, and curtailed movement. There was besides that constant bombardment; not to speak of the anxiety of hundreds in the city for their sons and fathers in the field.[43]

TWENTY-FIRST DAY OF SIEGE, JUNE 7

A cheerless, rainy day, darkened by heavy clouds. One of Waul's Texans, having been detached for special duty, pushed forward to Johnston's camps with this word from Pemberton: "I am still without information from you later than your dispatch of the 25th. The enemy continues to intrench his position around Vicksburg. I have sent out couriers to you almost daily. The same men are constantly in the trenches, but are still in good spirits, expecting your approach. The enemy is so vigilant that it is impossible to obtain reliable information. When may I expect you to move, and in what direction? My subsistence may be put down for about twenty days."[44] Pemberton would have chosen to say a good deal more; for, "Let it not be forgotten that an enormous responsibility rests on the shoulders of a commander in the field. . . . and that failure, even if he can plead that he only obeyed the orders of his Government, or that he was supplied with inadequate means, will be laid at *his* door."[45]

Night brought quiet, but no report from Johnston. That day, pursuant to Richmond's orders, Edmund Kirby Smith, the senior general west of the Mississippi, had directed minor diversions be tried by his commanders "to relieve the pressure on Vicksburg." So, at dawn, General Richard Taylor's little army of some four thousand men attempted (on the Louisiana side of the river) to break up Grant's base at Milliken's Bend. As noted, the base in question was twenty miles upstream from Vicksburg, on the right bank. But Taylor was soon driven away by Porter's gunboats; they were glad of an opportunity to deflect their tedious fire from the granite fortress on the left bank.

In Arkansas, General Holmes was similarly pressed to throw his weight on the scales of "Confederate diversion." He concluded to make the desired move by attempting the capture of the fortified position at Helena, in Arkansas. Helena was the Union base for the invasion of the eastern part of Arkansas, and Richmond thought that such a feint, if severely threatened, would cause Federal troops to be drawn away from Vicksburg. Holmes, however, instead of keeping his mission subsidiary to the main effort, was tempted to develop his undertaking out of proportion to the prize. As a result, the attack of Holmes, "not well made in concert," would be "repulsed with severe loss, on July fourth."[46]

Passing over the unavailing Confederate enterprise against Helena, Grant has devoted a paragraph of his *Memoirs* to Taylor's slash at Milliken's Bend, "with an eye to Vicksburg." It was a unique engagement, as will appear in a moment, the Federal leader thus relating the details: "On the 7th of June our little force of colored and white troops across the Mississippi, at Milliken's Bend, were attacked by about 3,000 men from Richard Taylor's trans-Mississippi command. With the aid of the gunboats they were speedily repelled. I sent Mower's brigade over with instructions to drive the enemy beyond the Tensas Bayou; and we had no further trouble in that quarter during the siege. This was the first important engagement of the war in which colored troops were under fire. These men were very raw, having all been enlisted since the beginning of the siege, but they behaved well."[47] On the Confederate side, Taylor's report reflects credit on no one. He writes: "At Young's Point, ten miles above Vicksburg, on the west bank of the river, the enemy had a fortified camp, and a second one four miles above Young's, both occupied by negro troops. Holding one brigade in reserve at the point of separation of the roads, Walker sent a brigade to Young's and another to the camp above. Both attacks were made at dawn, and, with the loss of some scores of prisoners, the negroes were driven over the levee to the protection of gunboats in the river.... The right of Grant's army rested on [a bend of the Yazoo], and here his supplies were landed, and his transports were beyond the reach of annoyance from the west bank of the Mississippi. As foreseen, our movement resulted, and could result, in nothing.... The time wasted on these absurd movements cost us the garrison of Port Hudson, nearly eight thousand men; but the pressure on General Kirby Smith to *do something* for Vicksburg was too strong to be resisted."[48]

TWENTY-SECOND DAY OF SIEGE, JUNE 8

Pemberton's diary entry reads: "Nothing more than the usual artillery practice and sharp shooting occurred on the lines today.—Our works are kept in good condition by the activity of the Engineers who are constantly engaged in constructing new batteries, traverses, rifle-pits, etc.—The enemy was very quiet until late in the afternoon, when our batteries opened on him, provoking a rigorous response—The works of the enemy are progressing rapidly and begin to assume a formidable appearance."

As the lengthening siege dragged on, none had a sharper eye than Pemberton in noting the growing decline in morale; it was all around him. And we cannot omit to note that, if only because of the galling stagnancy of these cramped days, Pemberton had to buffet much hectoring; for in the tightly hemmed-in district there now cropped up an unsuspected surplus of "born soldiers." Daily they sought the commanding general to glibly expound the strategy to raise the siege. It is as if we called up a picture of anxious relatives guiding a tormented surgeon through the intricacies of a cruel operation. In the circumstances, Pemberton heard them nearly all. It served no purpose. "You could only break him, for he would not bend." He continued to act on his own responsibility.[49]

During this eighth day of June Pemberton sent out four scouts with instructions "to penetrate if possible the enemy's lines." None succeeded. But that night one of the four managed to crawl back with the intelligence that a full division of Union troops had just arrived from Stephen A. Hurlbut's command, under General Sooy Smith, and that these reinforcements had been sent immediately to Haines's Bluff on the north. This news was not calculated to revive the spirits of its recipients.[50]

Twenty-Third Day of Siege, June 9

The ninth dawned without event and was a day of anxious waiting. The enemy's firing was continuous, if languid. At sunset the enemy opened an intense fire from his Parrott guns. There was, as always, constant sharpshooting.

Grant was manifestly aiming to isolate Vicksburg and its garrison, minimizing the danger of a stab in the back from Johnston's intervening army by the destruction of Johnston's railroad junction at Jackson. "Grant had thus provided a shield for his own rear, in fettering Johnston by virtual elimination of his railroad transportation."

Twenty-Fourth Day of Siege, June 10

In the morning there were some sputtering sorties upon Sherman's lines in the hopes of gathering up prisoners with possible information as to Johnston's whereabouts. One or two captured somewhat unconvincingly declared, "Johnston's army was still at Canton, 25 miles north of Jackson." They were right. The prisoners' questioning closed, another of Pemberton's couriers went forward to Johnston, carrying the same news, asking the same questions: "The enemy bombard day and night, from seven mortars on opposite side of peninsula. He also keeps up constant fire on our lines with artillery and sharpshooters. We are losing many officers and men. I am waiting most anxiously to know your intentions. Have heard nothing of you nor from you since May 25. I shall endeavor to hold out as long as we have anything to eat. Can you not send me a verbal message by a courier crossing the river above or below Vicksburg and swimming across again opposite Vicksburg?"[51]

Twenty-Fifth Day of Siege, June 11

No word from Johnston. "The morning opened with a heavy drenching rain, on account of which the firing was languid, with the exception of that from the mortar fleet which was rapid, heavy, and constant.—The enemy pushed his sap to within sixty-five yards of the outer works on the Grave yard road, and to about one hundred yards of those on the Jackson road."[52]

The labor at night was becoming severe and was beginning to tell upon the engineer working parties. The daily breaching of Pemberton's works by the enemy's heavy guns rendered the labor of repair very arduous.

Soberly examined, there was by now nothing in the least concrete—only hopes—to longer sustain the beleaguered army and its commander in those bleak days of discouragement. Pemberton could not help but feel it. Even should the Confederacy rescue him from Grant's tightening grip, he personally would find himself poised between the South, uncomprehending, and the North, where he had become an object of censure and abuse. Eyes opened to the fierce light upon him, he still kept at his task.

An hour before dusk on the eleventh the enemy breached Pemberton's works on the Jackson Road and ran their saps close up to his parapet. In consequence the commander hurried up a nine-inch Dahlgren gun and a nine-inch mortar—the only one he possessed and the position of which was changed almost nightly. Both were now rushed into place on General Forney's front. Toward midnight the Federal firing slackened.[53]

In a nibbling sort of way Grant was swallowing the outer sectors of the fortress, so that despite all Pemberton could do to pump new life into his weakened defenses, many were for surrendering on any terms. But of this Pemberton would hear nothing—backed as he was by the President's respected promise: "You [Pemberton] may expect whatever it is in my power to do for your aid."

Twenty-Sixth Day of Siege, June 12

At sunrise that morning a noisy demonstration disclosed an alarming contraction of the Federal envelopment, and noon brought no news from Johnston. Hard as it was on his pride to reiterate and reiterate his desperate plight, Pemberton's reluctance to do so passed almost as quickly as it came upon him; for the morning's observations had put a new and even worse face on affairs. "The enemy continues rigorously battering our works on the Jackson road, with their sharp shooters and mortar fleet occupied as usual—Eight transports filled with troops arrived in the bend above the city this morning," Pemberton recorded in his diary. An hour after midday he dispatched to Johnston: "Courier Walker arrived this morning with caps [20,000]. No message from you. Very heavy firing yesterday from mortars and on lines."[54]

About this time the garrison's provisions, particularly of meat, had become almost exhausted, and General Stevenson was instructed to impress all cattle in the city. The chief commissary was directed to issue for bread equal portions of rice and flour, four ounces of each. When even these staples ran short, the experiment was tried of making bread with equal parts of peas ground into meal, mixed with corn-meal. One who lived through the siege has written of this substitute, "It made a nauseous composition, as the corn-meal cooked in half the time the peas-meal did, so this stuff was half raw.... It had the properties of india-rubber, and was worse than leather to digest."[55]

Before the day was out, the works in front of Hébert and his Louisianians were nearly demolished; Smith's and Forney's fronts likewise "tottered under the destructive fire laid down against their entrenchments." As darkness came on it developed that on the Graveyard Road the Union diggers had pushed their work of sapping to within fifty feet of the Confederates. In an attempt to dislodge them, resort was had to hand grenades. They were ineffective, so the guardians of Vicksburg commenced a countersap.

TWENTY-SEVENTH DAY OF SIEGE, JUNE 13

Before it was quite light, Captain Sanders arrived from Jackson. He had been more than two weeks on his way from Johnston, from whom he brought disheartening information. The message, dated May 29, read as follows: "I am too weak to save Vicksburg. Can do no more than attempt to save you and your garrison. It will be impossible to extricate you unless you co-operate and we make mutually supporting movements. Communicate your plans and suggestions, if possible."[56]

It will be remembered that Pemberton had withdrawn to Vicksburg at the behest of, and not in defiance of, the President's desires—"To hold both Vicksburg and Port Hudson is necessary to our connection with Trans-Mississippi." When, during that crowded day, Pemberton found time and the heart to reveal the contents of Johnston's message to his resolute command, the outline he quickly gave as to his own ideas of their present duty—and their reaction to it—instantly enhanced his confidence in these brave men, and theirs in him. Surrounded as he was, could Pemberton make a supporting movement—unless Johnston contrived to relieve the pressure? In any aspect, Pemberton must first ascertain his would-be-

Left: *Entrance to gallery leading to the Union mine.* Right: *Abraham, who was "blow'd t'ree mile into de air." Defenders were underground counter-mining when the explosion occurred on June 25. The Negro was sketched by Theodore H. Davis for* Harper's Weekly, *August 8, 1863, shortly after his descent into the Union lines.*

The surrender of Vicksburg. One section of the Confederate line is coming out to stack arms in front of the defenses while General Grant rides by into the city. From Harper's Weekly, *August 1, 1863.*

Train with reinforcements for General Johnston running off the track in the forests of Mississippi. From the London Illustrated News, *August 8, 1863. The artist, who was riding on the train, wrote that the incident would give "an idea of the perils of traveling on a used-up military railroad."*

Southern women and children encamping in the woods near Vicksburg. The artist for the London Illustrated News, *in which this sketch appeared, August 29, 1863, reported that the country for forty miles around the city was covered with such small encampments.*

supporter's position: in the two days ensuing, he made re-newed attempts to do so.

Twenty-Eighth and Twenty-Ninth Days of Siege, June 14 and 15

Unless Pemberton could determine Johnston's whereabouts, the hope of getting relief or supplies was at an end; and that in the critical situation now existing would mean disaster. The results were too painful to contemplate. Pemberton de-clined to do so, but hastened in the morning of the fourteenth to send off this advice to Johnston:

> "Vicksburg, *June 14, 1863*
>
> "Last night Captain Sanders arrived with 200,000 caps, but brought no information as to your position or move-ments. The enemy is landing troops in large numbers on Louisiana shore above Vicksburg. They are probably from Memphis, but it may be from Yazoo; I cannot ascer-tain positively. On the Graveyard road the enemy has run his saps to within *25 yards of our works.* He will probably attempt to sink a mine. I shall try to thwart him. I am anxiously expecting to hear from you to arrange for co-operation."

Then, on the morning of the fifteenth, this message to John-ston quickly followed:

> "Vicksburg, *June 15, 1863*
>
> "The enemy has placed several very heavy guns in posi-tion against our works, and is approaching them very nearly by sap. His fire is almost continuous. Our men have no relief; are becoming much fatigued, but are still in pretty good spirits. I think your movement should be made as soon as possible. The enemy is receiving re-enforcements. We are living on greatly reduced rations, but I think sufficient for twenty days yet."[57]

THIRTIETH DAY OF SIEGE, JUNE 16

A Confederate river battery, earlier set up with great care, heavily shelled—and for a time silenced—two large Federal guns in position on the peninsula opposite the city. It was hoped that these particular Northern pieces had been dislodged, as their accurate fire had already killed and wounded many civilians, among whom were a number of women and children.[58]

THIRTY-FIRST DAY OF SIEGE, JUNE 17

There was nothing that day to vary or stay the uninterrupted progress of the Federal works. The long hours brought no more explicit news of Johnston.

THIRTY-SECOND DAY OF SIEGE, JUNE 18

The commander's diary entry is the same as for the day preceding.

THIRTY-THIRD DAY OF SIEGE, JUNE 19

Sometime after the preceding midnight, activity around Snyder's Mill had led Pemberton's army nearest that point to believe that Johnston might be near. A courier was accordingly entrusted with this report, coupled with instructions to do everything possible to locate Johnston or any part of his forces. Said Pemberton: "The enemy opened all his batteries on our lines about 3.30 o'clock this morning, and continued the heaviest fire we have yet sustained until 8 o'clock, but he did not assault our works. Artillery is reported to have been distinctly heard about 2 a.m. toward and east of Snyder's Mill, supposed to have been an engagement with your troops. On the Graveyard road the enemy's works are within 25 feet of our redan; also very close on Jackson and Baldwin's Ferry roads. I hope you will advance with the least possible delay. My men have been thirty-four days and nights in trenches, without relief, and the enemy within conversation distance. We are living on very reduced rations, and, as you know, are entirely isolated. What aid am I to expect from you? The bearer, Captain [G. D.] Wise, can be confided in."[59]

This Captain Wise, who could be confided in, was four days in locating and in reaching Johnston, whom he found at Jackson. The Captain was not to return to Vicksburg; nor was Pemberton to know for a decade the full details of this trusted courier's high adventure. Then, from Wise, since become a lawyer, Pemberton in October, 1874, received this historic letter:

"HOWARD & WISE
*Attorneys and Counsellors at Law
Corner Bank and 11th Streets*

Robert Howard
George D. Wise

Richmond, Va., *Oct. 13th—1874*

"GENL. J. C. PEMBERTON—

"My dear Sir—I have received your letter and have delayed the answer to refresh my memory as much as possible by a book, in which I recorded all important events in my military career. I find that I kept a regular account of the Vicksburg campaign up to the time of my departure from that place with the dispatch you allude to in yours to me.—I left Vicksburg Saturday night, the 20th day of June, 1863, and reached Genl. Johnston's headquarters at Jackson Wednesday morning June 24th. I am positive as to these dates; it is so written in my journal, but apart from that, my memory is fresh and distinct. Before leaving, I spent more than an hour at your headquarters in conversation with yourself. While it is a fact that I left you on the night of the 20th—I think it probable, that your dispatch bore date the 19th., because in the interview with you at the time you handed it to me to be borne to Genl. Johnston, you informed me that you had on the previous day been in consultation with 'the

Generals commanding divisions,' concerning the condition of the garrison. I have said that on the night of my departure from Vicksburg, I was with you for an hour or more. Maj. Genl. Smith was present at the same time.— You then informed me, that I had been selected for a duty surrounded with difficulties and danger, but that it concerned the welfare of the Confederacy that it should be performed, and enjoined upon me the utmost caution in its performance. You said that, reposing confidence in me, you would freely communicate to me everything for the information of Genl. Johnston. The dispatch as given in your letter is to the best of my recollection & belief correct, but you gave me verbally some directions for Genl. Johnston not contained in your dispatch, & you said that you thought it best not to commit them to paper, even in cypher. They were substantially as follows— that you had full & correct reports from all the departments under your command—the quarter-master, commissary & ordnance departments—that allowing to your men already enfeebled by their long service in the trenches, without relief & without adequate food, very reduced rations, you could not hold out longer than the 10th day of July.—That while there might be sufficient ammunition to meet the emergency of an assault, you could not permit your men to reply to the continuous fire upon them—that they were very weak & enfeebled, & you doubted if they could endure the fatigue of a march, much more if they could sustain the shock of a struggle with the overwhelming numbers of the enemy in an attempt to cut their way out. You urged me to impress upon Genl. Johnston the urgent necessity for speedy action on his part, if he could afford you assistance, & my memory is very clear, that you instructed me to tell him in what direction you thought it best for him to come to your assistance. I may be mistaken as to this, but I think you told me to tell him to approach Vicksburg by the Grave-yard road, & that when you heard his guns, you would endeavor to pop out by the Hall's ferry road.

I repeat, that I may be mistaken in the roads I have named, but I am distinct as to the fact, that you indicated to me the best route for him to come up, & the route by which you would attempt to go out, so that you & he might act with a perfect understanding. I am positive that you never said anything to me about propositions to be made either by yourself or Genl. Johnston to Genl. Grant about terms for the surrender of the place, but not of the troops. I never heard anything about a surrender until on the 27th day of June, when Genl. Johnston called me to his head-quarters in Jackson. He then informed me, that he was in no condition to make a movement in your favor; that he had not sufficient troops, and that he had been unable to obtain the requisite number of horses for artillery purposes & at the same to haul the necessary supplies for his army.—After thus explaining his own situation & his inability to strike a blow for the relief of the garrison of Vicksburg, he added—'tell Genl. Pemberton that the determination manifested by him, and Genl. E. Kirby Smith's expected co-operation, encourages me to hope that something may yet be done to save Vicksburg; but if it should become necessary to surrender, that he (meaning yourself) should make propositions to Genl. Grant, as my making them would be an impolitic confession of weakness.' At the same interview he told me that I would soon be a prisoner of war, & handing me an open letter addressed to Major General McPherson, U.S.A., told me to keep it & present it in person to Genl. McPherson & that it might be of service to me. Upon leaving his head-quarters I read the letter & found it to be a simple request, that Genl. McPherson would do what he could, consistently with his duty as a soldier, to lessen the burdens of my imprisonment.—If I can give you any fuller information, it will afford me pleasure to do so, because, though not brought often into personal contact with yourself, as an humble Captain under your command I learned to admire the courage and patriotism which you exhibited in behalf of the cause I loved so well. And I shall never forget the spirit and energy you displayed in defense of Vicksburg. With best wishes I am—

> "Yrs truly,
> "GEO. D. WISE.

"P. S. I forgot to say—that when on the 27th day of June, 1863, Genl. Johnston spoke of a surrender, he added after telling me substantially what he represents was his dispatch to you, "tell Genl. Pemberton to consider himself authorized by me to surrender"—I am positive that he used those words."[60]

THIRTY-FOURTH DAY OF SIEGE, JUNE 20

It was becoming clearer with every fresh development— the extension of Union mines and trenches, the increased fire from the enemy gunboats and mortars—that the siege had reached an advanced stage. And that the Federal activities were not localized was plain from the repercussions on all fronts of the defender's forces. They were being pinched inevitably, with their boundaries shrunken day by day. In Pemberton's diary is written, "At 3 o'clock this morning the enemy opened a tremendous artillery fire along his whole line, which was continued for six hours without cessation—The Gun boats also participated and the storm of shot and shell was terrific, greatly exceeding in severity anything yet witnessed since the commencement of the siege—The remainder of the day was comparatively quiet, but the heavy fire of the morning seriously injured our works on the right—the enemy has commenced mining on the left of the Halls ferry road, and within two hundred yards of our works."

THIRTY-FIFTH DAY OF SIEGE, JUNE 21

The morning passed off rather quietly, but by mid-forenoon two couriers arrived with duplicate advices from Johnston to Pemberton:

"June 14, 1863

"All that we can attempt is to save you and your garrison. To do this, exact co-operation is indispensable. By fighting the enemy simultaneously at the same point of his line, you may be extricated. Our joint forces cannot raise the siege of Vicksburg. My communications with the rear can best be preserved by operating north of railroad. Inform me as soon as possible what point will suit you best. Your dispatches of the 12th received. General Taylor, with 8,000 men, will endeavor to open communication with you from Richmond."[61]

To the above, Pemberton at once replied:

"...If it is absolutely impossible, in your opinion, to raise the siege with our combined forces, and that nothing more can be done than to extricate this garrison, I suggest that, giving me full information in time to act, you move by the north of the railroad, drive in the enemy's pickets at night, and at daylight next morning engage him heavily with skirmishers, occupying him during the entire day, and that on that night I move by the Warrenton road by Hankinson's Ferry, to which point you should previously send a brigade of cavalry, with two field batteries, to build a bridge there and hold that ferry; also Hall's and Baldwin's, to cover my crossing at Hankinson's. I shall not be able to move with my artillery or wagons. I suggest this as the best plan, because all the other roads are too strongly intrenched and the enemy in too heavy force for a reasonable prospect of success, unless you move in sufficient force to compel him to abandon his communication with Snyder's, which I still hope we may be able to do. I await your orders. Captain [J. M.] Couper understands all my views, and will explain further."[62]

THIRTY-SIXTH DAY OF SIEGE, JUNE 22

There was little firing this day. The Southern pickets were posted at night within a few feet of the Federal lines. It being discovered that a sap had reached within forty yards of his works on the railroad road, Pemberton directed a raid to break up its further extension. In execution of this order, a party from Cumming's Georgia brigade of Stevenson's division made a midnight sortie. They brought in a heavy haul of captures: one lieutenant colonel, twelve men, a quantity of intrenching tools, some fine blankets, and several brand-new canteens with alcoholic contents. For a time vigilance was relaxed among one small group of jaded outposts.[63]

THIRTY-SEVENTH DAY OF SIEGE, JUNE 23

The sum total of Johnston's four dispatches received by Pemberton since manning the Vicksburg lines on May 17 were not calculated in quantity or content to make the beleaguered commander "very sanguine of relief." The one that now arrived with greater promptness than its despairing forerunners (it was dated June 22) was not of a nature to increase the confidence of its recipients. "Your dispatch of the 15th received," Johnston wrote. "General Taylor is sent by General E. Kirby Smith to co-operate with you from the west bank of the river, to throw in supplies, and to cross with his force, if expedient and practicable. I will have the means of moving toward the enemy in a day or two, and will try to make a diversion in your favor, and, if possible, communicate with you, though I fear my force is too small to effect the latter. I have only two-thirds of the force you told Messenger Sanders to state to me as the least with which I ought to make an attack. Scouts report the enemy fortifying toward us and the roads blocked. If I can do nothing to relieve you, rather than surrender the garrison, endeavor to cross the river at the last moment if you and General Taylor communicate."[64]

Pemberton never received any communication from Major General Taylor on the subject of co-operation; nor had he any knowledge of his whereabouts or of his forces. Of far greater consequence in its after effects was the fact that Pemberton had no other single word from Johnston until near a week after Vicksburg's fall. On July 10 Pemberton for the first time received Johnston's dispatch of July 3, in which Johnston said he hoped to attack Grant on July 7. The bearer had been for several days a prisoner to the Federal authorities.[65]

THIRTY-EIGHTH DAY OF SIEGE, JUNE 24

The mortar fleet of Porter, strangely silent for the past three days, opened with a vengeance and kept up until long after dark. Outside word came on an average but once a week. Perhaps this was just as well; all news from the quarter of the distracted rescue party was by now dismal and brought small hope. Johnston's dispatch of June 22 had rendered it painfully apparent that the siege could not be raised. To cross the Mississippi River as he suggested, in the face of the enemy's gunboats and land batteries, was beyond all possibility of even partial accomplishment.[66]

Once more a fair opportunity for Confederate success had been suffered to slip out of hand. "By late June and early July, whatever opportunity to raise the siege that existed in May had passed. Grant was too strong in numbers, in position, in equipment and material, to be attacked with any hope of success, either from inside or outside his double fortified line."[67] For long days the people and the army of Vicksburg had been promised by implication, at least, that an attack would be made "at the right time." It was difficult to hearten men by dramatizing their resistance to the relentless pressure of their enemies. "There is a mental, as well as a moral, hazard in the defensive; and not alone among the harried fighting ranks." Could the Federal challenge be met for many more days unless Johnston's counterblows were imminent? There were no such indications.

THIRTY-NINTH DAY OF SIEGE, JUNE 25

Only a few brief days before, things were so quiescent the soldiers of the two sides conversed banteringly across the narrow barriers between them; "sometimes they exchanged the hard bread of the Union soldiers for the tobacco of the Confederates; at other times the [Southerners] threw over hand-grenades, and often the [Northerners], catching them in their hands, returned them unexploded."[68]   But under this date, Pemberton has noted in his diary of the siege: "The morning opened with a heavy bombardment from the mortar fleet and the Parrott batteries on the Peninsula.   It was kept up with great violence until 4 P.M., when the enemy's guns along the whole line swelled the chorus and turned upon the city a most murderous and concentrated fire.—Late in the afternoon the enemy exploded a mine on the left of the Jackson road [under the parapet of General Forney's works], which however caused but little damage—He immediately attempted to charge our works, but was heavily repulsed—Our loss was eighty-eight killed and wounded."   General Forney reported that at dark "work was resumed by the enemy and by us, they mining and we countermining."

Grant has related of this affair that a colored man, underground and at work when the explosion took place, was thrown into the air, coming down on the Union side, alive and for the most unharmed.   "He was not much hurt, but terribly frightened.   Some one asked him how high he had gone up.   'Dun no massa, but t'ink 'bout t'ree mile,' was his reply."

At this point, one is reminded of Douglas Freeman's recital of a similar incident at the later Battle of the Crater before Petersburg, Virginia, July, 1864.   Captain Featherston asked, "How high did they blow you?"   "I don't know," the man replied, "but as I was going up I met the commissary officer coming down, and he said, 'I will try to have breakfast ready by the time you get down'."

FORTIETH TO FORTY-FOURTH DAY OF SIEGE, JUNE 26 TO JUNE 30

To those closest around him, Pemberton appeared still as cool as arctic ice, and as solid. Holding to his contracting ground, he refused to believe "he was forsaken by his comrades in arms."[69] Of the dreadful strain of these dark days, his diary, strictly factual, gives no hint: "There was the usual heavy firing from Admiral Porter's mortar fleet, the Peninsula batteries, and the heavy guns of the enemy in the rear of the city."

About this time Vicksburg's stock of bacon having been almost exhausted, the experiment was tried of using mule meat as a substitute. It was issued "only to those who desired to use it," and Pemberton was gratified to find that both officers and men considered it "not only nutritious, but very palatable, and in every way preferable to poor beef."[70]

Unbeknown to Pemberton, the Confederate government had by now concluded that its confidence in Johnston as the savior of Vicksburg had been misplaced. They were therefore after him, hammer and tongs, to bestir himself, Secretary of War Seddon telegraphing him categorically—"I look to attack in the last resort. . . . I rely on you for all possible to save Vicksburg."

Prodded into action by higher authority, Johnston hurried off to Pemberton an intimation that something might yet be done to save Vicksburg:

"June 27, 1863

"Your dispatch of the 22d received. General E. K. Smith's troops have been mismanaged, and have fallen back to Delhi. I have sent a special messenger, urging him to assume direct command. The determined spirit you manifest and his expected co-operation encourage me to hope something may yet be done to save Vicksburg, and to postpone both the modes suggested of merely extricating the garrison. Negotiations with Grant for the relief of the garrison, should they become necessary, must be made by you. It would be a confession of weakness on my part, which I ought not to make, to propose them. When it becomes necessary to make terms, they may be considered as made under my authority."[71]

This word, so long awaited, of Johnston's purposed move to aid the stricken fortress was entrusted to none other than Captain Wise. It was he who had carried to Johnston, Pemberton's dispatch of June 19. Unhappily perhaps, the Captain failed in accomplishment of his return mission to Vicksburg: it was not until August 20 in Gainesville, Alabama, that the dispatch he carried was received by Pemberton. "Nor had I," says Pemberton, "the most remote idea that such an opinion was entertained by General Johnston."[72] The courier's fate is cleared up in Grant's *Memoirs,* where we find: "At this time an intercepted dispatch from Johnston to Pemberton informed me [Grant] that Johnston intended to make a determined attack upon us in order to relieve the garrison at Vicksburg."[73] As a matter of fact, the dispatch in question fell short of such an avowal of intended audacity: Johnston had committed himself to no such program. What he actually projected was more airy—"The determined spirit you manifest ... encourage[s] me to hope something may yet be done to save Vicksburg. ..."

Forty-Fifth Day of Siege, July 1

In the morning "Johnston's advanced troops came up and spent the next three days in vainly exploring Sherman's front for a weak point." Meantime, "the doubly demoralizing sensation of isolation from outside and emptiness within had done its work." The citadel was truly undermined and sapped of its strength, while the man sent to save the day for the

THE SIEGE OF VICKSBURG

Confederacy realized day by day that it was useless "to sacrifice two armies for an illusory hope of saving one."[74]

"Loss of hope is worse than loss of men and land." When
Pemberton learned that such was Johnston's frame of mind,
he felt satisfied that the time had arrived when it was necessary either to evacuate the city and cut his way out or to
capitulate upon the best terms obtainable. His own inclination led him to favor the former.[75]

On May 25, thirty-seven days previous, Johnston had informed Pemberton that on the arrival of an expected division
from Bragg's army he would move to Vicksburg. Pemberton
supposed the move would be made with his co-operation to
raise the siege. No subsequent dispatch from Johnston sustained this understanding, all such, without exception, speaking "only of the possibility of extricating the garrison."[76]

The time had come for Pemberton to unmask, to run up
his flag of truce. Often in recent days his hidden troops were
compelled to undergo hours of shelling in stubborn silence.

From his rust-encrusted dugout in a near-by hillside, the
"forsaken" master of the waiting game of siege addressed to his
division commanders, Generals Stevenson, Forney, Smith, and
Bowen, the following communication:

"HDQS. DEPARTMENT OF MISSISSIPPI
AND EASTERN LOUISIANA,
Vicksburg, *July 1, 1863.*

"GENERAL: Unless the siege of Vicksburg is raised or
supplies are thrown in, it will become necessary very
shortly to evacuate the place. I see no prospect of the
former, and there are many great, if not insuperable,
obstacles in the way of the latter. You are, therefore, requested to inform me with as little delay as possible as to
the condition of your troops, and their ability to make the
marches and undergo the fatigues necessary to accomplish
a successful evacuation. You will, of course, use the ut-

most discretion while informing yourself through your subordinates upon all points tending to a clear elucidation of the subjects of my inquiry.

"Very respectfully, your obedient servant,

J. C. PEMBERTON,
Lieutenant-General, Commanding."[77]

FORTY-SIXTH DAY OF SIEGE, JULY 2

The courage of the men who had so long defended Vicksburg under Pemberton was near drained to the end; yet mercifully, so was their time of testing. Promptly, Pemberton received reply from the officers of whom he made his fateful inquiry of the day before. That of General Forney follows, differing only in its phraseology from those of Generals Stevenson, Smith, and Bowen.

"DIVISION HEADQUARTERS,
Near Vicksburg, *July 2, 1863.*

"GENERAL: In reply to your confidential note of yesterday, requesting to be informed as to the condition of my troops and their ability to make the marches and undergo the fatigues necessary to accomplish a successful evacuation, as heartrending as the reply may be, I have to state that I concur in the unanimous opinion of the brigade and regimental commanders, that the physical condition and health of our men are not sufficiently good to enable them to accomplish successfully the evacuation. The spirit of the men is still, however, unshaken, and I am satisfied they will cheerfully continue to bear the fatigue and privations of the siege. I inclose herewith for your further information the brigade reports.

"I have the honor to be, very respectfully, your obedient servant,

JNO. H. FORNEY,
Major-General."[78]

Pemberton has stated that, so far as he knew, not a solitary brigade or regimental commander favored the scheme of cutting out; and only two, whose views were presented to him, intimated the possibility of making more than one-half of their commands available for that purpose. With this unanimous opinion of his senior officers against the practicability of a successful evacuation, and no relief in sight from General Johnston, a surrender with or without terms was the only alternative left him.[79]

As this portion of Pemberton's official report reveals, more than hunger was involved. "The assertion that the surrender of Vicksburg was compelled by the want of subsistence, or that the garrison was starved out, is one entirely destitute of truth. There was at no time any absolute suffering for want of food among the garrison. That the men were put upon greatly reduced rations is undeniably true; but, in the opinion of many medical officers, it is at least questionable whether under all the circumstances this was at all injurious to their health. It must be remembered that for forty-seven days and nights these heroic men had been exposed to burning suns, drenching rains, damp fogs, and heavy dews, and that during all this period they never had by day or by night the slightest relief. The extent of our works required every available man in the trenches, and even then they were in many places insufficiently manned. It was not in my power to relieve any portion of the line for a single hour. Confined to the narrow limits of a trench, with their limbs cramped and swollen, without exercise, constantly exposed to a murderous storm of shot and shell, while the enemy's unerring sharpshooters stood ready to pick off every one visible above the parapets, is it strange that the men grew weak and attenuated? They had made a most heroic defense. Many had met death with a smile upon their lips, all had cheerfully encountered danger, and almost without a murmur had borne privations and hardships well calculated to test their manhood. They had held the place against an enemy five times their number, admirably clothed and fed, and abundantly supplied with all the appliances of war. Whenever the foe attempted an assault, they drove him back discomfited, covering the ground with his killed and wounded, and already had they torn from his grasp five stand of colors as trophies of their prowess, none of which were allowed to fall again into his hands. Knowing the anxious desire of the Government to relieve Vicksburg, I felt assured that if within the compass of its power the siege would be raised, but when forty-seven weary days and nights had passed, with the knowledge I then possessed that no adequate relief was to be expected, I felt that I ought not longer to place in jeopardy the brave men whose lives had been intrusted to my care. Hence, after the suggestion of the alternative of cutting my way out, I determined to make terms, not because my men were starved out, not because I could not hold out yet a little longer, but because they were overpowered by numbers, worn down with fatigue, and each day saw our defenses crumbling beneath their feet. The question of subsistence, therefore, had nothing whatever to do with the surrender of Vicksburg. With an unlimited supply of provisions, the garrison could not, for the reasons already given, have held out much longer."[80]

It is of more than purely military interest to note that Pemberton's feat in holding Vicksburg secure against Grant's crushing numbers for near nine months would not be matched throughout the war—until Grant's collision with Lee at the siege of Petersburg, where the Union commander was held off by Lee but little longer.[81]

Wootten-Moulton

Statue of General Pemberton in the National Military Park at Vicksburg, erected in 1917, pursuant to an act of Congress, by the Vicksburg National Military Park Commission. Edmond T. Quinn, sculptor.

Generals Pemberton and Grant under the oak tree—the tree which "furnished as many cords of wood, in the shape of trophies, as 'The True Cross'." From a contemporary drawing.

CHAPTER XVII

The Surrender

ON THE FORTY-SEVENTH day of siege, July 3, 1863, Pemberton opened negotiations with Grant for the surrender of Vicksburg and its defending army. To Grant went this letter.

"HEADQUARTERS,
Vicksburg, Miss., July 3, 1863.
"MAJ. GEN. U. S. GRANT,
   Commanding United States Forces:
"GENERAL: I have the honor to propose to you an armistice for several hours, with a view to arranging terms for the capitulation of Vicksburg. To this end, if agreeable to you, I will appoint three commissioners to meet a like number, to be named by yourself, at such place and hour today as you may find convenient.

"I make this proposition to save the further effusion of blood, which must otherwise be shed to a frightful extent, feeling myself fully able to maintain my position for a yet indefinite period.

"This communication will be handed you under a flag of truce by Maj. Gen. John S. Bowen.

"Very respectfully, your obedient servant,
                     J. C. PEMBERTON,
          Lieutenant-General Commanding."[1]

Grant, with somewhat unlooked-for vividness, thus describes what followed: "On the 3d about ten o'clock A.M. white flags

appeared on a portion of the rebel works. Hostilities along
that part of the line ceased at once. Soon two persons were
seen coming towards our lines bearing a white flag. They
proved to be General Bowen, a division commander, and
Colonel Montgomery, aide-de-camp to Pemberton, bearing
[Pemberton's] letter to me. . . .

"It was a glorious sight to officers and soldiers on the line
where these white flags were visible, and the news soon spread
to all parts of the command. The troops felt that their long
and weary marches, hard fighting, ceaseless watching by night
and day, in a hot climate, exposure to all sorts of weather, to
diseases and, worst of all, to the gibes of many Northern
papers that came to them saying all their suffering was in
vain, that Vicksburg would never be taken, were at last at an
end and the Union sure to be saved.

"Bowen was received by General A. J. Smith, and asked to
see me. I had been a neighbor of Bowen's in Missouri, and
knew him well and favorably before the war; but his request
was refused. He then suggested that I should meet Pemberton. To this I sent a verbal message saying that, if Pemberton
desired it, I would meet him in front of McPherson's corps at
three o'clock that afternoon."[2]

Sunk deep in reverie, sleepless all through the night before,
Pemberton waited for Bowen to return—and perhaps for his
own exit from the stage of war. Now, still morning of July
3, "the thermometer gave warning of another torrid day." In
the week that had gone before, June had run towards its end
under breathless and blazing weather, broken by thunder-
storms which left the country unrefreshed and steaming in
the heat, "too lovely a country to lie under the hoof of war."

Fate in these hours had contrived to present a stirring pag-
eant—not alone at Vicksburg. "One o'clock in the stately
house in Richmond where Davis, sick and anxious, looked up

expectantly for a telegram from Lee [at Gettysburg] whenever
a knock came at his door; noon along the Mississippi, as Pemberton with heavy heart was penning a letter asking terms of
General Grant for the surrender of Vicksburg; tea time in
London, and a sealed letter on the desk of John Bigelow,
telling Secretary Seward he was satisfied that Lee's invasion
of Pennsylvania had been made in concert with J. A. Roebuck's
proposal to the House of Commons that Her Majesty's government enter into negotiations with foreign powers for the
recognition of the Confederacy."[3]

On the Vicksburg battlefield without the Southern lines, the
silence had become almost complete. At last, looking grey and
worn, Bowen returned and waited to make his report.[4] First
off, he handed Pemberton this letter from the Union leader:

"HEADQUARTERS DEPARTMENT OF THE TENNESSEE,
     In the Field, near Vicksburg, Miss., July 3, 1863.
"LIEUT. GEN. J. C. PEMBERTON,
     Commanding Confederate Forces, &c.:
GENERAL: Your note of this date is just received, proposing an armistice for several hours, for the purpose of
arranging terms of capitulation through commissioners to
be appointed, &c.

"The useless effusion of blood you propose stopping by
this course can be ended at any time you may choose,
by an unconditional surrender of the city and garrison.
Men who have shown so much endurance and courage
as those now in Vicksburg will always challenge the respect of an adversary, and I can assure you will be treated
with all the respect due to prisoners of war.

"I do not favor the proposition of appointing commissioners to arrange terms of capitulation, because I have
no terms other than those indicated above.

"I am, general, very respectfully, your obedient servant,
                    U. S. GRANT,
                         Major-General."[5]

By this time, the atmosphere was electric with expectancy; and the wildest rumors raced through camp and city. Everyone had the air of knowing something vital. In the lull of waiting for Grant's letter to be read by all his senior officers, Pemberton talked quietly in a corner with General Bowen and with Colonel L. M. Montgomery, his aide-de-camp. Both gave Pemberton the same impression, which he has thus recorded: "Upon the return of General Bowen with this letter, I understood that it was the desire of Major-General Grant to have a personal conference with me...."[6]

The morning was getting late as Pemberton, "reduced to the ignominy that awaits a defeated leader," rode on the way to rendezvous with his conqueror. In 1863 bewildered Union armies were taking part in victory after victory, but never conquest. They would do so now.

With Pemberton rode Bowen and Montgomery. As they proceeded to the ordeal of loaded parley with their foes, the damp mists breathed up by the Mississippi swamps reluctantly dissolved beneath a sullen sky. Half to himself, the two with Pemberton heard him say, "I feel a confidence that I shall stand justified to my Government if not to the Southern people.... Should it be otherwise—the consolation of having done the only thing which in my opinion could give security to Vicksburg and to the surrounding country ... will be reward enough."[7]

Between him and the appointed meeting spot, several small streams "twisted through the intervening gulleys like dark green serpents." The road, hideously gashed and gutted, slowed the horses to a limping pace. Grant's *Memoirs* run so: "... between the Big Black and the Yazoo all bridges were to be destroyed and the roads rendered as nearly impassable as possible. . . . There were eight roads leading into Vicksburg, along which our ... batteries advanced; . . ."

But Pemberton in thirty years as soldier had traversed far worse thoroughfares, though never with a heart so heavy.

Called on to hold New Orleans against the British in 1814, General Jackson told the President in Washington: "A real military man, with full knowledge of the geography of... this country... would march direct to the Walnut Hills [the site of Vicksburg]...and make this country an easy conquest."[8]   Now it was Grant who came to do the bidding of that famed soldier-statesman who had named Pemberton to West Point. The worsted Southern "volunteer," still deep in his thoughts, rode on. Many things bulked large in his mind—and in his imagination. The happiest were not to be; for Grant was prepared to be near adamant.

The three in grey had by force of circumstance and country traveled in a roundabout way. "At three o'clock," Grant relates, "Pemberton appeared at the point suggested in my verbal message, accompanied by the same officers who had borne his letter of the morning. Generals Ord, McPherson, Logan, and A. J. Smith, and several officers of my staff, accompanied me. Our place of meeting was on a hillside within a few hundred feet of the rebel lines. Near by stood a stunted oak-tree, which was made historical by the event. It was but a short time before the last vestige of its body, root and limb had disappeared, the fragments taken as trophies. Since then the same tree has furnished as many cords of wood, in the shape of trophies, as 'The True Cross'."

"Pemberton and I had served in the same division during part of the Mexican War. I knew him very well, therefore, and greeted him as an old acquaintance."[9]

On the other hand, to most of Grant's officers and men Pemberton was a stranger and "of course the chief attraction." So notes the Pittsburgh *Evening Chronicle,* and then continues, in its issue of July 14, 1863: "In appearance, Pemberton is a tall, lithe built and stately personage. Black hair, black eyes, full beard, and a rather severe expression of countenance.... He is, you know, a native of Philadelphia ... and a trusted friend of the President, who, it is thought, would have spared nothing of men or means to aid him in this extremity...."

Pemberton "soon learned that there was a mutual misunderstanding in regard to the desire for this interview."[10] Consistent with the impression he had gained from Bowen and Montgomery as to the nature of Grant's "verbal message," Pemberton asked what terms Grant proposed to give his army if it surrendered. Grant had none.

When "the conference" gave every indication of unhappy collapse, three or four of the younger officers present got together "during which time, Pemberton and Grant moved a short distance toward the Vicksburg lines, in conversation." After some minutes Pemberton and his escort departed, with the understanding that Grant would communicate with them by 10:00 P.M. About that hour the following letter came into the Southern lines under flag of truce.

"HEADQUARTERS DEPARTMENT OF THE TENNESSEE,
          Near Vicksburg, Miss., July 3, 1863.

"LIEUT. GEN. J. C. PEMBERTON,
          Commanding Confederate Forces, Vicksburg, Miss.:

"GENERAL: In conformity with agreement of this afternoon, I will submit the following proposition for the surrender of the city of Vicksburg, public stores, &c.:

"On your accepting the terms proposed, I will march in one division as a guard, and take possession at 8 a.m. to-morrow. As soon as rolls can be made out, and paroles signed by officers and men, you will be allowed to march out of our lines, the officers taking with them their side-arms and clothing, and the field, staff, and cavalry officers one horse each. The rank and file will be allowed all their clothing, but no other property. If these conditions

are accepted, any amount of rations you may deem necessary can be taken from the stores you now have, and also
the necessary cooking utensils for preparing them. Thirty
wagons also, counting two two-horse or mule teams as
one, will be allowed to transport such articles as cannot
be carried along.

"The same conditions will be allowed to all sick and
wounded officers and soldiers as fast as they become able
to travel.

"The paroles for these latter must be signed, however,
while officers are present authorized to sign the roll of
prisoners.

"I am, general, very respectfully, your obedient servant,
U. S. GRANT,
Major-General."[11]

Pemberton's "own inclination was to reject these terms,"
but with one exception, every one of his brigade and division
commanders urged him to acceptance. Brigadier General
Baldwin, without offering any objections to the surrender proposals, insisted upon holding out, but assigned no reason for
it.[12] When each of these officers had had his say, Pemberton
only added, "Gentlemen I have done what I could";[13] then he
dictated his decision to Grant.

"HEADQUARTERS,
Vicksburg, Miss., July 3, 1863.

"MAJ. GEN. U. S. GRANT,
Commanding United States Forces, &c.:

"GENERAL: I have the honor to acknowledge the receipt
of your communication of this date, proposing terms of
capitulation for this garrison and post.

"In the main, your terms are accepted; but in justice
both to the honor and spirit of my troops, manifested in
the defense of Vicksburg, I have to submit the following
amendments, which, if acceded to by you, will perfect the
agreement between us:

"At 10 a.m. to-morrow I propose to evacuate the works in and around Vicksburg, and to surrender the city and garrison under my command, by marching out with my colors and arms, stacking them in front of my present lines, after which you will take possession.

"Officers to retain their side-arms and personal property, and the rights and property of citizens to be respected.

"I am, general, very respectfully, your obedient servant,

J. C. PEMBERTON,
Lieutenant-General, Commanding."[14]

On parting, the opposing commanders had agreed that hostilities should not be renewed until their correspondence broke off. Yet Pemberton and his officers hoped for more than this fleeting interlude of "cease firing." Almost shockproof as had become the Confederates, each inwardly offered an unspoken prayer that Grant would not strike to whittle down the "ultimatum" presently submitted by their leader.

By the hands of General Martin L. Smith, Pemberton's proffer of near complete submission went forward in the first few minutes after midnight of the third. Perhaps the clearest story of what took place behind the scenes before the sealing of this offer comes from the pen of General Thomas. This brigadier, a colonel through the siege, then commanded a brigade of Louisianians. To a friend he wrote in later years: "During the siege of Vicksburg ... I was present at a conference of General officers. ... At that meeting [on July 3, 1863], it was ascertained that our entire effective force was but a little over eleven thousand men; that we would in a few days be out of ammunition; that the troops had been for weeks subsisting on rations barely sufficient to sustain life; that the men were physically unable to undergo exertion; that we were entirely without artillery horses.

"General Pemberton read his correspondence with General J. E. Johnston, by which it appeared that General Johnston never at any time entertained hopes of compelling the enemy to raise the siege. The most he expected to accomplish was to occupy the enemy, and enable us to cut our way out. No communication had been had with him for many days; he had not made the promised diversion. That expedient, it was admitted sorrowfully and reluctantly by all, was now impracticable, if not utterly impossible, for the reasons before enumerated. We could not cut our way out.... I recollect, at that meeting, I thought that General Pemberton had met with improper treatment. Time has but strengthened the opinion then entertained. In view of these facts, succor being hopeless—our capture was but a matter of time, and could be delayed but a few days at best—it was deemed unnecessary to sacrifice further the lives of the gallant men, who, from simple rifle-pits, had repulsed for forty-eight days, the combined attack by land and water of a force more than ten times their number, that was replete with every appliance of modern warfare.... The capitulation was, therefore, universally assented to; and I am sure that there was not an officer present—and there were not a few who were heroes of many hard-fought fields—but was convinced that General Pemberton had done all that the most exalted patriotism, or the most punctilious soldierly honor, could have demanded...."[15]

This very night, while Pemberton and his senior generals were preparing for the morrow's surrender, "the largest capture of men and material ever made in war up to that time,"[16] Johnston was between Brownsville and the Big Black. From there he sent to Pemberton this note:

"CAMP NEAR BIRDSONG FERRY, *July 3*, [*1863*]
"Your dispatches of the 28th were destroyed by messenger. He states that General Smith's troops were driven back to Monroe. This statement and his account of your

condition make me think it necessary to create a diversion, and thus enable you to cut your way out if the time has arrived for you to do this. Of that time I cannot judge; you must, as it depends upon your condition. I hope to attack the enemy in your front the 7th, and your co-operation will be necessary. The manner and the proper point for you to bring the garrison out must be determined by you, from your superior knowledge of the ground and distribution of the enemy's forces. Our firing will show you where we are engaged. If Vicksburg cannot be saved, the garrison must."[17]

Johnston had been playing dead these many weeks of siege. His long deferred response now came too late: this news of his unhatched good intentions was not to reach Pemberton until July 10.[18]

Before sunrise of "that momentous Fourth," General Smith delivered into the hands of U. S. Grant the proposals he carried from Pemberton for Vicksburg's delivery to the Union. It was not long before he hurried back to the fortress with Grant's "absolutely final conditions," slightly modifying what Pemberton had put forth:

"HEADQUARTERS DEPARTMENT OF THE TENNESSEE,
        Before Vicksburg, Miss., July 4, 1863.
"LIEUT. GEN. J. C. PEMBERTON,
        Commanding Confederate Forces, Vicksburg, Miss.:
"GENERAL: I have the honor to acknowledge receipt of your communication of July 3. The amendment proposed by you cannot be acceded to in full. It will be necessary to furnish every officer and man with a parole signed by himself, which, with the completion of the rolls of prisoners, will necessarily take some time.

"Again, I can make no stipulations with regard to the treatment of citizens and their private property. While I do not propose to cause them any undue annoyance or loss, I cannot consent to leave myself under any restraint by stipulations. The property which officers will be allowed to take with them will be as stated in my proposition of last evening; that is, officers will be allowed their private baggage and side-arms, and mounted officers one horse each.

"If you mean by your proposition for each brigade to march to the front of the lines now occupied by it, and stack arms at 10 a. m., and then return to the inside, and there remain as prisoners until properly paroled, I will make no objection to it.

"Should no notification be received of your acceptance of my terms by 9 a. m., I shall regard them as having been rejected, and shall act accordingly. Should these terms be accepted, white flags should be displayed along your lines to prevent such of my troops as may not have been notified from firing upon your men.

"I am, general, very respectfully, your obedient servant,

U. S. GRANT,
Major-General."[19]

In response to the foregoing final conditions Pemberton immediately dispatched the following acceptance:

"HEADQUARTERS,
Vicksburg, Miss., *July 4, 1863.*

"MAJ. GEN. U. S. GRANT,
Commanding United States Forces, &c.:

"GENERAL: I have the honor to acknowledge the receipt of your communication of this day, and in reply to say that the terms proposed by you are accepted.

"Very respectfully, your obedient servant,

J. C. PEMBERTON,
Lieutenant-General."[20]

Grant had relinquished his first demand for unconditional surrender. In the end he had agreed that the defeated garrison might be paroled at Vicksburg, thus waiving their imprisonment in the North or elsewhere. He had not demanded that prisoners be sent to the nearest regular station for exchange.[21]

The exultant Union army had but a short march down the road—to reach their Vicksburg goal. In the end, the task had proved too great for Pemberton alone. Vicksburg and Gettysburg, July 4, 1863. But for these, the course of American history—and of the Western world—might have been other than it was. One cannot help playing with the "ifs" of history.

A burning sun brightened the scarred pinnacle of the city's courthouse. The neighboring streets were thronged with crowds, milling and uneasy. It was July 4, 1863, in Vicksburg.

Around the corner, close by the public square, Lieutenant General John Clifford Pemberton was riding up for a last review of the troops in grey. Northern man or no, this soldier looked the gladiator: tall, immaculate, erect, the Yankee's appearance was striking. Though his stern, sober look of determination suggested hauteur, his calm dignity commanded respect. The manner, darkly serious at this hour, was assured; the voice was rich, the diction flawless.[22]

Not under the siren spell of his Virginia wife had Pemberton cast in his fortunes with the Confederacy; but because he felt the North was wrong, the South right, he yielded to the strangers' call and threw away an inheritance. At this moment he dismounted quickly and for the last time passed down the faded ranks of those with whom he'd stood the siege. Was there with some of them a wordless sympathy for him who came so far to serve, and then to lead them?.... "Lieutenant-General J. C. Pemberton.... Excuse the liberty I take in addressing you this letter. The privilege was not given me of grasping your hand, as you passed, and looking into your face after your long and heroic defense of Vicksburg. I trust that you may soon be restored to command and that the Army of the West will be in the field again.... If I can be of any service

in organizing and drilling the men as they arrive at Demop-
olis, I am ready to obey the summons to leave....The 46th
Georgia are your friends and desired to call in a body upon
you at Jackson. It numbers eleven hundred and thirty-three
men.—P. H. Colquitt, Colonel, Commanding General Gist's
Brigade."[23]

At 10:00 A.M. General Steele's division marched into and
garrisoned the city, the bands playing national airs. The flag
of the Union was seen floating above the buildings where of
late only rebel ensigns met the breeze; and Vicksburg was
in loyal possession once more. Not long after, Colonel Mark-
land made his entrance and took possession of the Post Office,
at once proceeding to establish Federal mail routes with the
rest of the world (*Missouri Democrat,* July 9, 1863). Now hear
Grant:—"At the appointed hour the garrison of Vicksburg
marched out of their works and formed line in front, stacked
arms and marched back in good order....I rode into Vicksburg with the troops, and went to the river to exchange congratulations with the navy upon our joint victory....the fate
of the Confederacy was sealed when Vicksburg fell....Really,
I believe there was a feeling of sadness just then in the breasts
of most of the Union soldiers at seeing the dejection of their
late antagonists."[24]

"No event of the Siege," runs a recent Vicksburg paper,
"does Mrs. Ella Strother Powell recall quite as vividly as the
sight of two men on horseback riding towards the Court
House. The one in grey, Pemberton, the one in blue, Grant.
Breathlessly she watched them pass, saw Grant dismount,
climb the Court House steps and stand until the changing of
the flags. Slowly the Confederate colors were lowered from
the mast and in their stead...."[25]

In exchanging congratulations with the navy upon their
joint victory, Grant then said, and later wrote: "The navy

under Porter was all it could be, during the entire campaign. Without its assistance the campaign could not have been successfully made with twice the number of men engaged. It could not have been made at all, in the way it was, with any number of men without such assistance."[26]

The streets of Vicksburg were not garlanded for Grant's approach; they were sacked. The victory parade, from all accounts, looked upon shattered houses and hospitals, upon gutted schools and piles of wreckage. "Grant beheld the desolation of a proud city, fiercely attached to the landmarks and mansions of the unforgotten past." No doubt he glimpsed the bitter faces of the people crushed under his army's weight. Perhaps, as he gazed upon the vast destruction, his triumph was darkened by the spectacle of ruin.

In the preceding April Lee had explained that, in his opinion, the Confederacy had to choose between maintaining the line of the Mississippi and that of Virginia. "When it came to a final choice between advancing into Pennsylvania or detaching troops from Lee to do battle on the Mississippi, the President and all members of the Cabinet except Postmaster-General Reagan favored a new invasion of the North."[27] The day had now come for Grant to claim the price of this choice. It was a large one: 31,600 prisoners were surrendered, 172 cannon, approximately 60,000 muskets. Also counted in the cost was a great amount of ammunition.[28] Despite there being an effective fighting force of but eleven thousand men among the thirty-one thousand accounted prisoners, still and all, "the captures by this capitulation were the most important of the war."[29]

At the city's fall fifty-six hundred persons appeared by the records to be under medical care. Most were sheltered in private houses. At least a hundred homes had been set up as hospitals in the emergency. During the siege, losses among the combatants and noncombatants exceeded six thousand. No place within the city was really safe; almost every dwelling suffered shelling or was shattered; and there was not "a whole pane of glass to be found anywhere."[30]

In a great many places, "the streets were soon plowed up beyond further use as such, while enormous craters near the size of a hogshead were to be seen everywhere. Countless dwellings had their corners or their sides blown out. As a result, most of the four thousand citizens then besieged were driven to the caves earlier dug in the banks of earth." Old inhabitants recall close to five hundred of such "holes," and state that "as many as fifteen people at a time often crowded into one of these shelters during the worst hours of bombardment." It is likely some such cavern was hewn out for use as Pemberton's headquarters in times of intensest shelling. However, it is known positively only that he made use of the residence of Lieutenant Ludwell Blackstone Cowan for the duration of the siege. Cowan's home stood on the south side of Crawford Street, opposite the Convent.[31]

What Grant saw in Vicksburg, he never forgot. Returning there in 1880, from his tour around the world, he was asked if he cared to look around. He said, "No;" but added, "I would like to visit the National Cemetery."[32] Lying there are 16,822 Union soldiers who lost their lives in and around Vicksburg. The names of 12,719 to this day remain unknown.[33]

The day after the surrender found Sherman writing to his wife, "You will have heard all about the capitulation of Vicksburg on the 4th of July, and I suppose duly appreciate it. It is the event of the war thus far. Davis placed it in the scale of Richmond, and pledged his honor that it should be held even if he had to abandon Tennessee."[34]

The coincidence of Vicksburg's fall and the Confederate defeat at Gettysburg followed within less than two months the death of Stonewall Jackson. Taken together, these three disasters "raised for the first time a doubt of Confederate victory." Even so, Lee "was no more prepared to admit a crushing defeat than Meade was to claim one." Not till four days after Gettysburg did Pemberton learn of it. That day (July 8, 1863) his Philadelphia boyhood playmate, now Major General George Gordon Meade, wrote to his wife, "I never claimed a victory, though I stated that Lee was defeated in his efforts to destroy my army."[35] Meade had also been a friend and comrade of Robert Edward Lee—before the war.

Within a few short months of the Union's double celebration of that year's July Fourth, there was to take place a formal christening, a christening of that vast slaughterhouse where "many of the dead were so carelessly buried that the plows of Pennsylvania farmers were catching in their bones." November 16, 1863, was appointed to make official the Union burial of the Union dead. All others had died in vain. That day, in Lincoln-music, was made immortal the test on a great battlefield of war—whether a nation conceived in liberty could long endure. The Gettysburg Address was so soaring in its eloquence few weighed its towering irony—that implicit in these deathless words is the claim that Robert E. Lee and his warriors had dedicated *their* lives and *their* honor to the proposition that "government of the people, by the people, for the people" *shall* perish from the earth. It may be permitted to us to doubt that such was the South's ambition or intent.

CHAPTER XVIII

Aftermath of Surrender

AT THE FALL of Vicksburg General Grant "paroled" Pemberton and issued instructions requiring him to report to his superior—still General Johnston. After an interval, Pemberton found the officer designated, "sitting on a cleared knoll on a moonlight night surrounded by members of his staff." Unheralded, and of a sudden coming up the hill towards him, Johnston observed "a tall, handsome, dignified figure." He sprang up to greet the officer now recognized, extended his hand, saying the meantime, "Well, Jack old boy, I am certainly glad to see you." The proffered hand, unclasped, was slowly lowered as Johnston's staff saw Pemberton salute his senior officer punctiliously, pause for the barest second and reply, "General Johnston, according to the terms of parole prescribed by General Grant, I was directed to report to you, sir!" Both stood motionless, and in silence. Then Pemberton saluted once more and turned away.[1] It was the last meeting for these two. In April, 1861, at the start of war—in Richmond—they had been friends. Pemberton in point of fact had served as Johnston's chosen adjutant and chief of staff. One is sadly reminded of the last meeting between Lee and Pickett.

By July 11, just one week after the surrender, the task of

paroling the army was completed, and the Confederate garrison marched out of Vicksburg. Many deserted.[2] With the remnant, "the Lieutenant General commanding remained, attending to their wants, and shared with them the hardships of the march to Enterprise [Mississippi], where the army of Vicksburg was dissolved on parole."[3]

Within a few days (July 16, 1863) Pemberton heard from the President: "Yourself and the general officers whose names were sent on here have been discharged from their parole and can enter at once on duty."[4]   But, surveying his career in the sunless light of defeat, Pemberton had cause to pause and wonder whether he was not essentially unsuited longer to serve the Southern people; whether he would not always be subject to their censure in his failure.   All the same, such moods seldom got the upper hand in him.   From every point of view his prospects looked black—and still he kept on.   Moreover he actually benefited in one respect from his anguish of feelings: the spectacle of his own career disposed him to a certain new tolerance towards those who differed in thought or capacity.

Soon the Nation—North as well as South—saw a sight nearly unprecedented. The world of military men, the people, and the press hurled themselves upon one solitary figure. "It was not so much that he had surrendered the fortress—that was recognized as inevitable after brave resistance—as that it had been done on July fourth." This, to some, proved that he had been a traitor to the South from the beginning, and had gone with the Confederacy just to humiliate the South and glorify the Union by surrendering Vicksburg on July Fourth.[5]

Nonetheless, the loyalty of a few warmed the Lieutenant General's heart; he contrived to face it through. Said Secretary of War James A. Seddon: "I feel deep regret and sympathy that —— has aspersed you, whose efforts and sacrifices in

our cause are as meritorious as they have been illy rewarded."[6]
Pemberton's champions ruefully, courageously, pointed out his
merits, his sacrifices. It was no use; a scapegoat simply had
to be provided. "Our cause is dim in Europe, if it be true,
as the Northern papers report, that the Confederate loan has
sunken from par to 35 per cent. discount since the fall of Vicksburg." So reads the diary (August 20, 1863) of the Rebel War
Clerk, Jones; and according to one pre-eminent in matters
Confederate, the diary had real value in that it held up a
mirror to the hopes and the fears of the city of Richmond, in
which Jones labored.[7]

As Pemberton commenced the tedious and roundabout journey to Gainesville, Alabama, where he was to remain until
the August following and the completion of his official report,
stories flourished that he was passing out of army life. The
tales were untrue. The soldier whose reputation was all that
remained of his worldly estate hoped to disarm malice and
silence scandal by unostentatious diligence in the duties of a
subordinate position.[8] In those days he had no doubt that
"at some calmer period in the future justice will be done me,"
or so he wrote a friend, and continued, "I am content to wait
for the vindication of my military reputation until the country
shall be at rest, and my public defense shall have been successfully accomplished."[9] The Southern world in those days stood
incredulous before such silent resignation, Davis heading those
urging Pemberton to defend himself.

To return to the *casus belli* that set off the explosion around
and about Pemberton—that matter of his having surrendered
on July 4. Twenty years after Vicksburg, people still wanted
to know more of what took place just before the surrender.
What did Pemberton say, and what were Grant's answers?
In consequence of this extended public curiosity, the *Century
Magazine* in August, 1887, printed the absorbing Pemberton-

Grant correspondence which is reprinted as an appendix in this book.* The subject is still dynamite; but here are the versions of Pemberton, of Grant—and a new one.

Pemberton's account: "If it should be asked why July 4 was selected as the day for the surrender, the answer is obvious. I believed that upon that day I should obtain better terms. Well aware of the vanity of our foes, I knew they would attach vast importance to the entrance on July 4 into the stronghold of the great river, and that to gratify their national vanity they would yield then what could not be extorted from them at any other time. This question of time was also discussed by a council of my general officers, and my views concurred in."[10]

As to this, Grant in effect says, "poppy-cock." In his view Pemberton couldn't hold out a day longer; the surrender just happened to fall on July 4.[11]

And then comes this voice from the blue:

"BATTLE McCARDLE   Telephone Maine 1999
Attorney at Law
Suite 613 New York Life Building
                    Kansas City, Mo., May 27th. 1937.
"JOHN C. PEMBERTON,
     New York.
My dear Mr. Pemberton:
"Some days ago I read with interest that you had visited the battle fields of Vicksburg and there had met a grandson of General Grant. The meeting must have been of interest to both of you.

"I was born at Vicksburg and my father, Colonel Wm. H. McCardle, was in the Confederate army and during the siege of Vicksburg was on the staff of your grandfather, General Pemberton. You are aware of the storm of criticism that broke over General Pemberton's head by reason of his surrender of Vicksburg on July 4th. It gives

* See "The Terms of Surrender," p. 281.

me pleasure to tell you that up to his death in 1893 my father never permitted a word of criticism of General Pemberton to go unchallenged. He was his steady advocate.

"When I was a small boy my father told me that when further resistance became useless a council of war was held and that at that council he, my father, proposed that surrender be had on July 4th. His words were that 'Those fellows will be so elated to get in here on July 4th., that they will give us better terms.' He added that better terms were thereby obtained.

"I have never seen the above in print but my father was a prominent man in Mississippi where he lived and was loved for fifty years, and I never knew his lips to be the messenger of a lie. You realize that after criticism began General Pemberton would not impute the idea of surrender on July 4th. to a subordinate.

"I have lived in Missouri for forty years and for some years have been Judge of the Jackson County Court at Kansas City.

"With best regards,

M.E.   I am, Very truly yours,

BATTLE MCCARDLE."[12]

Through the barrage of invective leveled at him, Pemberton's superiors renewed their evidences of unshaken faith, both openly and in private. But as regards the world at large, these graceful gestures of steady support were unconvincing, were in fact wasted. Thankfully Pemberton was singularly independent of the general run of popular opinion; and it is the measure of his detachment that at least outwardly he continued on the even tenor of his way. Making terms with his difficulties, he reaped no later rewards for his real courage. But it hardly mattered—he was "that rare phenomenon, a genuinely independent personality."

In their fantasies about Pemberton, gossipers asserted he had sought a million Yankee dollars for the surrender of Vicksburg. Such rumors were persistent in the North.[13] Curiously enough, considering all the mendacities with which the history of this war is studded, such a lie direct one finds of rare occurrence. Except for his mother's later generosity, Pemberton, literally devoid of worldly goods, would have been a charge upon the bounty of his adopted state, Virginia. Another diverting bit of defamation circulated by Jones avowed that Pemberton and Sherman during the siege's progress gave evidence of their mutual esteem through the pleasant exchange of beautiful bouquets! Confederate bouquets Sherman had indeed received; but the donors were two young Vicksburg majors. By brief and considerate suspension of his army's accurate artillery fire, Sherman had foreborne to interrupt a social gathering given by these young bloods the night before. The youthful hosts were grateful—and next morning sent Sherman flowers. Carl Sandburg's *Lincoln* supplies the details of this strange incident of men at war.

In Montgomery (Alabama), while awaiting the Court of Inquiry by him solicited from the President, Pemberton was cheered to receive this handsome appreciation and good advice from the chief magistrate.

"Unofficial

"Richmond, Va.
August [?], 1863.

"LT. GENL. PEMBERTON,

My dear Sir:

"Maj. Memminger handed to me yours of the 29th ult. and I intended to reply by the same medium, but he left sooner than I expected and I must adopt the less safe channel of the public mail.

"The article to which I called your attention bore internal evidence of its origin, and indicated some points which should be noticed in your report, it was therefore that I wished you to read it. I did not expect, or desire, that you should reply to articles found in the press.

"The statements in relation to operations connected with the battle of Baker's Creek sufficiently warn you of an attempt to place on you the responsibility for all which preceded, and followed that event, and it indicates the points to be covered.

"To some men it is given to be commended for what they are expected to do, and to be sheltered when they fail by a transfer of the blame which may attach; to others it is decreed that their success shall be denied or treated as a necessary result and their failures imputed to incapacity, or crime—

"The test of success therefore, though far from just, is one which may be accepted in preference to the popular delusion so readily created by unscrupulous men who resort to the newspapers to disseminate falsehood and forestall the public judgment. Genl. Lee and yourself have seemed to me examples of the second class, and my confidence in both has not been diminished because 'letter writers' have not sent forth your praise on the wings of the press.

"I am myself no stranger to the misrepresentation of which malignity is capable, nor to the generation of such feeling by the conscientious discharge of duty, and have been taught by a disagreeable experience how slowly the Messenger of Truth follows that of Slander. The court which has been ordered to inquire into the campaign in Missi. & E. La. will I trust develop the real causes of events, and give to the public the means of doing justice to the actors.

"I thank you for the information in relation to my Brother for whose safety I have been very anxious.

"With my best wishes for you and your family, I am very truly & respectfully yrs.   JEFFERSON DAVIS."[14]

Idle as he was in Montgomery until the crucial Court of Inquiry could launch those hearings of whose future findings he was so confident, these random passages from the press of those days typify the sort of thing Pemberton read in the painful weeks of waiting for the judgment of his military peers: "... Pemberton's planning and Federal gold had more to do with the final result of that campaign than all of Grant's planning.... Pemberton made the defense of Vicksburg the most memorable of modern times.... Joseph E. Johnston desired to have him for Chief of his Staff.... Beauregard declares that there is not a truer man or a braver soldier in the Confederate service.... We cannot understand what occasions the storm of hatred against Pemberton except his Northern birth, and perhaps the strict discipline he has kept up in his camps. ... for the Big Black, Pemberton received all the blame, although a portion of his troops shamefully abandoned him, saying that he had sold them and Vicksburg.... At Vicksburg Pemberton made one of the stoutest and noblest defenses of which there is any account in history, bringing Vicksburg the fame of Saragossa.... General Stephen D. Lee writes this newspaper: 'I am glad to add this testimonial to Pemberton's loyalty and patriotism for he was indeed in a most delicate position—President Davis advising one course and General Johnston ordering another....' ...General Early maintains those who know Pemberton best, know him only to love and honor him...."[15]

The Court of Inquiry was not held at Montgomery; nor at Atlanta as planned for the ensuing fall. The reason in both cases was the same: "When the time arrived for the Court's assembling, and when the officers composing it reached Montgomery, and in later months Atlanta, a dispatch arrived from Richmond stating that the exigencies of the service required all officers—including those summoned as witnesses—to report for duty in the field." And the Court was broken up.[16]

That same month Pemberton sought out his wife and children in Gainesville, Alabama. He had not seen them since the siege. The family had remained in Jackson until Grant crossed the river and commenced his march to take the state capital. Then Mrs. Pemberton and children hurriedly departed, happy to get off on freight cars, and in total darkness. Pemberton soon made out the busy little figure of his oldest daughter, playing in the yard of an unpretentious dwelling to which he was directed. Patty was then thirteen. Who was that soldier coming through the gate? The child had left her father's side but five months earlier. Yet, on looking up from play, she failed to recognize him now. His black hair had turned a solid gray, and to her he "looked like an old man." Before—she had always thought him young.

CHAPTER XIX

The Vicksburg Campaign in Review

WITHOUT RAKING UP the back yards of history, we may agree with Pemberton's sharpest critic in this: "General Johnston was of practically no assistance to General Pemberton—General Pemberton and his army would probably have done better if Johnston had never appeared on the scene.... as I said in my *American Campaigns,* I repeat here, General Johnston did nothing in the Vicksburg Campaign that entitled him to any fame."[1]

There is no denying that Joseph Eggleston Johnston had an aversion to attack that was cloudily profound. By nature and in practice he shrank from attack, never taking a strong line of action with his opponents, McClellan, Grant, or Sherman. Intransigent, and in his own eyes the rightful head of the army by seniority and by ability, he neither acknowledged nor heeded authority above him.[2] A devouring egotism caused him to reject and scorn all ideas and strategy not his own. Finally, he made it a matter of conscience to withhold his needed co-operation if any risk attached. Would Lee, in Johnston's place, have failed to raise the siege of Vicksburg?*

* In a letter to the author, dated March 19, 1941, Lieutenant Colonel John W. Thomason, Jr., says: ". . . it is obvious that Grant's success depended upon an absolutely supine attitude in Joe Johnston—who by every standard ought to have pitched into him. But Johnston wasn't a fighter. . . . I've never been able to ac-

The foremost Confederate biographer has written: "Once again it must be said that it is beyond the function of a biographer of Lee to criticise the skill of Lee's opponents. But in reaching a fair appraisal of Lee's place as a soldier the shortcomings of his adversaries must sometimes be taken into account. . . . the student of war is apt to ask himself, How was it that Grant exposed his right . . . ?" Then, Lee's biographer without troubling to further explain the function of a biographer, takes up the cudgels in earnest: "Grant did not hold literally to his boast 'I never manoeuvre.' He did manoeuvre, but he did not manoeuvre well." Next, he quotes Lee:— "Grant's talent and strategy . . . consisted in accumulating overwhelming numbers."[3]

To return to Johnston—with the inestimable advantage of hindsight. Manifestly, his tidbits of advice, his belated orders, his want of all aid were insuperable handicaps to Pemberton; and it is clear that he was more concerned to see that his own plans worked properly than to upset Grant's envelopment of Vicksburg. Note in Johnston's official report that he was "convinced of the impossibility of collecting a sufficient force to break the investment. . . ."[4] Of this Confederate, Sherman observed, "Johnston's falling back before us without a serious battle, simply resisting by his skirmish-lines and by his rearguard. But his friends proclaimed that it was all *strategic*."[5]

Again, as the end of the winter of 1863-64 approached, Johnston, then in command of the Army of Tennessee, "did not believe he should take the offensive until he was reinforced and supplied with more transportation." By the end of April, 1864, he was "still unprepared to take the offensive in the

count for the high reputation he enjoyed. . . . Have you heard the story that Davis' plans for 1863 included the despatch of Jackson to the west? If Jackson, or Lee, or even Longstreet—any of the killers—had been sent out there Grant wouldn't have been free to starve out fortresses."

West.... President Davis had discovered in the winter of 1861-62 the proclivity of General Johnston for retreating.... Johnston, [Lee] thought, should send his cavalry against Sherman's communications and accept the risks of battle."[6]

Yet on more than one occasion both Grant and Sherman referred to Johnston as their ablest adversary. But so spoke Lee of McClellan; not of Grant or of Meade. Said Lee to Longstreet: "We [McClellan and I] always understood each other so well. I fear they may continue to make these changes [of Union Generals] till they find some one whom I don't understand."[7] To quote Jeb Stuart's dazzling biographer, "General Lee, on brief reflection, decided there was no more harm in McClellan." Hence, when Cassius Lee asked his cousin R. E. Lee to name the ablest general he had opposed, General Lee "did not hesitate a moment for the answer: 'McClellan, by all odds,' he said emphatically."[8]

On August 2, 1863, which he states was the earliest moment compatible with the performance of other and very pressing duties, Pemberton presented his official report to the Secretary of War in Richmond. Something over a month later, September 30, 1863, he had a personal conference in Richmond with Secretary Seddon. Of part of this meeting we have a report from the pen of the Adjutant General of the State of Virginia. Addressing Major General Francis H. Smith, Superintendent of the Virginia Military Institute, Richardson wrote: "I have just had occasion to visit the office of the Sec'y of War, where Gen. Pemberton happened to be and where I sat for some time listening to a conversation between them, illustrated on his part by frequent references to his report. It was very interesting and never did I hear a more soldier like and conclusive vindication of his course by any man. Not one word too many, no undue excitement—tho manifestly a strong sense of unmerited censure, tho refraining himself from throwing any upon his superior in command, Gen. Johnston, who certainly (tho mildly vindicated by the Sec'y) appears to me from facts and dispatches to have enforced Gen'l Pemberton into a course opposed to his own judgment and inclination. The discussion concluded with an undoubting conviction upon my mind, that the Confederacy has not a truer, more gallant, and few more gifted soldiers, and that no officer was ever more shamefully and unjustly censured. I never saw him before, was not introduced, there being others present, but I felt that what I had heard, if known to the whole country would make his calumniators hide *their* heads, and place *him* high among the bravest and the best. Gen. Johnston seems to have been in the sulks when he went out there and to have been by no means hearty in the cause. I take it he is an unfortunate tempered man and it seems to me has fallen short of his duty."[9]

Irrespective of the quality of Pemberton's performance, the ultimate authority has sketched within the limits of one crisp paragraph the mission assigned him: "[Pemberton's] first assigned duty was to keep Grant from [Vicksburg]....It is debatable whether the Confederate administration was right in insisting that [Vicksburg] be held at any price, but there can be no disputing the fact that in the summer of [1863] this was the fixed policy of the government. [Pemberton] was forced to subordinate everything to that or else should have resigned his commission."[10] But this sharply analytical conclusion has been taken from Freeman's life of Lee, not of Pemberton! Where "Pemberton," "Vicksburg," and "1863" appear in brackets, "Lee," "Richmond," and "1864" occur in the original text. Perhaps "military circumstance is [not always] incommensurable"; for the device of transposition, to which confessed resort has just been had, reveals a striking similarity in what Pemberton confronted in 1863 at Vicksburg and Lee in 1864-65 at Richmond.

After Gettysburg, Lee reported to the President: "With the knowledge I then had, and in the circumstances I was then placed, I do not know what better course I could have pursued."[11] Pemberton might have claimed the same immunity.

Now, in the afterlight of operations long past, what can it be said Pemberton *should* have done? Today, to Pemberton's biographer, bound to him by ties of blood and greatest sympathy, these appear his faults and errors:

Throughout the war, Pemberton was the West Pointer, the professional soldier; except when pressed by Davis he rarely attempted conciliation. Aloof, formal, and a stranger among those he led, Pemberton failed to secure support behind the lines and at the front to the extent his ability and character warranted. Like his famed West Point sponsor, Pemberton had two sets of manners: one for the drawing room and one for "the service." He never allowed the South fair opportunity to glimpse his actual self. It may be that later pages of this story will in a measure reveal him behind the scenes.

As for Pemberton's military mistakes: Trained for a lifetime in the profession of arms, firm in character, with guts and spirit, nonetheless at Edward's Depot, where every second demanded stern, unyielding decisions, Pemberton perhaps erred in submitting to the judgment of the majority of his officers. In consequence, he abandoned his chosen field of battle and marched to cut Grant's lines of supply, then believed near Dillon's. There, well capable of devising his own strategy, he once more surrendered his own judgment. This time it was in obedience to changed orders from the remote Johnston; and he had to reverse the whole army's march. Better would it now appear had Pemberton stood his ground at Edward's and risked the consequences. For, if Freeman is right in his view of Lee's deferring to Longstreet at Gettysburg ("It is scarcely too much to say that on July 2 the Army of Northern Virginia was without a commander");[12] by the same token was the Confederate army handicapped in the few confused and crowded hours before Champion's Hill was fought. In these fateful moments it is likely Pemberton conceded too much to the views of others in lieu of adhering to his own well-considered plans.

However, the achievements to his credit are large. Miraculously, in one way or another, he month on month halted, shattered, or trapped what was then counted the largest army on earth. So long, in fact, did Pemberton stall the Union steam roller, that Sherman was driven nearly insane and almost out of the army.[13] Grant in the meanwhile had seen himself the target of acrid critics noisily demanding his removal from command.

Finally, in the construction of Vicksburg's fortifications Pemberton made a major contribution to the art of war. "The reader who can appraise the conditions under which he fought can appraise the man."

The refraining from throwing any censure upon his superior in command, so much admired in Pemberton by the Virginia adjutant, prevailed for sixteen years. Then in 1879 Pemberton sat down and wrote this letter.

"To the Editor of THE [RICHMOND] TIMES:
    "An article appeared in the WEEKLY TIMES of January 25, 1879, which purports to be 'A Hitherto Unpublished Report of General Joseph E. Johnston to the Confederate Government.' If that article be compared with the official report made by General Johnston in 1863 to his government, of which some two thousand copies were printed and issued at the time, the two will be found to be identical—a few clerical and typographical discrepancies excepted. Whatever value, therefore, is to be attached to the original report as an historical document is neither enhanced nor diminished because 'the manuscript recov-

ered from an unexpected source' has been 'revived by
General Johnston.' This re-publication has, however, accomplished the object which was no doubt intended. It
has revived 'the issues between the officer who surrendered
Vicksburg and his superior officer.' Many of my friends,
who have knowledge of the facts upon which hinge some
of the most important points in controversy between General Johnston and myself, have strongly urged that I have
not the right to decline a discussion so persistently pressed
upon me. I have finally reached the same conclusion,
and shall, therefore, after an absolute silence of more than
twelve years, endeavor to show that neither General Johnston's official report, nor the pages of his 'Narrative of
Military Operations,' which he has offered as his 'contribution of materials for the use of the future historian of
the war between the States,' are worthy of the high purposes to which he would have them applied—where they
have relation to the Mississippi campaign of 1863.

"J. C. PEMBERTON,
Philadelphia, March 21, 1879."[14]

Pemberton's answer to Johnston's renewed charges against
him was addressed to President Davis's historical assistant,
Major W. T. Walthall. It was unfinished and never published.
Here printed as an appendix, the document has in the past
decade been accorded interested comment by military men and
historians.*

In summing up the Vicksburg Campaign, Liddell Hart remarks: "There is a curious parallel between Vicksburg and
Gallipoli half a century later, not only because each controlled
the bloodflow along a vital economic artery. In time and in
method the Union effort to open this artery anticipated the
British effort to open the Dardanelles—above all, in arousing
the defender's anticipation of the move."[15]

There is perhaps a further analogy between Vicksburg and

* See pp. 289-319.

Wolfe's siege of Quebec: "Wolfe initiated a starvation campaign against Montcalm, sending detachments to lay waste the country round. . . . More important still was Wolfe's move to cut off their [the French] main supplies which came . . . downstream from Montreal. . . . Now because he had got so many of his ships up river, he perplexed the French command, wearing out their troops with ceaseless marching and countermarching until he made a choice of landing spots on the opposite shore at the Foulon Cove. . . ."[16]

CHAPTER XX

New Duties

GENERAL PEMBERTON, left by the fall of Vicksburg without a command, reported from Montgomery to Richmond "for duty in the field." He came as soon as the difficulties over his parole were ironed out with the Federal officer charged with the duty of exchange of prisoners.[1] At the time, there was no corps or station commensurate with Pemberton's rank as lieutenant general. He accepted the snub and was willing to bide his time.

Before long Davis handed Pemberton the following letter, addressed to General Bragg.
"*Unofficial*

"Richmond, Va.

Oct. 4, 1863

"GENL.

"This will be handed to you by Genl. Pemberton who goes to confer with you as to the propriety and advantage of being placed on duty with your army. He will speak to you freely and will after an exchange of views be able to decide whether or not it is desirable that he should remain.

"I have had much occasion to regret that which I regard as unjust criticism of him by persons in Missi and have heard of opposition to him by some of the troops he commanded. The latter surprised me more than the former, because the troops had opportunity to know how zealous and gallant his services were. Many of the officers have borne testimony to his capacity and good conduct, and I have no means of measuring the degree of opposition existing among the troops. He would not desire to command men who distrusted him nor would it be for the public interest that he should.

"My own judgment places him among the ablest of our Generals, but as you knew him in early life and have enjoyed sufficient opportunity to judge of his recent career it is needless to say more on this subject.

"His manly character and just appreciation of what is due to others even where he is the party most concerned will render your conference easy and I hope satisfactory.

"Should a corps now organized or to be organized be indicated, it might be well for General Pemberton to converse with the Division, and other Commanders as the means of judging before hand how far he would be acceptable to them and might rely on their cordial support of him.

"As ever Very truly yours,

"JEFFERSON DAVIS

"GENL. B. BRAGG

   Commanding"[2]

In later years Davis was to write to Bragg of these after-Vicksburg days: "I then as now held him [Pemberton] in high estimation and regarded him as an officer most unjustly censured. Being about to visit the Army under your command, I invited Genl Pemberton to accompany me* under the hope that some duty appropriate to his rank might be

* Davis evidently changed his mind about sending Pemberton alone and asked the General to accompany him on his visit to Tennessee, October 9, 1863.

found and his desire for active service gratified.... Then when I inquired whether Genl Pemberton could be advantageously employed, you said you would have to make inquiry before expressing an opinion."[3]

Bragg was personally attached to Pemberton—his West Point classmate—and had, so he reported to Davis, "confidence in his worth." In spite of these personal sentiments, Bragg subsequently informed the President that after consultation with officers he thought Pemberton's appointment to a command in that district "would not be advisable."[4]

After Bragg was driven away from Chattanooga, he disciplined several of his generals, notably Lieutenant General ("Bishop") Polk; and Davis doubtless hoped that Polk's suspension from the command of his corps might result in Pemberton's being named as Polk's successor; in fact such was Davis's suggestion.[5] But as Albert Sidney Johnston bravely wrote in the dark hours that came before the disaster at Shiloh, "the test of merit in my profession is success"; and Pemberton's name could not longer command confidence after Vicksburg. "It would be untrue to say that a defeated general can never regain the confidence of his soldiers; but unless he has previous successes to set off against his failure, to permit him to retain his position is dangerous in the extreme."[6] Such was the opinion of Stonewall Jackson. And of course the fall of Vicksburg had served to efface the memory of Pemberton's unbroken series of earlier repulses—of Grant, and of the baffled Sherman.

Back in Richmond, Pemberton waited for the call to duty that surely could not much longer be denied him. Yet the months dragged on and on, until at the coming of that cool and greening March month of '64, the still undaunted soldier could no longer stand by in silence, inactive and ignored. He wrote the President for answer to his fate:

"BOYNTON, MUHLENBURG CO., VA.
March 9 '/64

"HIS EXCY
JEFFERSON DAVIS.
Mr. President.

"As the spring campaign must soon open, and as there is no prospect that the Court of Inquiry will be reconvened during active operations may I not hope to be assigned service in the field, or in any capacity in which you think I may be useful?

You are so thoroughly acquainted with the circumstances of my position that I need refer neither to them, nor to the causes which have brought them about—but I can not help thinking that there is much less prejudice against me now, than there was when you offered me a command (conditionally) in Gen*l* Bragg's Army.

I feel very deeply the position of inactivity in which I find myself & can not refrain from asking you to relieve me from it.

"Most resp*ly* y*r* ob*d* servt

J. C. PEMBERTON.
Lt. Genl."⁷

Responding at once Davis considerately replied:

"Richmond, Va., *March 11, 1864.*

"DEAR SIR:

"You correctly suppose that your position is not due to a want of confidence or appreciation on my part. The circumstances which deprived you of a command belong to the chances of war.

"I thought and still think that you did right to risk an army for the purpose of keeping command of even a section of the Mississippi River. Had you succeeded none would have blamed, had you not made the attempt few if any would have defended your course. [Author's italics.]

"If it has not since been found expedient to place you in command of a corps, it has not been that I regarded

you as unequal to such position, but because of considerations which I could not control.

"Your devotion to our country's cause has enabled you
to rise above personal and professional pride; and in the
manner you have borne disappointment I find proof of
the injustice of the prejudice which has existed against
you, and sincerely hope you rightly believe that it is subsiding.

"Very respectfully
& truly yours
"JEFFERSON DAVIS

LIEUT. GENL. J. C. PEMBERTON
   Richmond,
   Virginia"[8]

On May 9, 1864, there were 479 instead of 480 generals of
different rank in the service of the Confederacy.[9] That day
Pemberton had resigned his commission as lieutenant general
and expressed his willingness to serve in the ranks.[10] The
President would hear none of it. Remaining adamant as regards Pemberton's insistence that he be permitted to resign
altogether his services as an *officer,* Davis conferred on him
the rank of lieutenant colonel in the artillery corps—this being
Pemberton's former branch of the service in the army of the
United States. Comment that followed was favorable from
most quarters, or lacking in hostility, no matter how looked at.
A sample editorial of the press read:

"An Act of Public Devotion

"The *Whig,* of yesterday, thus appropriately notices a
remarkable act of unselfishness and patriotism in an officer holding a high military position: 'General Pemberton
yesterday resigned his commission as Lieutenant General
in the Provisional Army of the Confederate States, and
went into active service in the field as Lieutenant Colonel
of Artillery. This action on the part of General Pemberton exhibits a highly laudable spirit, and goes far towards

sustaining all that his friends have claimed for him as a man of patriotism and honor. It is no time now to criticise the military conduct of unsuccessful Generals, who, whatever errors they may have committed, manifest, as in the case of General Pemberton, so much unselfishness at this critical period of the country's history. The magnanimous people of the Confederacy will remember, to his credit, his present conduct; and those who have felt bitterly towards him will be strongly inclined to mitigate their animosity. We have no doubt that General Pemberton will render valuable and efficient service to the cause in the present emergency.' "[11]

But if the Southern papers as a whole had no doubts that General Pemberton would render "valuable and efficient service to the cause" as a lieutenant colonel of artillery, the Rebel War Clerk, for one, could not be so deluded. His diary was adorned with this comment as regards the President's latest blunder: "Gen. Pemberton has resigned his commission; but the President has conferred on him a lieutenant-colonelcy of artillery. Thus the feelings of all the armies and most of the people are outraged; for, whether justly or not, both Pemberton and Bragg, to whom the President clings with tenacity, are especially obnoxious both to the people and the army. May Heaven shield us! Yet the President *may* be right."[12]

Perhaps Jones should be pardoned his venom—war works such devastation in most men's characters.

Before long "Pemberton really had command of all the batteries defending Richmond," a development which sorely distressed the Rebel War Clerk.

Soon to be included in Pemberton's command were Stonewall Jackson's youngsters, the cadets from "the West Point of the South." West Pointers generally managed to get along, regardless of their nativity; they understood, expected, and responded to strict discipline.

The corps of splendid Virginia Military Institute Cadets, of Lexington, first joined Lieutenant Colonel Pemberton on October 27, 1864. They were at once encamped at Poe's farm as an infantry support for a near-by battery. Poe's farm lay near the intersection of the Williamsburg Road and the intermediate line—the front there having been placed under the command of Jackson's "right arm," Lieutenant General Dick Ewell.[13]

And now Jones took two last snaps at Pemberton's heels. Under date of January 9, 1865, we find this entry: "General Pemberton has been relieved *here* and sent *elsewhere*." But the wish with Jones was father to the stillborn fact. Pemberton had been promoted inspector general of artillery with headquarters at Charleston.[14] To the dismay of the diarist, this but seldom carried the Yankee out of Richmond. With one final bleat, the jaundiced clerk noted: "Congress has passed an act organizing the artillery force of Lee's army—submitted by Gen. Pendleton (Episcopal clergyman), who writes the Secretary that Col. Pemberton (Northern man and once lieutenant-general) is making efforts to induce the President to withhold his approval of the bill, which he deprecates and resents, as the bill is sanctioned by the judgment of Gen. Lee. From this letter I learn we have 330 guns and 90 mortars under Lee; enough to make a *great noise* yet!"[15]

Surprisingly, Grant would have agreed that the South still "had enough to make a great noise yet." But he did not say so until his *Memoirs* came out more than a decade later. Then one could read this amazing might-have-been recorded by the deliberate strokes of the Union leader's pen: "Anything that could have prolonged the War a year beyond the time that it did finally close would probably have exhausted the North to such an extent that they might then have abandoned the contest and agreed to a separation."[16]

Knowing little of this defeatist spirit in the North, all things now ran down quickly to the end for the Confederate States of America, and for their artillerist, Lieutenant Colonel Pemberton. His remaining war days are mirrored in this final letter to a chief and champion who never failed him. It is the last one of which there is a record.

"NEAR WARRENTON, FAUQUIER CO., VA.

August 28th, /66.

"MY DEAR SIR—

"A day or two since I had the pleasure of meeting the Reverend Mr. Barton who informed me that if I entrusted a letter to him, he would deliver it in person—Although I do not design to say anything which the most rigid official could take exception to, it is not the less pleasant to know that your friends can address you without the intervention of such persons, and convey to you the assurance of their respectful regard and sympathy—

"I hope and believe, it is unnecessary for me to say how frequently my thoughts have been with you, and how deeply I have felt the wrongs which have been done you. I can never forget the uniform kindness and consideration with which you honored me even to your own prejudices and which manifested itself most, when I was most under the ban—neither need I tell you how sincerely I have deplored the effect upon your health of the long and cruel incarceration you have suffered for our common cause; we can only hope that a speedy trial—which we know you earnestly desire, and which can only result to your high honor—may restore you to health and to such freedom as we now possess.

"After the evacuation of Richmond, I made two efforts to join you: the first, whilst you were still at Danville; but the Fedl. Cavalry under Stoneman had destroyed a portion of the R. R. near High-bridge, and I was compelled to return to Salisbury, where I witnessed the capture of our last piece of Arty. and narrowly escaped the same fate myself—The second occasion was, on learning that you were in Charlotte, N. C., when I confidently hoped to have tendered my services in any way in which they might be useful; but I was again disappointed; for on reaching that place I found you had left the day previous. My horse had cast three shoes on the route from Newton, and the confusion consequent upon Johnston's surrender was so great, that I failed to get them replaced, though I made every exertion to do so. This apparently trivial obstacle alone, prevented me from endeavoring to overtake you to share your fortunes—After consultation with Genl. Cooper I returned to Newton, N. C., where I remained with my family until Feby. when, through my mother, I was enabled to purchase a small farm of 200 acres near Warrenton, Va., where we are now striving against inexperience, and many adverse circumstances, to earn a frugal support—I do not regret the course I conscientiously took, and only lament the results as they affect our country and yourself—

"Mrs. Davis has the heart-felt sympathies of my wife, as I believe she has of every noble lady in the land. Mrs. Pemberton unites with me in respectful regards which we beg you will present to her, and accept from both of us our earnest wishes for your own health and future happiness.

"Most truly yr friend,
"J. C. PEMBERTON.
"HON. JEFFERSON DAVIS."[17]

CHAPTER XXI

The Last Years

To THAT FARM she had provided for him, and of which the General's letter to Davis speaks, the mother quickly came as first visitor. It was the summer of 1866. Except for the ancient matron's generosity her "Rebel" son confronted dire need—perhaps even hunger. Her "dear John," no longer facing death in battle or long years of prison—she at once expanded, thawed out, and rapidly became the personality so long revered by all her own. At her bidding the farm was dubbed "Harleigh," after an old homestead near Philadelphia, which had belonged to some rather distant but impressive ancestor. "Harleigh" cost $5,000. That part of the country had been occupied, successively, by both armies, and the house had suffered accordingly. Bacon, hung from the rafters, had soaked through the pine flooring; not a window was intact; the porch railing had been torn off for firewood; the fences were down; the barn was overrun with rats. In short, the whole place was utter dilapidation. The entire family eagerly set to work to rehabilitate it. General Pemberton himself scraped and painted the woodwork; his little boys scrubbed floors; while Mrs. Pemberton did what she could to contrive curtains and pillows out of next to nothing. At this juncture the United States government, custodian of the few articles of furniture shipped five years earlier from Fort Ridgely, Minnesota, returned them all free of cost; and with this nucleus the family began its adventures to survive. The only thing in this meager collection that mattered greatly was a square piano, "like sweet bells jangled, out of tune and harsh" now, but destined to play a large part in cheering both parents and children for many a long day. All lovers of music, with good voices, the five children gathered around that old piano every evening while Mrs. Pemberton accompanied them through the songs of Stephen Foster and the Negro spirituals. During these nightly performances the Negroes, from field hands to babes in arms, gathered at the back entrance, listening, enthralled, to their own lovely hymns.

Irrespective of ethics which they were too young to appreciate, the youngsters' preference was their father's spirited rendering of

> Mynheer Van Dunk,
> Though he never got drunk,
> Took whisky and water freely,
> And quenched his thirst,
> With a quart of the first,
> To a pint of the latter daily,
> Saying, O, that a Dutchman's thirst should be
> As deep as the rolling Zuyder Zee, &c.

Mark Twain's *Innocents Abroad* was a nightly diversion, the General frequently interrupting his reading to chuckle, "By George this is equal to *Pickwick*." And no one could listen unshaken to his dramatic recital of Monk Lewis's "Alonzo the Brave." His Biblical stories also took on a Shakespearean eloquence that many pulpit interpreters might well have envied. Result: the children had an intimate acquaintance with David's wail over his lost Absalom, and a mental

General Pemberton in 1879 at the age of sixty-five. The picture was taken in Philadelphia where the General was then living.

F. Gutekunst

Martha Thompson Pemberton, General Pemberton's wife, from a picture taken in Norfolk, Virginia, when she was about thirty years of age.

vision of Daniel as a second Androcles. The mother supplied
the religious element.

General Pemberton leaned to tragedy, except in his musical
efforts. There the memory of West Point frolics colored the
old songs and gave a youthful dash to most of them, even
after he was an elderly man. Cases of this dare-deviltry never,
in all the years, failed to elicit the children's demands for
encores.

> He that wears a regimental suit,
> Is oft as poor as any raw recruit,
> But what of that?
> Girls will follow when they hear the drum,
> To view the tassel and the waving plume,
> That decks his hat.
> O, vive l'amour, cigars and cognac,
> Huzzah, huzzah, huzzah, huzzah,
> For those who bivouac.
>
> When we march into a country town,
> Prudes may fly from us, and dames may frown,
> But that's absurd.
> When we march away, we leave behind,
> Prudes and dames that have been vastly kind,
> Pray take my word.
> Off, off we go, and say that we're on duty,
> Smoke our cigars, and flirt with some new beauty,
> Huzzah, huzzah, huzzah, huzzah,
> For those who bivouac.

Strangely enough, music, except the rhythm of a march,
never seemed to appeal to one whose love of poetry, drama,
and finished prose was so great that his knowledge of each
of these departments of literature might well have fitted him
for quite a different career than the army.

History, ancient and modern, was at his finger tips, but he
had not the faculty of imparting what was so familiar to him.

Always the lack of responsiveness, or an inability to grasp what appeared to him easily within reach, meant impatience on his part and discouragement to the less alert mind.

General Pemberton, from all that his grandchildren have heard of him, was just two things—a soldier and a scholar. His children were still children after the war and remember him most clearly in the post-war period, when he attempted unsuccessfully to be a farmer in Virginia. He loved Latin and read it continually. A nephew of his tells that his boyhood recollection of Uncle John was that he covered his oatmeal with cayenne pepper, and immediately after breakfast sat down to read Virgil in the original. Anna, General Pemberton's youngest daughter, once, being irked by her father's absorption in his Virgil, said to her mother, "Come on Mama let's go to bed and leave Papa with his Virgins."

It was the custom to have family prayers every morning, and it was Mrs. Pemberton's part to offer the prayers and the General's, to read a chapter from the Bible. This he did so dramatically that his children were enraptured. His rendering of St. Peter cutting off the ear of a servant of the High Priest was so realistic that they were about as thrilled as the modern young one is in seeing a fight at the movies. He also sang continually and had a collection of most ridiculous songs, all of which were sung so feelingly the absurd verses became the recital of a tragic history. He could not turn a tune, so he was actually declaiming.[1]

The visit of Pemberton's Quaker brother, with the Biblical name Israel, was an outstanding event. He was the General's most congenial brother; the two were privately set down as "fossils" by the younger ones, both their literary tastes running on classic lines. Israel and John, very near in age, had shared all boyhood adventures and were always intimate. In so big a family, many years intervened between the elder and younger members, and the General's two brothers who "fought North" were born while he was at West Point. But brothers and sisters alike completely buried the hatchet after the war; and all were visitors to Harleigh at one time or another.

"I reckon you never been down so fa' amung 'secess' befo', M'am; have you," remarked a genial farm hand. He was dining with the family, in his shirt sleeves, after a day's work in the fields. The old lady (Pemberton's mother) bore up nobly against the shock of the queer word. She had determined to eschew politics, and the children had been instructed by their mother not to sing "The Good Old Rebel" during her sojourn. She had also brought along a small Philadelphia grandson. His coming South impressed upon him that to sing "Hang Jeff Davis on a Sour Apple Tree" would entail a good ducking in Cedar Run Creek. Once this understanding was established, the children's rival camps speedily sank their differences and all went well. Indeed, this small boy became so infatuated with farm life he was henceforth sent down to Virginia every summer. In later years other Northern cousins fought for this rare privilege.

Israel Pemberton was the "Major Pendennis" of the clan, known not alone to his nieces and nephews but to the world at large as "Uncle Is." He was a most likable old scalawag, kindhearted, selfish, worldlywise, an ornament in Society. To the end, he regarded his married brother, his junior by barely a year, as "a lamb of innocence," to be shepherded to strictly male suppers. From these, Is, the shepherd, was apt to return the worse for the banquet. He never failed to assert that the *bread* had disagreed with him! The General's wife, aware of the importance Is attached to the table, suffered some perturbation before his arrival as to the limitations of Harleigh's menus; but as good luck would have it, his visit took place in a gala year for mushrooms. They were brought in from the fields—literally by the bushel. Nothing could exceed the epicure's satisfaction. His twinkling blue eyes gleamed benedictions upon his relieved hostess. He expatiated on the rarity and expense of the dish at the Philadelphia Club ("sink of iniquity," she confided to others) and would have forgiven any other shortcomings of the diet sheet. On but one occasion was there ever a rift in the visit. Once, in the innocence of her heart, fearing monotony, Mrs. Pemberton provided some other delicacy and suspended the mushrooms. The curtain (dish cover) rose, and disclosed fried chicken. Alas! Brother Is's expression of benign expectancy vanished like the dawn of morning: "Good Lord, Patty!", he almost spat at her, "Have you no mushrooms?"

The politics of "Major Pendennis" accommodated themselves to his circumstances. At heart he went South; but for the rest of his body it would have been very inconvenient. So his head kept him where he was, and the divorce of head and heart was not suffered to incommode him—much.

Before Uncle Is's gift of a side saddle (and never had he done a more gracious deed) the General's girls had nothing except the "Mexican" article—for men. To this, they sought to adapt themselves and skirts, as best they could. Little did they dream that riding astride would ever conceivably become the fashion for any self-respecting female. As to anything in the shape of a carriage—that was beyond the family's fondest hope. They had only the farm wagon without springs, except for the oxcart. It would take untold time to do the four miles to "town." They seldom went.

General Pemberton kept a rough and ready diary of events jotted down without sequence, as this: "Jan. 3rd. Mr. Skinker here this morning.... Jan. 4th. Two chickens stolen last night." However, Mr. Skinker's ample dimensions exonerated him from any possible connection with an entrance to a foot-wide chickenhouse door. The diary further faithfully recorded the accouchement of each horse and cow and the achievement of Polly, the old sow—sixteen piglets at one go. Polly was the only animal who received the General's personal attentions. He visited her daily, with an ear of corn or an apple, and she came to know him and to welcome him noisily with a grunt. For a long time the General could not bring himself to a philosophic acceptance of pork at the table. (During the siege of Vicksburg he cheerfully ate alligator's tongue, but could not join in a meal where horse flesh was served; for, as he once confessed, "their eyes would have haunted me.")

As noted, the General both read and recited poetry exquisitely. One little daughter delighted to curl up in his arms and listen by the hour while the old soldier gave her long extracts from "The Burial of Sir John Moore." Mrs. Pemberton would protest, "Oh, John, don't recite that gruesome thing," and the child would whisper, "Go on, Papa." In his daughters Pemberton found always an appreciative audience.

Reading aloud in long winter evenings formed the staple entertainment of Harleigh life. The whole family gathered round the table, where evil-smelling kerosene oil lamps made darkness visible. One Mr. Homer, sharing the General's literary tastes, sent his friend a rickety old bookcase full of odd volumes: they ran all the way from early drama and Shakespeare to Bulwer, Thackeray, Dickens, and Dumas—and proved a mine of inexhaustible wealth. The "Madman's Manuscript" from *Pickwick* and Dumas' *Memoirs of a Physician* were listened to with rapt attention, though they sent the younger ones to bed scared to death.

General Pemberton had great facility for drawing; this was not an unalloyed blessing, for he endured a "well-meant" persecution because of it. In this subject he had passed first in his class at West Point, and his sketches were full of spirit; but he had never really studied art and well knew his limitations. This, neither wife nor children at all understood. Consequently they, and other less learned friends, thought it a case of buried talent and for years worried the life out of him. Eventually he allowed his family to collect odd materials. Thus, woodcuts, among other things, were always lying in ambush, grinning at him for his failure. The General was quite right. The things he sent—almost at the bayonet's point—for approval were pronounced to "lack sufficient technical finish for reproduction."

The ten years' struggle of the soldier-scholar to make a livelihood out of farming was an uphill battle, the kind of battle Pemberton had fought from the very day he became a Virginian and then a Confederate. Not that he was sorry for this step that blasted his career—"I do not regret the course I conscientiously took, and only lament the results as they affect our country and yourself," he had written to Davis in the summer of 1866. Still and all, Warrenton had afforded "a welcome retreat from the harassments of the unsettled state of public affairs in those times." Nor had the pensive warrior ever found so many treasured opportunities to lose himself in books.

Towards the end of 1875 Pemberton was finally won over by his brothers' call to return to his birthplace. Yearly their entreaties grew more insistent, and that year the family in Philadelphia would no longer be denied. Moreover, the health of the Pennsylvania Confederate was failing.

And so—though it brought but a small portion of its hard cost ten years before—the farm was sold.

Among the small company of his soldier comrades, these three Confederate friends of Warrenton years would most sorely miss Pemberton's friendship and affection: Eppa Hunton, who was one of Pickett's colonels at Gettysburg; William H. Payne, a brigadier of the renowned Black Horse troop; and John Singleton Mosby, leader of Jeb Stuart's celebrated scouts. There was a most remarkable group of men who lived within the confines of the town of Warrenton at that time— a community of some twelve hundred people. In addition to Lieutenant General Pemberton, Brigadier General William H. Payne, Brigadier General Eppa Hunton and Colonel John S. Mosby, Warrenton also counted as citizens, Extra Billy Smith, Major General and twice Governor of Virginia; Major General L. L. Lomax; Major Taylor Scott; Captain Alex Payne—and Captain North of the Confederate Navy who earlier had been assigned to the construction of the *Alabama*.

First off, Pemberton, still not a citizen of the now single nation, took up his life in Philadelphia. Here were his brothers, his sisters, and their large devoted families. All was forgiven and the days were happy, if not yet prosperous. Then in 1879 the Congress in Washington, on the ninth day of May, "passed a bill removing General John Clifford Pemberton's political disabilities, and restoring to said citizen such property as might be lawfully his."

But Philadelphia continued a bit beyond the dimensions of the General's slightly more ample purse. So he moved with his family to Allentown. Of those years a local paper gives this account in part:

"He came to this city to become associated with the old Allentown Furnace Co. in the Sixth ward, then under the management of Samuel B. Lewis, father of ex-Mayor Fred E. Lewis. He took a residence on Union street, near Fourth, at what was known as 'Fry's spring property,' and resided here for about two years.

"The records of Grace Episcopal church, which have been searched by Rev. S. Franklin Custard, the rector, show that

Mrs. Pemberton transferred membership from her Warrenton, Va., church to Grace church, February 7, 1876. The records give no clue as to whether the general was a member of the church or not.

"The couple was accompanied by their beautiful daughter, Anna, and a son, William, and Mrs. Schaadt recalls the dignified and soldierly bearing of the general, who was a regular attendant at Grace church where she worshipped.

"General and Mrs. H. C. Trexler also recall the tall and dignified general whose arrival here caused quite a stir although the war was then more than ten years a matter of history. However, Pemberton found congenial company here, for while General Robert McAllister had served the Union he was not a vindictive character and in brotherly spirit received his former foe. They met frequently in that popular rendezvous, Zellner's cigar store.

"An interesting reminiscence of this exotic visitor to Allentown is afforded by Ben Zellner, one of the few surviving veterans of the Fighting Forty-seventh regiment.

" 'After the war, I worked for quite a time for Snyder and Hendricks, who conducted a livery stable at the southwest corner of Sixth and Maple streets,' Ben recalls.

" 'I remember Pemberton very well. He was always well dressed, carried himself well and was what I call mighty "spunky." There were lots of us soldiers around here then and many of us young fellows were ready to start an argument, but he always had good answers, took the teasing good-natured but didn't back up an inch.'

" 'He used to come to the stable to hire horses and carriages to take his wife and children for drives into the country. I used to harness the horses for him and I can tell you he wasn't stingy. I lost all track of him after he left Allentown, but I guess I never could forget him. To have a real live Rebel general here in Allentown to tease and pick at was something a young soldier was not likely to forget. But he was as we say in these days "a good sport" and you really couldn't get cross at him.' "[2]

In the Spring of 1881 Pemberton's health, which had been good beyond that of most men, failed badly; and, it continuing to decline, the old man picked himself up and tried a change of scenery—nearer Philadelphia. This time he chose Penllyn. The change made no difference; he had reached the last milestone along his road of life. "To every man, be he whom he may, there comes a last happiness and a last day": that of the General's was near. And though, unlike Stonewall Jackson, he failed to win "Death's royal purple in the foeman's lines," such was what he sought at Vicksburg, and twice again as artillerist at Richmond.

Adversity too has its heroism, but seldom fame.

At eleven minutes after five o'clock at Penllyn on the afternoon of Wednesday, July 13, 1881, Pemberton breathed out his life without a struggle. Clearly recognizing his approaching death, he said to his wife and children, "Except for leaving you—I am not sorry my time has come."

Under a plain marble marker—which records but his name, his date of birth and death—he lies in Philadelphia, next his mother and his wife, at Laurel Hill.

So ends the story of Pemberton, whom fame once beckoned, then passed by.

Was there no single word of tribute the South might pay him? There was a wait—then silence. As at Vicksburg, the now tired old soldier was forsaken—even to the end.

APPENDICES
NOTES

Appendix A

THE TERMS OF SURRENDER*

I. BY JOHN C. PEMBERTON, LIEUTENANT-GENERAL, C. S. A.

†PHILADELPHIA, June 12, 1875.

DEAR SIR.—I give you with pleasure my version of the interview between General Grant and myself on the afternoon of July 3, 1863, in front of the Confederate lines at Vicksburg.

If you will refer to the first volume of Badeau's life of U. S. Grant, you will find a marked discrepancy between that author's account of it and mine. I do not fear, however, to trust to the honest memory of any officer then present to confirm the statement I shall make.

Passing over all preceding events, I come at once to the circumstance that brought about the personal interview referred to.

Feeling assured that it was useless to hope longer for assistance from General Johnston, either to raise the siege of Vicksburg or to rescue the garrison,‡ I summoned division and brigade command-

---

* This correspondence appears here as it was printed in *Battles and Leaders of the Civil War*, III, 543-46. The rest of the footnotes in this section are part of the text as quoted.

† For this letter, addressed to Lieutenant-Colonel John P. Nicholson, the American editor of the Comte de Paris's "History of the Civil War," we are indebted to General Marcus J. Wright, Agent of the War Department for the Collection of Confederate Records. See General Grant's reply, addressed to General Pemberton, p. 545; also his paper, "The Vicksburg Campaign," p. 493.—EDITORS.

‡ Among General Pemberton's papers was found a copy of the following letter, accompanied by a note stating that the original had "miscarried and was never received, but General Johnston was kind enough to furnish me a copy":

"June 27, 1863. GENERAL PEMBERTON: Your dispatch of the 22d received. General E. K. Smith's troops have been mismanaged, and have fallen back to Delhi. I have sent a special messenger, urging him to assume direct command. The

ers, with one or two others, to meet in my quarters on the night of the 2d of July. All the correspondence that had taken place during the siege between General Johnston and myself was laid before these officers. After much consideration it was advised that I address a note to General Grant, proposing the appointment of commissioners to arrange terms of capitulation.

The following, having been read to the council and approved, was sent to General Grant under a flag of truce by the hands of Major-General J. S. Bowen, on the morning of the 3d:

"VICKSBURG, July 3d, 1863. MAJOR-GENERAL GRANT, Commanding United States Forces near Vicksburg, Mississippi. GENERAL: I have the honor to propose to you an armistice of —— hours, with a view to arrange terms of capitulation of Vicksburg. To this end, if agreeable to you, I will appoint three commissioners to meet a like number, to be named by yourself, at such place and hour to-day as you may find convenient. I make this proposition to save further effusion of blood, which must otherwise be shed to a frightful extent, feeling myself fully able to maintain my position for a yet indefinite period. This communication will be handed you under flag of truce by Major-General John S. Bowen. I am, General, very respectfully, your obedient servant, JOHN C. PEMBERTON, Lieutenant-General Commanding."

In due time the following reply was handed to me:

"HEADQUARTERS, DEPARTMENT OF THE TENNESSEE, NEAR VICKSBURG, July 3d, 1863. LIEUTENANT-GENERAL JOHN C. PEMBERTON, Commanding Confederate Forces, etc. GENERAL: Your note of this date is just received, proposing an armistice for several hours for the purpose of arranging terms of capitulation through commissioners to be appointed, etc. The useless effusion of blood you propose stopping by this course can be ended at any time you may choose, by an unconditional surrender of the city and garrison. Men who have shown so much endurance and courage as shown now in Vicksburg, will always challenge the respect of an adversary, and I can assure you will be treated with all the respect due to prisoners of war. I

determined spirit you manifest and his expected co-operation encourage me to hope that something may yet be done to save Vicksburg and to postpone both of the modes suggested of merely extricating the garrison. Negotiations with Grant for the relief of the garrison, should they become necessary, must be made by you. It would be a confession of weakness on my part, which I ought not to make, to propose them. When it becomes necessary to make terms, they may be considered as made under my authority.—J. E. JOHNSTON, General."

do not favor the proposition of appointing commissioners to arrange the terms of capitulation, because I have no terms other than those indicated above. I am, General, very respectfully, your obedient servant, U. S. GRANT, Major-General."

I at once expressed to General Bowen my determination not to surrender unconditionally. He then stated that General Grant would like to have an interview with me if I was so disposed, and would meet me at a designated point between the two lines at 3 P. M. that day. I was not aware that the suggestion had originated with General Bowen, but acceded to the proposed meeting at the joint request of my four division commanders.

On reaching the place appointed, accompanied by Major-General Bowen and Colonel Montgomery, then temporarily serving on my personal staff, I found General Grant and a number of his generals and other officers already arrived and dismounted. To the general himself, with whom my acquaintance dated as far back as the Mexican war,—as well as to several of the group who surrounded him,—I was formally introduced by General Bowen.

After a few remarks and inquiries on either side, a pause ensued, which was prolonged on my part in expectation that General Grant would introduce the subject, the discussion of which I supposed to be the object of our meeting. Finding that he did not do so, I said to him that I understood that he had expressed a wish to have a personal interview with me. He replied that he had not. I was much surprised, and, turning to General Bowen, remarked, "Then there is a misunderstanding; I certainly understood differently." The matter, however, was satisfactorily explained to me in a few words, the mistake, no doubt, having been my own. Again addressing General Grant, I said: "In your letter this morning you state that you have no other terms than an unconditional surrender." He answered promptly, "I have no other." To this I rejoined: "Then, sir, it is unnecessary that you and I should hold any further conversation; we will go to fighting again at once"; and I added: "I can assure you, sir, you will bury many more of your men before you will enter Vicksburg." General Grant did not, as Badeau represents, reply, "Very well," nor did he "turn off." He did not change his position, nor did he utter a word. The movement to withdraw, so far as there was any movement, was on my part, and was accompanied by the remark that if he (General Grant) sup-

posed that I was suffering for provisions he was mistaken, that I
had enough to last me for an indefinite period, and that Port Hudson was better supplied than Vicksburg. General Bowen made
no suggestion whatever in regard to a consultation between any
parties during this interview, as he is represented to have done by
Badeau; but General Grant *did* at this time propose that he and
I should step aside, and on my assenting, he added that if I had no
objection, he would take with him Generals McPherson and A. J.
Smith. I replied, certainly, and that General Bowen and Colonel
Montgomery would accompany me. General Grant then suggested
that these gentlemen withdraw and see whether, on consultation,
they could not arrive at some satisfactory arrangement. It will be
readily understood that I offered no objection to this course, as it
was, in fact, a withdrawal by General Grant from the position he
had so unqualifiedly assumed, to wit, unconditional surrender—
and it really submitted, as I had desired it should, the discussion of
the question of terms to a commission, although that commission
was now necessarily an *impromptu* one.

Pending the interchange of views by the officers named, General
Grant and I remained apart from them, conversing only upon topics
that had no relation to the important subject that brought us together. The terms which this commission agreed to propose were
in the main those that were afterward proffered by General Grant,
and eventually accepted by me. During this discussion I stated
to him that as he declined to appoint commissioners when invited
to do so by me, it was now his part to propose the terms. He agreed
to this, and said I should hear from him by 10 P. M. When about
to part I notified General Grant that I held myself in no manner
pledged to any agreement, but should consult my division and
brigade commanders. He replied that I must understand him in
the like manner, and that he, too, should consult his corps commanders. With this our interview ended.

Mr. Badeau's statement is a misrepresentation of the facts as they
occurred, and, whether intentional or otherwise, conveys false im-
pressions to his readers. If he was present at the interview he
knows, if he was absent, he could readily have ascertained, that
after General Grant's verbal declaration that he had no other terms
than unconditional surrender, all suggestions and all overtures look-

ing to terms arose directly from General Grant himself, and neither directly nor indirectly from me or my subordinates. There was no display by General Grant as to the result of this interview, nor did he feel indifferent. On the night of the 3d of July a dispatch was intercepted by my signal-officer from Admiral Porter to General Grant. The former inquired as to the chances of a surrender on the 4th. General Grant replied through the same medium, mentioning in a general way the terms offered, stating that the arrangement was *against his feelings,* but that his officers advised it on the ground that it would free his river transportation for other important uses, etc., etc. If this message was sent it should be found in the reports of the signal-officers. Will you have it looked up? No doubt both these gentlemen remember the circumstances. I am, Colonel, very truly yours,

J. C. PEMBERTON.

II. BY ULYSSES S. GRANT, GENERAL, U. S. A.

THE following letter, dated New York, November 30th, 1884, and printed for the first time in "The Century" magazine for August, 1887, was addressed to General Marcus J. Wright, Agent of the War Department for the Collection of Confederate Records, by whose permission it is here given, from the original manuscript.—EDITORS.

DEAR GENERAL: Herewith I send you General Pemberton's account of the surrender of Vicksburg. As the written matter [printed above] is "Copy," and supposing you have what it has been copied from, I do not return it, though I will if you inform me that you want it.

A gentleman from Philadelphia sent me the same matter I return herewith, last summer. I probably left the paper at Long Branch, but do not know certainly. All there is of importance in the matter of the surrender of Vicksburg is contained in the correspondence between General Pemberton and myself. The fact is, General Pemberton, being a Northern man commanding a Southern army, was not at the same liberty to surrender an army that a man of Southern birth would be. In adversity or defeat he became an object of suspicion, and felt it. Bowen was a Southern man all over, and knew the garrison of Vicksburg had to surrender or be captured, and knew it was best to stop further effusion of blood by surrendering. He did all he could to bring about that result.

Pemberton is mistaken in several points. It was Bowen that proposed that he and A. J. Smith should talk over the matter of the surrender and submit their views. Neither Pemberton nor I objected, but we were not willing to commit ourselves to accepting such terms as they might propose. In a short time those officers returned. Bowen acted as spokesman; what he said was substantially this: The Confederate army was to be permitted to march out with the honors of war, carrying with them their arms, colors, and field-batteries. The National troops were then to march in and occupy the city, and retain the siege-guns, small-arms not in the hands of the men, all public property remaining. Of course I rejected the terms at once. I did agree, however, before we separated, to write Pemberton what terms I would give. The correspondence is public and speaks for itself. I held no council of war; hostilities having ceased, officers and men soon became acquainted with the reason why. Curiosity led officers of rank—most all the general officers—to visit my headquarters with the hope of getting some news. I talked with them very freely about the meeting between General Pemberton and myself, our correspondence, etc., but in no sense was it a council of war. I was very glad to give the garrison of Vicksburg the terms I did. There was a cartel in existence at that time which required either party to exchange or parole all prisoners either at Vicksburg or at a point on the James River within ten days after captures or as soon thereafter as practicable. This would have used all the transportation we had for a month. *The men had behaved so well that I did not want to humiliate them. I believed that consideration for their feelings would make them less dangerous foes during the continuance of hostilities, and better citizens after the war was over.*

I am very much obliged to you, General, for your courtesy in sending me these papers. Very truly yours,

U. S. GRANT.

III. CORRESPONDENCE BETWEEN GENERAL PEMBERTON AND GENERALS GRANT AND BLAIR

*General Pemberton to General Grant:**

WARRENTON, FAUQUIER, VIRGINIA, January 30, 1874. His Excellency, U. S. GRANT, PRESIDENT OF THE UNITED STATES. SIR: A state-

* On the 19th of January, 1874, General Pemberton addressed a letter, substantially to the same effect, to General Frank P. Blair, whose reply follows General Grant's.—EDITORS.

ment of some historic significance and of considerable interest to me personally, has lately come to my notice in a way that induces me to address you as the single individual competent to confirm or refute it. I am aware that I have no claim to your special consideration; should you, however, deem it not improper to respond to my inquiry, I shall feel myself indebted to your kindness. The statement I refer to was from a general officer of the Army of the Tennessee, and was in the words following:

"It was generally understood in our army that General Johnston's courier, conveying dispatches to you previous to the battle of Baker's Creek or Champion Hills, betrayed his dispatches to General Grant, and also your answers to General Johnston's orders. I do not know positively from General Grant these facts, but the matter was spoken of by the officers of our army in such a way as to leave no doubt in my mind."

Permit me to add that this information has tended to confirm my own suspicion, excited at the time by the (otherwise) inexplicable delay in the receipt of General Johnston's dispatch of the 14th of May, which, as you, sir, are probably aware, was not handed to me until after 5 P. M. on the 16th, when my army was in full retreat. My inquiry is confined simply to two points: first, the truth (or reverse) of the facts discussed by the officers of the Army of the Tennessee; second, the correctness (or the reverse) of my surmises as to the dispatch of the 14th, above referred to. I am, sir, most respectfully your obedient servant,

J. C. PEMBERTON.

General Grant to General Pemberton:

EXECUTIVE MANSION, WASHINGTON, January 31, 1874. GENERAL J. C. PEMBERTON, Warrenton, Virginia. General: Your letter of yesterday was duly received this morning, and the President authorizes me to say that the statement of the officer to which you refer was correct, and he thinks you are also correct as to your surmises in regard to the delay in receipt of your dispatch. He says the dispatches were brought in our lines and given to General McPherson, and by him immediately brought to headquarters. I have the honor to remain, sir, your obedient servant,

LEVI P. LUCKEY, Secretary.

288   APPENDICES

General Blair to General Pemberton:

St. Louis, January 24, 1874. General J. C. Pemberton, Fauquier County, Virginia. Dear General: I take pleasure, in answer to your letter of the 19th of January, in saying that it was generally understood in our army that General J. Johnston's courier, conveying dispatches to you previous to the battle of Baker's Creek or Champion Hills, betrayed his dispatches to General Grant, and also your answers to General Johnston's orders, so that, in fact, General Grant had the most precise information as to your movements and those of General Johnston. I do not know positively from General Grant these facts, but the matter is spoken of by the officers of our army in such a way as to leave no doubt in my mind. Very respectfully, your obedient servant,

Frank P. Blair.

Appendix B

The following unfinished letter, written in pencil by General Pemberton, was found in 1931 by his family among other papers. The letter was undoubtedly addressed to Major W. T. Walthall, Jefferson Davis's historical assistant; the manuscript is referred to in the General's letters to Major Walthall (Rowland, *Jefferson Davis, Constitutionalist*, VIII, 156, 195, 338, 346).

Dear Sir:

Before entering into details of the operations immediately preceding the Siege of Vicksburg and of other matters connected therewith referred to by President Davis in his private note to you I think it will be well for us to take a general view from my standpoint of the status of the Dept of Missi. & E. Lou *a* when I was assigned to the command of it and of the army—that is to say on the 14th Oct 1862 which date is in fact that of the organization of the Depar *t*. This may be briefly stated as follows. Nominally, the Depar *t* embraced the State of Missi. and that part of Lou *a* east of the Missi. Riv.—practically the enemy was in possession of Lou *a* to the north shore of Pontchartrain and beyond Baton Rouge with undisputed control of the Missi to within gunshot range of Port Hudson, on the north he held Memphis and West Tennessee, controlled the R.R. to the east and the Missi. to the gates of Vicksburg. Van Dorn spite of his own gallantry and that of his men, had just been disastrously repulsed at Corinth, and was then reorganizing at Holly Springs an army badly equipped, and whose numerical strength including all arms did not exceed 24,000. Vicksburg had a garrison of 5500—Port Hudson 1500—on the line of the J & N.O. R.R. At Jackson, Columbus and various other localities there were possibly 2500 more. A very considerable part of these troops may be properly characterized as irregular, having little organization and less discipline. But few depots of subsistence had been established and not one of them had a sufficient supply on hand in the event of an emergency. The Q r, Mst r, Ordnance and Medical Departments were in no better condition, and above all the deficiency of guns for water defence was extreme both as to number and character. [end p. 1 MS] Within the geographical limits of the Department about to be organized, there was scarcely an earth work worthy the name of a defence. I conclude this exhibit of its general condition by calling attention to the fact that when on or about the 17 th October, 1862 I passed hurriedly from Port Hudson to Holly Springs to asume in person the command of the army there, I found its wagons packed & every preparation made to fall back at once behind the Tallahatchie. Van Dorn having then reason to believe that Grant was already advancing upon him with a greatly superior force.

I sent last summer to my friend Col. McCardle of Vicksburg a somewhat detailed statement of the operations within the Dep t up to the repulse of Sherman on the Yazoo in Dec b 1862. There may possibly be matter in that which might be of service to you, though I do not know that it will come within the scope of the work you have in hand—probably it will not. However that may be, as all our operations looking to the defence of the Department were entirely successful up to the middle of April 1863, I need not dwell more on events anterior to that period, only noting that a personal inspection of our condition at Port Hudson on Oct. 15/62 satisfied me that if we intended to hold it, no time should be lost in greatly strengthening the defences and increasing the garrison. To effect the latter, the only resource was to draw on the army under Van Dorn. This I did immediately on my arrival at H. Spring to the extent of about 3500 men, noting further that between the 24 th De r and 5 th of Jany, the Depart. was strengthened by about 13000 Infy & Field Arty., and weakened during the same period by the withdrawal under Gen l Johnston's orders of at least 3/4 of all its cavalry—a procedure which in my judgment was not only a remote but also a great proximate cause of all our misfortunes. [end p. 2 MS] A remote cause because at an eventful period it compelled the diversion of a large force of Infantry to distant points that should and would have been available in conjunction with Bowen's command to repel Grant on his first landing. A great proximate cause because without cavalry I was entirely unable to make a reconnaissance in force, and to prevent the enemy from obtaining from the adjacent country those supplies without which he could not have reached Jackson, fought the battle of Baker's Creek or sat down before Vicksburg. These are not afterthoughts on my part, as my correspondence with Johnston at the time will sufficiently show, nor is the opinion I have expressed mine alone. Major Jacob Thompson, then a member of my staff, a gentleman doubtless well known to you, writing officially to me from Enterprise, Missi. under date of July 21, 1863 speaking of events immediately preceeding the Battle of Baker's Creek says "The almost total want of cavalry not only kept you in ignorance of his (enemy's) movements, but deprived you of all means of annoying or retarding him in his movements." The letter from which the foregoing is an extract may be found in full in Mrs. Sarah Dorsey's memoirs of Ex. Gov r Allen.* Col. Wirt Adams who commanded what little cavalry there was in Central Missi. can speak with knowledge on this subject if disposed to do so. In a conversation with Gen l S. D. Lee in the fall of 1875, he stated emphatically to me that he thought the want of cavalry was the foundation of all my troubles. Altera parte, Gen l Johnston asserts—foot of page 223 of his "Narrative" that because "At the time in question Gen l Grant had no garrison to be surprised nor depots to be destroyed," therefore "no disposition [end p. 3 MS] of Confederate Cavalry would have been less inconvenient to him (Grant) than that by which his opponent fancies that he would have been defeated." This to my mind is unfair reasoning, for if it be true, to quote his own language, that "In its march from Bruinsburg by Port Gibson to Jackson, and thence to Vicksburg, the Federal Army drew its supplies from the country" would not "a moderate cavalry force at my disposal" have enabled me to prevent the army from obtaining these supplies, gathered as they necessarily must have been by small foraging parties from plantations generally widely separated & off the line of march? Again, if cut off from other source of subsistence for men and animals, would not the army have been forced to depend upon its communications with the Missi? To say that "it did not in the least depend on them" is therefore to beg the whole question in dispute, since I claim that with a moderate force of cavalry I could have prevented the march from Bruinsburg by Port Gibson to Jackson and thence to Vicksburg by depriving the enemy of the sole means that enabled him to make that march. It is however by no means absolutely true that Grant had no communications to

* General Pemberton was here referring to the *Recollections of Henry Watkins Allen*, published in 1866.

maintain. There were many indispensables to an invading army that the country did not and could not supply—for instance it certainly could not have replaced expended or unserviceable ordnance stores. Be good enough to refer again to pages 222 & 223 of Johnston's Narrative. You will readily see the connection of the text with some remarks I am about to make. I positively deny that the whole or the largest part of my correspondence with Gen *l* Johnston in the month of April /63 [end p. 4 MS] indicated that I was more apprehensive of predatory incursions than of the formidable invasion preparing under my eyes. That of the first half of the month mainly referred to the transfer of troops from my Depart. to Gen *l* Bragg. About the 16 *th* or 17 *th* April simultaneously with the passage of the Vicksburg batteries by the enemy's gunboats I learned that several columns of Fed *l* cavalry starting from different points were making inroads into the northern part of Mississippi and that one of them under Col. Grierson was apparently strong enough and bold enough to push on perhaps to the southern limits of the Depar *t*. Strong enough to defy any cavalry that I could oppose to it & to destroy my depots with their large accumulation of subsistence and Q *r* Mr*s* supplies, the workshops of the Depar *t*. as well as the Railroads, and to break up or interrupt to our serious detriment the communications of the latter unless protected by a sufficient force of infantry. Then indeed I was "apprehensive," not "of predatory incursions." Purposes of plunder had nothing to do with the preparation or execution of Grierson's movement, but I did fear, and not without reason, that it was part and parcel "of the formidable invasion preparing under my eyes." It had indeed so effective a share in the combined operations that it compelled the diversion of Loring's entire Division to the line of the Mobile & Ohio, and other railroads, when its presence was most needed to aid in repelling "the formidable invasion" not only "preparing" but actively progressing at another and distant point. That I was not negligent of, and that I did not undervalue the extent of the threatened danger while it was yet only threatened may be shown by a portion of one of many telegrams to Gen *l* Loring then engaged as above described on the line of the Mobile & Ohio R.R. *On* the 23 *rd* April I said to him—"Operations on your line are minor to those on the Missi. River. Therefore you must not [end p. 5 MS] be out of reach by telegraph, nor must your troops be so disposed as to be unable to move in this direction (towards the Missi.) at a moments notice." One of the effects of what Gen *l* Johnston is pleased to denominate "predatory incursions" may also be understood by a short dispatch from Gen *l* Loring, then with his troops and under orders to move west as rapidly as possible. From Lake Station Ap *l* 29 *th* he telegraphs me, *"Troops have been delayed here all day.* Only sufficient transportation for portion of one regiment has reached the break up to this hour-night. Repairing break is very slow." The Superintendent of the Road explained—"Many of our trains are east of the break." What did occur at Lake Station and at divers other points, would have been universal but for the protecting presence of Infantry. Unfortunately however the brigades of that veteran division could not be separated on the railroads and concentrated on the River at one and the same time. I have given documentary proof enough elsewhere I think to satisfy the unprejudiced of the injustice of Johnston's interested criticisms. If it were worth the candle I could produce eleven telegrams from him between the dates of April 18 *th* and May 6 *th* which will conclusively show that not a man of Roddys or of any other brigade of Cavalry from Bragg's Army ever entered my Depart. from the time that Johnston withdrew Van Dorn up to the day that I was forced into Vicksburg. It is impossible that I can be mistaken in this matter. I therefore positively deny that Roddy encountered the very troops from Corinth that I wished to meet. At the date referred to, he was serving in Alabama, where for all I know to the contrary he may have been contending with thrice threefold of the enemy. The first of the series of telegrams just referred to informs me that "a superior force from Corinth is in front of Col. Roddy at Tuscumbia" and suggests that I should send troops "from Columbus, Missi. or elsewhere" to *assist him.* The last *remarks* are assurance [end p. 6 MS] that "Roddy has been ordered into Missi." No doubt he was ordered, but there is also no doubt that he did not go. I know nothing of the why nor wherefore. Had Col. Roddy been in Missi., and under my control, he would have encountered the well organized Federal Cavalry led by Col. Grierson that started from La Grange Tenss *ee* on the 17 *th* April with the express object, as stated by Gen *l* Grant in his official Report to his Government, "of destroying railroads and other public property for the purpose of creating a *diversion* in favor of the army moving to the attack of Vicksburg,"—a purpose that was clear to my mind at the time, for on the 20 *th* April three days after the column left La Grange I urged Gen *l* Johnston by telegraph to make "a demonstration on it's rear if only for fifty miles," giving as my reason for the request that "The enemy is endeavoring to force a diversion of my troops to Northern Missi."

This appeal was renewed on the 21 *st,* without avail. The truth is that from the 16 *th* of April, the correspondence between Johnston and myself very clearly indicates that he was much more apprehensive of predatory incursions into *Alabama* than of the formidable invasion of Missi., giving no regard whatever to the latter, though he was kept fully informed by me of its preparation and rapid progress to consummation, while on the other hand my whole thoughts and energies were devoted to efforts to prevent or repel it. I take the liberty of again calling yr. attention to Mrs. Dorsey's memoir of Col. Allen as affording much written evidence of the correctness of my statement. I can not of course bring to yr. consideration or to that of the public 1/50 part of the correspondence of that eventful period. My papers do not show, nor do I remember to have received from Johnston even a suggestion as to my proper course in reference to the threatened invasion until after he was informed of the battle of May 1 *st* [end p. 7 MS] beyond an intimation that it would be well to invite the cooperation of Gen *l* Kirby Smith, advice that was unnecessary, as I had already done so of my own instance on the 17 *th* & 18 *th* April the two days immediately succeeding the night in which the gunboats passed the Vicksburg batteries. I specially invite yr. attention to that portion of my correspondence with Johnston between the 17 *th* & 29 *th* April together with remarks thereon by myself, which you will find in Mrs. Dorsey's book. Particularly remember pages 183, 194, 197, 202, 211, 213, 214 also 219 & following. The correspondence is very unsystematically arranged (through my fault not Mrs. Dorsey's) Still I think it better to refer you to it as it stands rather than attempt to rearrange or enlarge it. Col. McCardle has the printed official reports of Johnston and myself. They can be obtained from him should you need them. In mine or its supplement I think you will find the full text of all the correspondence between us from the date of his arrival in Jackson to that of the surrender of Vicksburg. The fact that two vessels of Farragut's squadron had succeeded in passing our batteries at Port Hudson from below on the night of 15 *th* March, in the estimation of Gen *l* Johnston "greatly reduced the value" of that port & of Vicksburg. I was at the time and am still of a different opinion. The passage of these ships was undoubtedly a great temporary disadvantage to us, but as long as we continued in possession of the two ports the navigation of the Missi. was cut off, as before to the merchant marine of the U.S., and a permanent tenure of them by us would have compelled such war vessels as had been run by the batteries either to repass them or eventually to surrender. [end p. 8 MS] Meanwhile, a fleet however numerous occupying the river between the two ports, could not have opened it to free navigation to the Northern people, although it might effectually close it for the time to ours. As it was, large supplies continued to be brought from the Trans Missi Dept. to within a few days of the evacuation of Grand Gulf. If it was wise & proper in Gen *l* Johnston on the 2 *nd* & 3 *rd* of May after a battle had been fought, to order me, as he claims he did order me, to unite all my forces—including the garrisons of Vicksburg & Port Hudson—to beat Grant if he landed, it would certainly have been eminently proper to have issued similar instructions two weeks earlier, when he was first notified that Grant was accumulating forces on the West shore of the river & that he had the means of crossing there. But he failed even to offer a suggestion, not only then, but on the various other occasions between the 17 *th* and 30 *th* of April, when the practicability of the threatened invasion was brought to his attention. The portion of Johnston's "Narrative" that has reference to this period is a confused and garbled statement which does not however avail to conceal his neglect of the many premonitions he had received of the enemy's probable designs. Be good enough to read the last paragraph of Page 168 of his Narrative and also what purports to be a telegram from me on the following page. One would naturally suppose from these preceding remarks that April 30 *th* was the date of the telegram. While in fact it is a combination of two of my dispatches, one of the 28 *th*, the other of 29 *th*, with an important part of the latter omitted. The full dispatch was in these words—"Apl. 29 *th* very heavy firing at Grand Gulf. Enemy shelling our batteries from above and below. The wires are down. Do not know *whether the enemy has made a landing on this side Mississippi river* if not Grierson's cavalry has cut them. All the cavalry I can raise is close on their rear, and was skirmishing with them last night." It was perhaps not advisable to call the readers attention [end p. 9 MS] to the language of this telegram as it would naturally induce the inquiry why was not "the reply dispatched immediately" to Pemberton, telling him "If Grant's army lands on this side of the river, the safety of Missi. (not of *the* Missi. as given in the text, and which bears a very different signification) depends on beating it, &c &c," instead of delaying your suggestion, or advice, or order, as you may please to consider it, for three days, in fact until after you had been informed that "a furious battle had been going on since daylight &c on this side of the river." It would be easy to point out many instances where Johnston's book is discrepant from facts and from ingenuous narrative. To some few of them I shall be compelled to invite y r attention hereafter. After the passage of the gunboats on the night of the 16 *th* April the Federal forces had undisputed possession of the immediate country West of the River—it was not within the limits of my Depart, and if it had been, our relative positions would have made it manifestly impossible for me to contend there with Grant. I had the greatest difficulty—so closely was the line of his intended operations guarded, in obtaining any reliable information of his strength, movements or disposition of his troops. Gen *l* Johnston and doubtless many others seem to suppose that I ought to have had an intuitive knowledge of all these matters, and of the objective point on this side of the river, that is to say—of his intended landing. From the 17 *th* up to the 29 *th* April the Federal fleet, or such portion of it as had passed the Vicksburg batteries was lying between that place and Grand Gulf, while two large bodies of troops— the one above and the other below Vicksburg were occupying the West bank of the river. It was difficult even to approximate their relative strength. They were supposed however from all the information I could get to be about equal. Gen *l* Johnston (Page 171, N) whether on his own authority or that of Federal official Reports I know not, [end p. 10 MS] asserts that Sherman's "15th Corps *and* a Division" were left at Milliken's Bend to divert my attention. Gen *l* Grant in his Report mentions only Sherman's Corps and "To prevent heavy reinforcements going from Vicksburg to the assistance of the Grand Gulf forces" he says "I directed Sherman to make a demonstration on Haines Bluff &c &c." The corps in question I suppose to have been not less than 20,000 strong. If there was another Division the entire force at his command was probably in the neighborhood of 25,000 men. This may be an exaggerated estimate but I think not. Be that as it may, it must be acknowledged by Gen *l* Johnston himself that up to the 2 *nd* of May at best, he had given me no intimation that under any circumstances that might arise I should abandon Vicksburg and its outposts to unite all my forces for any purpose elsewhere. With my estimate of its importance to the success of the Confederate cause I should have been in heart a traitor to that cause had I so weakened the place and its flank defences while still in doubt where Grant might attempt a landing by concentrating all my army at Grand Gulf or at Bruinsburg or Rodney and thus permitting Sherman's large force (large certainly relatively with mine it being at least 2/3 of my entire strength) to change the demonstration he was directed to

make on Haines Bluff into a real and very possibly a successful
attack. Loring's Division of 6500 veterans, which I was constrained
to distribute along the several lines of railroad to protect communications, depots of subsistence, workshops &c, because I had no
cavalry to meet that of the Federals in the field would, but for this
necessity, have been with Bowen on the 30 *th* April and May 1 *st*
to resist a landing or at least to delay an advance of the enemy until
[end p. 11 MS] he could be encountered east of the Big Black by
my whole force. On the night of the 3 *rd* May, nine full brigades
were concentrated west of that river at Hankinson's Ferry. (to wit
2 of Loring's, 2 of Bowen's, 4 of Stevenson's, and one of Smith's).
Four of these—viz Green's & Cockerell's (Bowen's entire Div *n*)
Tracy's (of Stevenson's Div.) and Baldwin's (of Smith's Div.)
had taken more or less part in the battle of May 1. Three others,
viz—Tilghman's and Buford's (of Loring's Div.) and Reynold's
(of Stevenson's Div.) joined Bowen on the 2 *nd*. But that gallant
officer, having been overpowered by numbers the preceding day &
thereby losing the advantage of position, it was decided after consultation by Generals Loring & Bowen, that this advantage could
not be recovered with the combined forces at their disposal, and
that it was necessary to retire either toward Edward's Depot or
across the Big Black at Hankinson's Ferry. The movement was
determined by the receipt of instructions addressed by myself to
both Generals (as I was at the time uncertain whether they had
united) to maintain their position on this side Bayou Pierre if possible until the arrival of reinforcements then hastening to their assistance—but "if compelled to fall back on Grand Gulf, to abandon
that position and recross the Big Black." Featherstone's, the only
remaining brigade of Loring's Divis *n* which had been held at
Grenada for the protection of the railroad &c in that direction, was
united two days later to the nine brigades heretofore mentioned,
and Moore's one of the two brigades composing Forney's [?] Divis *n*
then near Warrenton, was also available, in case Grant had attempted to cross the Big Black. But the advantageous position the
latter occupied, holding the bluffs & commanding the bridge, made
it absolutely impracticable for me to attack him there by recrossing
the river at any point south of the railroad bridge. Hall's ferry
was strongly guarded [end p. 12 MS] and the topographical features of the respective banks of the river there were nearly as adverse
to a successful passage of the stream as at Hankinson's. If attempted by Baldwin's Ferry, the enemy through his great superi-
ority in cavalry would have ascertained the movement by the time

I could begin the necessary preparations there, and would most undoubtedly have foiled the design by attacking me in the act of crossing. By the 5 *th* or 6 *th,* Sherman's corps had been united to the other two. The foregoing exposition of the circumstances sur﹀ rounding me is I think a sufficient refutation of Gen *l* Johnston's criticism (see foot of page 216, also 217 of his Nar.) on my milt *r* conduct in the first two instances he cites as "misapprehension of the principles of the warfare I was directing"—namely my failure "to assail the Federal troops with at least three Divisions instead of two or three brigades on the 1 *st* May while they were divided in the passage of the Missi.," and 2 *nd* in not attacking McPherson's & McClernand's corps with all my forces, near Hankinson's Ferry where they waited for Sherman's until the 8 *th*. By the way they did not wait for Sherman until the 8 *th*. Gen *l* Grant in his official report says—"Whilst lying at Hankinson Ferry waiting for wagons, supplies and Sherman's Corps which had come forward *in the meantime* demonstrations were made &c &c." and immediately after adds—"On the 7 *th* of May an advance was ordered" and he then gives the line of March pursued by that as well as by the other two corps. Gen *l* McPherson, possibly only referring to his own corps, though that is unlikely, says "The command remained in camp at Hankinson's Ferry three days from the 4 *th* to the 6 *th* inclusive xxx at 10 o'clock a.m. on the 7 *th* marched to Rocky Springs &c &c." We may therefore at least strike out two of the 5 days or 2/5 of the entire period during which Johnston says the enemy could have been attacked "near Hankinson's Ferry" [end p. 13 MS] with such marked advantage to us as to make the neglect to do so worthy of special reproach. The third occasion on which I am represented to have particularly shown my "misapprehension of the warfare I was directing" was in failing "to fall upon McClernand's corps on the 12 *th* when *it was between* Fourteen Mile Creek and my camp near Edward's Depot, *and Sherman's and McPherson's* corps were *at and near Raymond."* (see page 217, N) Now it happens, 1 *st* that the only camp I had at Edward's Depot on 12 *th* May was that of a guard from Bowen's Division—Col. Gates Regiment I think— Nine tenths of the army was west of the Big Black during the entire day, and was moved into position at Edwards in that night and ensuing day. But it happens 2*ndly* that McPherson's corps alone was on the 12th at and near Raymond, and that McClernand's and Sherman's Corps both crossed Fourteen Mile Creek on that day and but a short distance from each other. In his Official Report, Grant says—"All the ferries were closely guarded (this refers to

his march from Hankinson's ferry—J C P) until our troops were
well advanced. It was my intention here to hug the Black River
as closely as possible *with McClernand's and Sherman's Corps,* and
get them to the Railroad at some place between Edward Station
and Bolton. McPherson was to move by Utica to Raymond and
from there into Jackson &c &c. Orders were given to McPherson
accordingly. Sherman was moved forward on the Edwards Station
road *crossing Fourteen Mile Creek at Dillon's Plantation.* McClernand was moved *across the same Creek,* further West, sending one
Division of his Corps by the Baldwin's Ferry road as far as the
river. At the crossing of Fourteen Mile Creek *both McClernand
& Sherman* had considerable skirmishing with the enemy to get
possession of the crossing." Later, Grant says—"On the *night of
the 12 th* May *after* orders had been given for the Corps of *McClernand and Sherman* [end p. 14 MS] to march towards the railroad
by parallel roads the former in the direction of Edwards Station
and the latter to a point on the railroad between Edward's Station
and Bolton, the *order was changed and both* were directed to move
towards Raymond." The foregoing is a verbatim extract from
Grant's Report, and yet Gen *l* Johnston in a note (page 217, N)
cites this Report as authority for, and as corroborative of the correctness of his assertion that "my disasters were due to my own misapprehension of the principles of the warfare I was directing." It
may be true that they were due to that cause, but Gen *l* Johnston
has in this instance at least selected a bad witness to prove it, for by
his testimony it is clearly shown that the alleged opportunity to fall
upon McClernand's corps at a specified time and while separated,
did not in fact exist. After the 3 *rd* of May when I was satisfied in
my own mind that I could not with due regard to the safety of
Vicksburg, concentrate a sufficient force east of the Big Black to
effectually resist an advance of the enemy towards Jackson, I determined to defend the line of the Big Black, believing that it could
be held against any attempt to force it, while at the same time
Haines bluff and the approaches on the right flank of Vicksburg,
as well as Warrenton on the left, could be more readily supported
in case a coup de main should be attempted. My whole army including most of the garrison of the city would be thus held under
control for ready concentration. This "disposition of the troops"
was considered "judicious" by Gen *l* Johnston, as he informed me
by telegraph on May 9 *th* from Tullahoma in these words—"Your
dispatch in cypher rec'd. Cannot decypher about Port Hudson.
Make entirely new cypher of that part. Disposition of troops as

far as understood judicious. Can be readily concentrated against Grant's Army." As he made no further call for information except "about Port Hudson," it is to be inferred that he fully understood that disposition of the troops immediately under my command which had been minutely explained to him and that he meant to pronounce it judicious, and to express his opinion that they could be readily concentrated against Grant's Army. [end p. 15 MS] I feel that I have the right to claim that this approval of my action given before any controversy had arisen between us, should stand side by side with some of his later interested & vindictive criticisms. During a period throughout which, *according to his Official Report,* I left him absolutely without information, and disregarded all his instructions, the fact is shown that he expressed his approval of my disposition and that I had so far conformed *to his idea* of the principles that ought to govern me in the warfare I was directing as to earn from him the acknowledgment that the troops were so arranged by me that they could be "readily concentrated against Grant's Army." Information received on the 11 *th* and 12 *th* particularly on the latter day though not altogether reliable, was of a nature to induce the belief that the main body of the Federal Army was advancing on Edwards Depot or on the Railroad bridge, and that a considerable force would probably move upon Jackson at the same time. The uncertain character of the reports upon which I was compelled to act, through want of cavalry to make the proper reconnaissances, may be better estimated now than it could possibly be at the time. From among those which chiefly influenced my movements a few sent to Mrs. Dorsey will be found in her book. I also ask yr. attention to my instructions to Genls Loring & Gregg & others between the 10 *th* & 13 *th*. I was very loth to cross the Big Black until the arrival at Jackson of Gregg's & Maxey brigades from Port Hudson & of the reinforcements promised me from other Departments, and especially of a large body of cavalry. The necessity of covering Jackson, however and my communications there with the east against what I supposed would be at the most only a strong detachment, induced me to advance Gregg's Brigade, which had just arrived from Port Hudson, to Raymond on the enemy's main line of communications should he approach the Capitol. It was my intention to occupy these positions only long enough to concentrate the coming reinforcements there, and with the hope that enough would reach Gregg, before the advance of the enemy, to enable [end p. 16 MS] him or his successor in command, to hold it. In this I was disappointed. A fight at Raymond was however unnecessary and was not under the circumstances in accordance with my orders. My instructions to Gregg were to fall back on Jackson in case the enemy should advance upon him in "too strong force." Otherwise to meet him. (see Mrs. Dorsey's book). Gen *l* Johnston says (Page 16, of his O.R.) Gregg was "defeated and driven back by overwhelming numbers of the enemy"—for this *defeat* I was not responsible. The battle at Raymond was however fought on the 12 *th* for precisely the same reasons that induced Gen *l* Johnston two days later to fight at Jackson & with the same results—defeat and retreat. But if Johnston had not been in Jackson the consequences of defeat would have been different. I should under the change of circumstances—brought about by the necessity of evacuating that place—have taken measures at once to unite all the reinforcements then arrived with my army at Edward's Depot. This could have been readily done at any time by making a short detour to the north of the Southern Railroad for all the operations of the enemy were on, or south of it—every man with Johnston might have been with me at Baker's Creek, had *"his health* permitted." My army crossed the Big Black and took position at Edward's Depot on the night of 12 *th* & during 13 *th,* with three main objects in view—to wit—the protection of the communications of Vicksburg with the east by the Railroad bridge, which I had floored & prepared for the passage of troops & wagons, 2 *nd* to be nearer the arriving reinforcements & to facilitate their juncture with my army, and 3 *rd*—to compel Grant to attack me in a strong position, or to be himself attacked in rear and flank, if he should attempt to advance on Haines Bluff [end p. 17 MS] by crossing the Railroad to the north; or, if a favorable opportunity offered, to assail him in like manner should he return to his base at Grand Gulf. Meantime, as few wagons were required for the service of the army in position at Edward's, because of its location on the railroad, nearly all of them were available, and were diligently engaged in hauling supplies into Vicksburg from the Yazoo. To abandon the line of the railroad was to compel the withdrawal of a large part of them from this service, which would have a direct effect upon the length of time we should be able to hold Vicksburg, if unfortunately defeated in the field and forced to retire within its defences. Such were "the matured plans" I had formed, when they were utterly annihilated by the receipt at 9.10 a.m. on the 14 *th* of Gen *l* Johnston's note of the 13 *th,* dated from Jackson almost immediately after his arrival there from Tennessee, before he had any consultation with me, in ignorance of my surroundings, without knowledge of the enemy's strength, or of the disposition of the greater part of his troops, and apparently without consideration or regard for the fate of Vicksburg. I had hoped indeed, but hardly expected, to be able to keep the enemy out of Jackson by employing the arriving reinforcements to that end until a sufficient force should be formed on Gregg's brigade as a nucleus, when I intended either to unite them by a direct movement to my army at Edward's, or if a favorable opportunity should offer, to make with them a combined effort against the enemy. My instructions to Gregg & Walker show that they were not advanced from Jackson to Raymond with the expectation or desire that they should resist "an overwhelming force" but that they should retire before it. It was only in the event of an attack on the position at Edward's Depot that they were directed to cooperate with me, by coming up on the enemy's rear. Loring was ordered in the same contingency to advance with his whole force against the Federals should they turn upon the troops from Raymond. [end p. 18 MS] Gregg's and Walker's brigade had not been detached from my army, for they had never joined it. Gregg's brigade had reached Jackson on the 10 *th* from Port Hudson, and on the 12 *th* was some miles nearer to Edward's depot than to Jackson. The whole of Walker's brigade had not got into Jackson on the 13 *th* when Johnston himself arrived there. When that ————[?], so severe on the shortcomings—real or imaginary—of others, ascertained early on the morning of the 14 *th* that he could not save Jackson and its communications with the east, "he could and should" to use one of his own favorite expressions, have united those two brigades to my army by a short detour to the north. Instead of marching towards Canton on the 15 *th,* he should have marched towards Edwards. Had he done so he might have joined in, or prevented the battle of Baker's Creek, which began by 9 in the morning and continued until 4.30 p.m. of the 16 *th.* His health prevented it. He knew early on the 14 *th* that the *cooperative* movement he had instituted on paper the preceeding afternoon could not be executed. I did not know it until 7 a.m. on the *16 th,* about 48 hours later. During this long interim I was ignorant that he had been driven from Jackson. Where in fact was Gen *l* Johnston and the 6500 men with him while my army was fighting a battle brought about by an attempted obedience to his orders? I learn from his own statement (Page 179, Nar) that he spent that entire day in camp at Calhoun Station on the Canton R.R. I learn also from a dispatch of his dated "8½ a.m. May 15, 1863 Canton road ten miles

from Jackson" that he had just rec'd my dispatch dated 5.40 p.m.
May 14 *th* in which he was informed of my intended movement
on the enemy's rear *as early as possible* on the *next day the 15 th,*
and of the route I should take that he might cooperate with me.
And then I find, that instead of marching towards me on the 15 *th*
to cooperate or unite with me, he continued [end p. 19 MS] to
march on the Canton road, and that he encamped that night at
Calhoun Station; at least nine miles farther from my army than
he was when he received my note, informing him of the movements I intended to make on that same day—and there, during the
whole of the following day the 16 *th,* he remained quietly encamped with two of the very brigades—Gregg's & Walker's—which
in page 217 of his Narrative he says "could and should have been
in the battle of Baker's Creek,"—a battle that was fought on this
same 16 *th.* To the "could and should" I may safely add *would,*
had Gen *l* Johnston directed them, either under his own immediate
command, or if too ill himself, under the senior Brig *r* Gen *l,* towards Edward's, instead of towards Canton. As soon as he was
satisfied that he was not strong enough to beat the forces advancing
on Jackson from Raymond and Clinton, by a slight detour to the
north, say as far as his first days march towards Canton, he could
have reached Edwards Station, or my army, with no more serious
interference from the Federal troops than that he met with on his
way to Calhoun Station. Please refer to my letter of the 14 *th* May,
dated at 5.45 P.M., in connection with the preceeding remarks—
it will be found in my Official Report. Also to Johnston's dated
8½ a.m. 15 *th.* Both of these were delivered in good time. Mine
to Johnston was put into the hands of Capt. Yerger and was given
to him by that officer. As Johnston at the moment of its receipt
was "on the way" *not to Clinton,* but to Canton, I must leave you
to consider whether it is probable he was greatly *discouraged* by
its contents (see Narr. Page 179)—and (keeping in mind his intention to *continue* "his march toward Canton" on the 15 *th,* as he
explained in his note to me of the 14 *th*) to satisfy yourself whether
he is justified in asserting in his Official Report that [end p. 20 MS]
"A junction (of his troops & mine) that might have been effected
by the 15 th was delayed" because I had not moved from Edwards
up to 5.45 on the afternoon of the 14 *th.* It is by such assertions as
these, together with the perversion of the true & intended meaning of dispatches, and the misrepresentation of facts that he first
excited, and has since diligently nurtured the public prejudice
against me. I have explained the reasons that induced me to take

position at Edwards Depot on the 13 *th*. As soon as I had determined to do so, before I had any information that Gen *l* Johnston
had been ordered to Missi., and before the army had crossed the
Big Black, I notified that General by telegraph on the 12 *th* that
"the enemy is apparently moving in heavy force towards Edward's
Depot," and that in certain contingencies named I should fight
him there. This dispatch he rec'd. en route to Jackson. The information it gave him was perfectly correct at the time it was sent.
The facts were then precisely in accordance with "the impression"
he says he derived from it (see Page 176, Nar) as to the disposition
of the several Federal Corps—but on the evening of the 13 *th* when
he was writing his order of that date to me to come up on the rear
of "the detachment" at Clinton, the disposition of these corps was
very different. It would be however easy to demonstrate that,
whether located as he supposed them [?] to be or as they were in
reality, the capture or destruction of my whole army must have
resulted from an attempt to obey what he says (Page 218, Nar)
was his order—viz, "to march seventeen miles to the east" no matter what may have been the "expressed object of his order." But
in truth he did not order me "to march seventeen miles to the east"
but to come up if practicable *on the rear* of a detachment, which
had just advanced from Raymond, and by a general course from
the southwest, and whose rear was therefore in that direction. Clinton itself was directly between Johnston & myself, and as both his
line of battle and [end p. 21 MS] mine were facing that place,
neither his face nor mine by moving directly toward it, would be
thereby coming up on the rear of troops occupying it. I have always however acknowledged, that at the moment, I believed his note
was *intended* to bear the construction I gave it—that is to say; a
movement directly to the east. I think very differently now, and am
satisfied that had I acted on that construction, I might have been
as justly accused of proceeding "[?] in violation of his orders" as
I am now unjustly accused by him because I assert that the unfortunate battle of Baker's Creek was the consequence of his order—
an assertion which is most undoubtedly true. But for the unwhole-
some effect produced on the mind of almost every general officer
by the knowledge that I had rec'd. from Gen *l* Johnston orders to
move upon the enemy, I should have disregarded as I had always
previously done the public clamor for an advance. When I reached
the army at Edwards about noon, some two & a half or three hours
after the recp *t* of the instructions, positive information was given

me that a considerable body of the enemy was on our right flank—
probably large enough to operate seriously upon our rear, or upon
Big Black bridge. I at once in my own mind relinquished the
idea of advancing directly upon Clinton by the shortest route, which
I had intended doing, (though I did not so express myself) when I
replied to Johnston's note in which I merely stated that I would
obey his order immediately (see my 1st letter of May 14 in Off *l*
Rep *t*). From the reports rec'd. upon which I believed myself justified in forming an opinion, I did not think it would be wise to
move at that time from the position we were occupying, but I
found the almost universal sentiment so eager for an advance that
backed as it was by Johnston's order, I thought it best to call the
Gen *l* Officers together, place my views before them and if possible
get their concurrence in them. This as you know I failed to do,
though I believe all, after considerable discussion, [end p. 22 MS]
in the end advocated the movement to which greatly against my
judgment I finally assented. Of this decision Gen *l* Johnston was
immediately notified by a dispatch sent by the hands of Cap *t*
Yerger, by whom also Johnston says (Page 179, Nar) he sent to
me his first note, that of 13 *th*. I do not know by whom he sent it.
I am very confident that Cap *t* Yerger did not deliver it to me. The
original is still in my possession—it is dated "Jackson May 13 *th*
1863—8.40 P.M."; is not in Gen *l* Johnston's hand-writing, but is
signed or purports to be signed by him, thus

"J. E. Johnston
General"

It was handed to me on my way from Bovina to Edwards by a
person I did not know who remained close by whilst I having dismounted wrote my reply by the wayside. I directed one of my
staff who was with me to get a reliable courier, when the individual
who had given me Johnston's dispatch spoke up, and saying he
would like to return at once to Johnston, asked to be permitted to
take my note to him. I accordingly gave it into his hands, having
no reason whatever to suspect his loyalty, he having come to me
apparently direct from Johnston. I have given the above details
from memory of course, but I believe them to be strictly correct.
I state also that to the best of my recollection and belief, I did not
see Cap *t* Yerger until I reached my H *d* Q *r* near Edward's Depot,
nor do I remember that he made any allusion to having been the
bearer of a dispatch to me, though it is possible he may have done
so. Gen *l* Johnston twice introduces the name of this officer as the

bearer of communications between us—(Pages 176 & 179 Nar) an
unusual, and one would suppose an unnecessary particularity. I
have shown that the note referred to was handed to me not "about
7 *A.M.* on the 14 *th*," but *two hours* later. There can be no mistake
about this, as my reply dated at "9.10 A.M." was written instanter
and on the spot—but observe (Foot of Page 179, Nar) was not
delivered to Gen *l* Johnston until "the afternoon of the 16 *th*"—
certainly not less than fifty hours after. There is good reason to
believe that both of these dispatches and probably Johnston's to
me of the 14 *th* were betrayed to Gen *l* Grant. [end p. 23 MS] see
(page 180, Nar). Gen *l* Johnston's cursory reference to the influence the information thus derived had upon the Federal General's
movements and, observe, casual as that reference is how materially
it affects his criticism (Page 219, Nar) "that I moved southward
to fight an army" &c. Some time during the winter of 1873/74.
I was told by a lady a native of Missi., and at the time of the events
referred to residing in the state, that on the night of the 13 *th*-
14 *th* of May /63, Cap *t* Yerger reached the residence of her sister,
whilst en route from Gen *l* Johnston with a dispatch to me—that
a heavy rain had so raised the waters of a stream in his way that
he could not pass it at the usual place and that he either knew of
no other crossing or else did not know the way to Edward's Depot
by any other road than that by which he had expected to reach me,
and that he had given the dispatch to another individual who had
either arrived with him at her sister's or had met him there. The
name of this person was also mentioned, but I can not recall it with
certainty. My informant further stated that the person referred to
had procured or had endeavored to procure from her sister a fresh
horse to accomplish what he had undertaken. I took no memo-
manda of this information at the time, hence I rely entirely upon
memory now. I am sure however that it was substantially as I
have narrated it. If the facts were as represented it is strong cir-
cumstantial evidence that Gen *l* Johnston's dispatch of the 13 *th*
was not delivered to me by Cap *t* Yerger. I was also told by the
same lady and by a brother of hers of certain statements made in
their presence & in that of several other persons by Gen *l* Frank P.
Blair, who had commanded a Division of the Fed *l* Army in the
Missi. campaign of 1863. I was not personally acquainted with
Gen *l* Blair, but took the liberty of addressing some inquiries to
him based on the representations I was told he had made. [end
p. 24 MS] His reply promptly given, is a sufficiently clear explanation of the whole subject. I copy it in full as follows.

"St. Louis, Jany 24 *th,* 1874

"Gen *l* J. C. Pemberton, Fauquier Co., Va.

"Dear General—I take pleasure in answer to your letter of the 19 *th*
"January, in saying that it was generally understood in our army
"that General J. Johnston's Courier conveying dispatches to you
"previous to the Battle of Baker's Creek or Champion Hills be-
"trayed his dispatches to Gen *l* Grant and also your answers to
"Gen *l* Johnston's orders, so that in fact Gen *l* Grant had the most
"precise information as to your movements and those of Gen *l*
"Johnston. I do not know positively from Gen *l* Grant these facts
"but the matter was spoken of by the Officers of our army in such
"a way as to leave no doubt in my mind.

"Very Respectfully, your ob *d* servant,
(signed) Frank P. Blair"

As Gen *l* Blair stated that he did "not know positively from Gen *l*
Grant these facts" I immediately addressed a note to the latter in
which I quoted the language of Gen *l* Blair, commencing with the
words "it was generally understood &c" but omitting the words
"so that in fact Gen *l* Grant had the most precise information as
to your movements and those of Gen *l* Johnston." In continuation
of my letter to the then President I said—"Permit me to add that
"this information has tended to confirm my own suspicions excited
"at the time by the (otherwise) inexplicable delay in the receipt
"of Gen *l* Johnston's dispatch of the 14 *th* of May, which, as you
"Sir are probably aware, was not handed to me until after 5 P.M.
"on the 16 *th* when my army was in full retreat. My inquiry is
"confined simply to two points
"1st. The truth (or reverse) of the facts discussed by the officers
"of the army of the Tenn *e.* [end p. 25 MS]
"2nd. The correctness (or the reverse) of my surmise as to the dis-
"patch of the 14 *th* above referred to."
I may mention that I did not use the name of Gen *l* Blair in my
letter to the Pres *dt,* but referred to him only as "a General Officer
of the army of the Tennessee." The next day I received the following reply through the Pres *dts* private secretary Mr. Levi P. Lucky,
dated "Executive Mansion, Washington, Jany 31 *st* 1874
"General—Your letter of yesterday was duly received this morn-
"ing, and the President authorizes me to say that the statement
"of the officer to which you refer was correct, and he thinks you
"are also correct as to your surmises in regard to the delay in receipt
"of your dispatch.

"He says the dispatches were brought in our lines and given to "Gen *l* McPherson, and by him immediately brought to Head "Quarters." In a subsequent letter of Feby 11 *th* acknowledging the receipt of a second from me to the Pres *dt* in which I asked his consent to the publication of the preceeding correspondence, Mr. Lucky says—

"He (the Pres *dt*) directs me to say that he thinks you will find in the first volume of Gen *l* Badeau's book a full history of the matter." Referring to the book named, I see in a footnote (Page 252, Vol 1) a somewhat curious story of a "national spy" having been entrusted by Gen *l* Johnston with one of triplicate originals of his order of the 13 *th* to me, and that this original reached Grant. As Gen *l* Johnston makes no mention anywhere, so far as I have seen, of having sent this dispatch in triplicate to me, and does very particularly name the person by whom he says he did send it, I think Badeau's account of the matter must be incorrect. In his letter of Feby 11 *th* the President also referred again to the 2 *nd* inquiry in my first to him—that is in relation to the delay [end p. 26 MS] in the delivery to me of Johnston's dispatch of the afternoon of the 14 *th,* which as before mentioned was not rec'd until 5.35 P.M. on the 16 *th*. Mr. Lucky says "With regard to the delay in the recep *t* by you of Gen *l* Johnston's dispatch the President says he supposes the delay was caused by the long detour necessary to be made around his lines by the person carrying the dispatch and that the one received by you (me) was one started after the one delivered to him. He does not *know* relative to that delay, but remembers *positively* of the receipt by Gen *l* McPherson of dispatches from Gen *l* Johnston to you." This is rather confused and leaves me in doubt whether the President had not in mind Badeau's version of triple dispatches from Johnston to me, and thus confounded the dates of the 13 *th* & 14 *th,* & whether that particular dispatch was or was not delivered to him, to ascertain which was the point of my 2 *nd* inquiry in my first letter. I cannot conceive of any sufficient legitimate cause why a messenger sent from Johnston's camp on the Canton road 7½ miles north of Jackson should consume fully forty eight hours in reaching my army, *not more* certainly, than forty miles distant from it. No "detour was necessary to be made around Grant's lines," unless the messenger had first intentionally or by accident gone within them, for his lines did not extend north of the Southern R.R., nor had he any troops on that road west of Clinton. As proof of this fact, Cap *t* Yerger delivered to Gen *l* Johnston at 8½ A.M. on 15 *th* a dispatch from me dated 5.40 P.M. on 14 *th* that is to say in less than one third of the time that it took Gen *l* Johnston's courier to reach me, though the route and the distance were the same, or not materially different. In fact the two messengers should have met midway on the road. Whatever may have been the cause of the delay in the delivery to me of Johnston's dispatch of the 14 *th* May, the consequences were not less disastrous to the Confederacy than were those resulting from the receipt by me of his hasty order of the preceeding night, the 13 *th*, because I should not have attempted to execute in any manner instructions of a prior date which were made manifestly impracticable by the events narrated in a letter of later date, and of which the entire tenor clearly [end p. 27 MS] proves the fact that Gen *l* Johnston had entirely ignored his own orders and plans, to *beat* a *detachment at Clinton or elsewhere,* or to effect an immediate union of his troops with my army, either by a *combined* movement against the enemy, or in any other manner whatsoever.

Again, my second note of May 14 *th* to Gen *l* Johnston dated 5.40 P.M., written after I had dismissed the Council of War at Edward's, plainly shows that my purpose in the movement there indicated, was by coming up on the enemy's rear, to draw him from Jackson and from the line of the Southern railroad, and by threatening his communications, to reopen our own, and thus by a cooperative movement of Johnston's troops and mine to unite them. Be it remembered that I was ignorant then and for thirty six hours after, that Johnston had already been driven from Jackson, and was marching north by the Canton road. I was ignorant that his order and my reply had been betrayed to Grant, and that therefore I was advancing upon the enemy's rear to fight his whole army, instead of a comparatively small portion of it as I had hoped.

My "intended movement" did not make the cooperation of Gen *l* Johnston's troops impossible, nor did it prevent reinforcements from reaching me (see Page 219 Nar). It did not "[?] defeat his purpose of uniting all the expected reinforcements with my army." On the contrary it made cooperation practicable and would have made a union comparatively easy had it been promptly undertaken immediately after his expulsion from Jackson, but he preferred to march to the north and waited until the 17 *th* before he turned his deliberate steps toward my army. [end p. 28 MS]

Gen *l* Johnston received at 8½ A.M. on the 15 *th* May my note of the preceeding evening informing him of the intended movement upon the enemy's line of communications as early as possible on the 15 *th*—he did not then consider my contemplated action to be "in violation of his order of the 13 *th.*" On the contrary he virtually acknowledges that it would be in conformity therewith; and that *had he* not been driven out of Jackson in the meanwhile, it might have effected the main purpose of that order. In his note of the 15 *th* written immediately on the receipt of mine just referred to, he says—"Your dispatch of yesterday just received. *Our being compelled to leave Jackson makes your plan impracticable,*" therefore had he not been compelled to leave Jackson my plan in his estimation would have been practicable. He continues in the same dispatch, thus—"The only mode by which we can unite is by your moving directly to Clinton informing me that we may move to that point &c &c." Why it was necessary that we should both move to Clinton to effect a junction has always been incomprehensible to me. If he had marched from Calhoun Station as directly toward Edward's Depot as the roads permitted we could have united readily. If I had been in position when this dispatch was received to move in accordance with its instructions "directly towards Clinton," and had so moved, within ten hours my army would have been captured or destroyed, and Vicksburg would have been in possession of the enemy probably in less than two days. This entire dispatch of the 15 *th* is an exposition of Gen *l* Johnston's over estimate of the importance of Jackson; of his indifference to the fate of Vicksburg, and of his ignorance of the strength and disposition of the enemy's forces. What for instance can surpass the absurdity of the instructions to me contained in its last paragraph? [end p. 29 MS] "Gen *l* Maxey (en route from Port Hudson—JCP) was ordered back to Brookhaven. You probably have time to make him join you. Do so before he has time to move away." Being a Mississippian Sir, you know the relative positions of Brookhaven on the J.N.O.R.R. and of Edward's Depot on the Southern road, and you probably know the fact that every man of Grant's army was at the time referred to within the southern angle formed by the two roads or on the line of the Southern R.R. There is a wonderful contrast between the daring generalship indicated in this order as well as in divers others that I had the honor to receive, and the very cautious procedure that marked all the movements of the troops under Gen *l* Johnston's immediate command.

The fourth and last dispatch I rec *d* from Gen *l* Johnston after his arrival in Jackson and previous to the occupation of the trenches around Vicksburg, is dated from "Calhoun Station 7 P.M. May 16 *th,* 1863." It will be found in full in my Supplementary Report, and also in Johnston's Narrative, Page 562. The withdrawal of the Federals from Jackson reported in that dispatch and their advance by the Clinton road toward's Edward's depot on the morning of the 16 *th* was in consequence of information Grant had rec *d* at 5 o'clock a.m. on that day of "the *position being taken up* by our army," and the "intention of attacking his rear." He learned this he says from two "employees on the Jackson & Vicksburg Railroad who had passed through my army on the night before." He "had determined" he says "to leave one Divis *n* of Sherman's Corps one day longer in Jackson, but this information determined him to bring his entire command up at once." It is evident therefore that Grant considered that I was following Johnston's peremptory orders "to march out from the direction of Vicksburg and attack our (his) rear" when [end p. 30 MS] he was informed of the positions being taken up by our army. But on the evening of the 14 *th* he says in his Report, "he learned that Gen *l* Johnston, as soon as he had satisfied himself that Jackson was to be attacked had ordered Pemberton peremptorily to march out from the direction of Vicksburg and attack our rear. *Availing* myself of this information I immediately issued orders &c &c." The effect of the orders Grant immediately issued in consequence of the betrayal of the correspondence between Johnston & myself was the concentration by the evening of the 15 *th* of all his troops (with the exception of that portion of Sherman's Corps at Jackson) within good supporting distance to meet my advance upon his rear by whatever route I might select for that purpose. The federal troops from Jackson did not get up in time to participate in the battle, and had no influence on the result, but would have had a share in it, if I had attempted on the 15 *th* "to *march 17 miles to the east*" to attack a detachment at Clinton. That I failed to do so Gen *l* Johnston says, "was very discouraging," and he asserts that I thereby "deferred a junction that might have been effected on the 15th." He, *Johnston,* was on that day marching to *the east of North* on the Canton road & encamped in the afternoon at Calhoun Station. But I have explained this point before. In his dispatch of the 15 *th* I was informed by Johnston that "The only mode by which we can unite is by your moving directly to Clinton, and informing me &c." In that of the 16 *th,* which was next in succession, he says "It is matter of great anxiety to me to add *this little* force (not the arriving reinforcements) to your army, *but* the enemy being exactly between us, and *consultation by* correspondence so slow, it is difficult to arrange a meeting &c." [end p. 31 MS] "I will take the route you suggest, however, if I understand it." In his book (page 180, Nar) he says the description I gave him of the route I intended to pursue was "minute and clear." He concludes this dispatch of the 16 *th* with this inquiry "Is the force between us too strong for you to fight if it interposes itself." In my note of the morning written from the battlefield, to which his is a reply, he was told "Heavy skirmishing is now going on in front."

Through circumstances not of my own seeking it had fallen to my lot to bear alone the responsibilities of the defence of the most important geographical district of the Confederacy during seven months of incessant attack. At the expiration of that period and at a moment fraught with the greatest peril to the Confederacy, at a moment when the wisdom or folly of the plans I had persistently pursued were in all probability about to be tested on a battlefield of my own selection with more points in our favor than had been or could be expected elsewhere, it was my great misfortune to be brought under the immediate command of an invalid general who in four consecutive days could utter four such documents as those addressed to me from the 13 *th* to the 16 *th* May inclusive.

Gen *l* Johnston has made several assertions in regard to the battle of Baker's Creek so unjust to me that I cannot pass them by without at least an attempt to refute them. It is always easy to make an accusation, but not so easy to rebut it when the nature of the case allows of only negative proof to that end. I think it unnecessary to quote from the "Narrative" the passages to which I particularly refer but ask you to turn to Page 219 of that book. Since "no other commander" has ever to my knowledge made the march I did make on the afternoon and night of the 15 *th* May/63 I can not disprove Johnston's positive statement that the said march "would have involved no other commander in a battle." I shall endeavor however to show that *I* in consequence of that march *was necessarily* involved in a battle. [end p. 32 MS] I would have justly invited Gen *l* Johnston's severest criticisms if, following the example of the French king who "first marched up the hill and then marched down again," I had felt myself free to return to the chosen ground near Edward's Depot (which ground, *by reason of his order, I had not* felt myself free to maintain, when on it) simply because I was *informed* at night of the presence of the enemy, whose proximity I was perfectly aware of, when at noon I abandoned that ground that I might compel him to attack me, or myself attack him as events might require. His presence so far from "frustrating the intention in such slow course of execution" met those intentions half way, and I accordingly found myself precisely in the position I had anticipated when "my chosen ground and matured plans" were abandoned that I might execute as far as was practicable Gen *l* Johnston's instructions, save only that the enemy's advance on the lower Raymond road had diminished the distance over which I had expected to march for the expressed object of fighting him. I deny positively that I was "informed at night that the camp of a strong body of Federal troops was near in the direction of Bolton" (see Nar. Page 181). I knew nothing of the presence of troops there. They were there, however, and others close by them. They were brought there moreover by the betrayal of the correspondence heretofore mentioned.

Is it true that I moved but three or four miles on the 15 *th*? Is it true that my "army could have marched to it (my chosen ground near Edward's Depot) in about an hour"? Gen *l* Johnston affirms, I deny, the truth of both propositions. Loring's Division led the marching column from near Edward's Depot about 1 P.M. on the 15 *th* and bivouacked near 10 P.M. with its advance on the Raymond road—some six to seven miles by the nearest practicable route from its point of departure. Bowen's and Stevenson's Divisions, the centre & left, were on the march until past midnight; the distance accomplished being about the same if estimated from the points of departure of each Division. [end p. 33 MS]

The Army was, from fortuitous circumstances explained in Official Reports, compelled to move on narrow country roads hedged in on either side for much of the distance by dense woods. These roads were in bad condition from recent and unusually heavy rains. The stalling of a single wagon would block the way to the rest and to the column in rear. These facts should explain the length of time consumed on the march. To regain the "chosen ground" near Edward's depot, it was necessary to reverse the column. The wagon trains which on the advance movement had been in rear, became the head of the column; the field artillery and the ordnance wagons of the several divisions could not move forward in the new direction until the road became wide enough to open a passage between or on the one or the other flank of the train. Gen *l* C. L. Stevenson's Report accompanying mine fully explains the difficulty, and shows in connection with Gen *l* S. D. Lee's, not only the incorrectness of Johnston's assertion that "my army could have marched to it (i.e. the chosen ground) in about an hour," but taken together these two Reports prove that "obedience" to Johnston's "third order again directing him (me) to march to the east to meet me (him), that our troops might be united, was not only not "easy" but that it was absolutely impossible. The retrograde movement necessary to the execution of said order had hardly commenced, when our cavalry pickets in front of Tilghman's brigade on the lower Raymond road were driven in, and the enemy's artillery opened at long range on what had been the head of our column, now become the rear. I must refer you to Gen *l* Stevenson's report for a full explanation of the modus operandi by which it was intended to effect obedience to Johnston's order. You will observe that the road (because of the obstacles before mentioned) was not open for the passage of the troops until about 9.30 A.M. and that meantime in accordance with the programme Reynold's brigade the left of Stevenson's division had moved off with the wagon train, while the skirmishers of S. D. Lee's brigade now became the head of the marching column were almost immediately engaged on the upper Raymond & Clinton roads. [end p. 34 MS] There is no need of argument to prove that the train of an army without cavalry and face to face with an enemy having a fair proportion of that arm, must be kept either in *juxtaposition* with the army itself, or be accompanied by an Infantry force sufficient for its protection if circumstances require even a temporary separation. As our train was thus practically separated while the movements were in progress which should enable it to take its proper place in the column under the new order of march, so also was the leading brigade necessarily separated from the division to which it belonged by the events that quickly intervened to prevent the rest of the army from continuing the march which had been thus begun, and thus Reynolds brigade moving on with the train was entirely cut off from participation in the battle. The onus of this separation, which was entirely a consequence of his own order of the 15 *th*, Gen *l* Johnston as usual desires to lay on my shoulders (See page 220, Nar. where he speaks of my "detaching Reynolds & *Vaughn's* brigades.") Vaughn had been left to guard the R.R. bridge when the army moved to the front; both of these bodies of troops would of course have formed part of my fighting force had I been permitted to retain the position near Edward's Depot.

But to proceed with the discussion in regard to the easy or impossible obedience to Johnston's order——

Lt. J. C. Taylor, one of my aide D. C. who had been sent forward to ascertain on what point the enemy was moving his heaviest forces states in an official paper prepared at the time that I was writing my Report in Gainesville, Ala. that "the skirmishing was equally severe on the *right* and *left* and no definite conclusion could be formed as to which was the advance of the bulk of the enemy's force"—a second time he went forward "conveying the order to Col. Adams (Wirt) when forced to retire, to fell back with his whole command in front of the strongest column of the enemy." At this time I should think about 9 *A.M.* I found Col. Adams with all his cavalry about, retiring on a bye road just to the left of the Raymond road. The Infantry skirmishers on this road, and on its right were ordered to retire as their flank was exposed by the withdrawal of the cavalry." This occurred about 9 A.M. and our right became the *rear* in the new order of march. [end p. 35 MS]

Now see Gen *l* S. D. Lee's account of events transpiring at about the same time on the extreme left, which had now become the head of the column. I will only remark first that I believe it to be rather a customary course to begin a battle with skirmishing especially when it is impossible from the nature of the field to ascertain the strength of your enemy.

Gen *l* Lee says—"By eight o'clock (that is while the train was being placed in a position to permit the passage of the troops— J C P) my brigade was in line of battle, and skirmishing on both roads (i.e. the Clinton & Middle Raymond roads)xx At about nine o'clock it was discovered that the enemy was massing troops on the left evidently for the purpose of turning our left flank, and getting between our army and Edward's depot. My brigade was at once marched under fire by the left flank for the purpose of checking the enemy xxx Similar movements were frequently made by me under fire throughout the day xxx As early as ten o'clock in the morning it became evident that the enemy was in heavy force and determined on battle as his skirmishers were bold and aggressive and *several divisions* of his troops were visible in front of our left." In a footnote (Page 182 Nar) Johnston quotes Grant as saying "the action commenced at eleven o'clock." What Grant does say is this "There had been continuous firing between Hovey's skirmishers and the rebel advance which by *eleven* o'clock *grew* into a battle. For some time this Division bore the brunt of the conflict, but finding the enemy too strong for them, at the instance of Hovey I directed first one and then a second brigade from Crocker's division to reinforce him. *All this time* Logan's division was working up on the enemy's left and rear, and weakened his front attack most wonderfully." Now I place the preceeding statements (and they are supported by many others as well Federal as Confederate) in opposition to Gen *l* Johnston's base assertion that "obedience to his order was easy, for the engagement did not begin until near midday, and in the meantime there was *but a division* of the enemy before him (me)."

One of the chief reasons why I was most anxious that a searching investigation should be made by a Court of Inquiry into the causes of Confederate disasters within my Depar t in 1863 was that a——[?] understanding should be reached in regard to the orders sent by me to Gen l Loring during the battle of Baker's Creek—the nature of those orders, the circumstances under which they were given; and the probable consequences that would have resulted from a prompt obedience on his part. [end p. 36 MS]

Johnston defends Loring's whole course, both during the action, and in subsequently abandoning the rest of the army when in retreat. (Pages 183, 184 Nar) I do not desire to discuss this matter otherwise than very briefly. Two of Johnston's misrepresentations are however so direct that I can not pass them over in silence. Not only *"after* bringing Bowen's troops into action" did I direct "Loring to join in it with at least a part of his," but the orders were first given simultaneously to both generals, Loring being directed to follow up Bowen's movement immediately with two of his three brigades. Loring failed to obey. Bowen meanwhile had gone splendidly into action and with such effect that to use the language of the Federal General McPherson, "The tide of battle was turning against us (the Federals)" (see his Off l Report). It was then at the moment of greatest hope *of a successful* issue to our arms that I renewed my order to Loring which Major Jacob Thompson says (see his letter) he delivered in these words—"General Pemberton desires you to come immediately and with all dispatch, to the left, to the support of Gen l Stevenson, *whatever may be on your front."* This order was given in the very *height of battle* by the commanding general to a subordinate in terms which while they left the latter no discretionary powers as to prompt obedience, relieved him from all responsibility for the consequences of obedience. It was apparent to me as soon as I found that the enemy's right was being pushed back from the direction of my intended march that our whole force should be thrown as quickly as possible upon that part of his line. The order was accordingly renewed to Loring "to come immediately, and with all dispatch to the left (of our line) whatever might be on his front." Loring could have reached the desired position had he moved at double quick as Bowen did, in fifteen minutes I think at farthest. The enemy on his front could not have changed his position to any advantage in twice that time.

Johnston says a prompt obedience by Loring would have made our "defeat certain," I say that I believe it would at least have enabled us to regain our position at Edwards Depot "my chosen ground" [end p. 37 MS] and not improbably would have given us a great deal more. Gen *l* Johnston defends the *inaction* of my subordinate Loring who constituted himself the judge of the propriety of the orders he had received and which were again and again repeated to him during the heat of the engagement. He excuses that officer's long delayed obedience, *not because* he considered that immediate obedience was *impracticable* but because Loring did not think it *advisable* to obey.

Gen *l* Loring's division of three brigades with an aggregate (according to his report of the 10 *th* May) of 6500 effective, took no active part in the battle of Baker's Creek. That battle was fought on the Confederate side by less than eleven thousand men—to wit—by three brigades of Stevenson's division aggregate 6600, and by the two brigades composing Bowen's division aggregate 4300. There were no other troops on the field, nor near it, except Loring's who as just mentioned was not seriously engaged. Including his three brigades, there should have been available for action in all 17400 men. I do not take into account in this statement the three or four hundred cavalry with Col. Wirt Adams for after the battle had well begun, from the nature of the country they could not be actively engaged with the enemy. After covering the retreat of Stevenson's and Bowen's Divisions across Baker's Creek, Gen *l* Loring failed to follow the movement with his own Division, but withdrew his entire command and marched to Jackson having previously recalled Col. Scott's Regiment which had crossed the west bank under instructions from Gen *l* Stevenson. This act of Gen *l* Lorings was the primary cause of our disasters in front of the Railroad bridge on the following morning, necessitating the abandonment of the Big Black as a line of defence, and the occupation of the trenches around Vicksburg as a last resort. I am not, except by inference, informed of the reasons that actuated Gen *l* Loring to pursue the course he did. I presume that Johnston has accepted as his own whatever may have been the version of the former in regard to the difficulties in his way. Johnston in his usual positive manner [end p. 38 MS] asserts that "by the time Stevenson's and Bowen's divisions had crossed Baker's Creek the Federal troops were so near the stream as to render its passage by Loring's division impracticable." *If* it was impracticable, there is of course no blame to be attached to Loring. My individual belief is that it was not only practicable, but that the passage of the creek would have been accomplished, had it been attempted, with a loss comparatively so insignificant that it should not have been permitted a place in the general's calculations. Maj. Gen *l* Stevenson who was in command of the troops on the spot and who was an eye witness of all that transpired thus narrates the circumstances in his Official Report—he says—"On my arrival about sunset at the ford on Baker's Creek I found that the enemy had crossed the bridge above and were advancing artillery in the direction of the road. One battery had already taken position and was playing on the road, but at *right angles* and *with too long range to prevent the passage of troops.* Here I found on the west side the brigades of Gen *l* Green and Col. Cockerell of Bowen's Division who had then halted and taken up position (this disposition was made by Gen *l* Bowen under instructions from myself J C P) to hold the point *until Loring's Division could cross.* I found Col. Scott of the 12 *th* Louisiana Reg *t* of Loring's Division halted about half a mile from the ford on the *east* side, and directed him to cross. I then addressed a note to Gen *l* Loring informing him of what I had done, telling him of the change I had caused Col. Scott to make in his position, stating that with the troops then there and others that I could collect, *I would hold the ford and road until his division could cross,* and urging him to hasten the movement. To this note I received no answer but in a short time Col. Scott moved off his Reg *t* quickly in the direction of his original position in obedience I was informed to orders from Gen *l* Loring. Inferring from this that Gen *l* Loring did not *intend to cross at that ford he having had ample time to commence the movement,* I suggested to Gen *l* Green & Col. Cockerell to move forward to the Rail Road bridge." [end p. 39 MS]

It has always appeared unaccountable to me that Gen *l* Loring's course at and after the battle of Baker's Creek has attract[ed] so little attention. I believe my Official Reports cover all I have to say in relation to the unfortunate affair east of the Big Black bridge on the morning of the 17 *th* May. The object I had in view in desiring to hold temporarily the tete de pont, I thought at the time and still think, was of sufficient importance to require the attempt.

(Gen *l* Johnston) [?] In various connections he uses in his book the word "attack" as if it were synonymous in meaning with "beat." In none of his instructions nor suggestions to me, did he ever employ the former term. The concentration of my whole force to *"attack* Grant if he landed on this side of the Missi." would not necessarily have given back what was abandoned to win success, for the attack might have been unsuccessful. Neither can it be said that "to attack such a detachment (as that supposed at Clinton on the night of May 13) would necessarily "be of immense value" for that attack also might have been unsuccessful. Instances are not infrequent I believe where the attacking party has been beaten—for example our own troops at Baton Rouge and Corinth, and Grant and Banks in their assaults on Vicksburg and Port Hudson. There would have been something ludicrous in his language had he said (Page 218 Nar) "The first (order) dated May 1 *st,* and repeated on the 2 *nd,* directed him to *beat* the Federal army with all his forces united for the purpose"—he therefore substitutes for *beat—attack* and tells his readers that he orders me to do that which he did not order me to do, persuading them that his order to *attack* was repeated on the 2nd only to be disregarded. [end p. 40 MS]

Pemberton's hitherto unpublished answer to Johnston's charges has evoked the following interested comment:

"I have looked over the letter of General Pemberton with much interest. It is certainly a historical document of much importance. ...[Pemberton's] moderate and reasonable statement in every way goes to confirm my impression of General Johnston and the decided weaknesses of character which unquestionably detracted from his great abilities and his genuinely patriotic spirit."—Gamaliel Bradford, March 30, 1931.

"From a first reading it [Pemberton's letter] appears most significant and I am particularly struck by several points that he makes....I intend to go through the records afresh in the light of the letter."—B. H. Liddell Hart, April 14, 1931.

"I have been particularly interested in the Vicksburg Campaign. ...During the past year I have paid several visits—in fact, three visits—to the battleground and have been reading up, mostly from the Union side.... To an old Cavalryman, General Pemberton's need of it and his expression of its value are most interesting.... What a dense fog of war General Pemberton was in without the Cavalry and without proper staff communications....I sympathize...in his lack of almost everything, including a Commanding General who tried to pass the buck, rather than support a loyal subordinate."—Major General Frank Ross McCoy, U. S. Army. May 25, 1931.

Notes

The Pemberton Collection of MSS, newspaper clippings, etc., is now part of the Southern Historical Collection of the Library of the University of North Carolina. All references to the *Official Records of the Union and Confederate Armies (O. R.)* are to Series I.

CHAPTER I. HISTORICAL POSITION

1. Letter from Colonel Matthew F. Steele to the author, November 27, 1937.
2. *Personal Memoirs of U. S. Grant* (2nd ed., New York, 1895), I, 475.
3. H. J. Eckenrode and Bryan Conrad, *James Longstreet* (Chapel Hill, 1936), p. 174.
4. William Freeman Vilas, *The Vicksburg Campaign* (Wisconsin History Commission, 1908), p. 53.
5. S. C. Vestal, ed., *One Hundred and Seventy-Five Battles* (Harrisburg, 1937), p. 187.
6. Letter from President Davis to General Pemberton, August 9, 1863, original in Pemberton Collection.
7. Howard Swiggett, ed., *A Rebel War Clerk's Diary* (New York, 1935), II, 43.
8. Robert Selph Henry, *The Story of the Confederacy* (New York, 1936), p. 113.
9. Letters of November 1 and 14, 1932, from Dr. Freeman to the author.
10. Henry, *Story of the Confederacy*, p. 264.
11. Preface, *ibid*.

CHAPTER II. FAMILY AND EARLY LIFE

1. *Pennsylvania Gazette*, XXXVI (October, 1937), No. 1.
2. Pemberton Collection.
3. *Report of June 12, 1882, of the Thirteenth Annual Reunion of the Association of Graduates of the United States Military Academy*, pp. 17 ff.
4. *Dictionary of American Biography;* G. W. Cullum, ed., *Biographical Register, Officers and Graduates, U. S. Military Academy*, Vol. I (1891).
5. Vicksburg *Daily Herald*, April 19, 1874, Pemberton Collection.
6. Cullum, ed., *Biographical Register . . . U. S. Military Academy*.
7. Pemberton MSS.

CHAPTER III. MEXICO AND THE FRONTIER

1. Grant's *Memoirs*, I, 124.
2. From a London news letter, published in a Vicksburg newspaper in 1870, Pemberton Collection.
3. Colonel U. S. Grant, 3rd, to the author, February 4, 1938.
4. Freeman, *R. E. Lee* (New York, 1935), I, 298.
5. *Ibid.*, p. 294.
6. *Report of June 12, 1882, of the Thirteenth Annual Reunion of the Association of Graduates of the United States Military Academy*, pp. 17 ff.
7. Pemberton MSS.
8. *Ibid.*
9. *Ibid.*
10. In May, 1937, while Colonel U. S. Grant, 3rd, was inspecting the Vicksburg defenses with the author, Colonel Grant remarked, "General Pemberton must have been an artilleryman, from the placing of these guns." Two attacks of Grant were repulsed with ghastly losses to his men.
11. Henry, *Story of the Confederacy*, p. 264.

CHAPTER IV. WHY PEMBERTON WENT SOUTH

1. *Report of June 12, 1882, of the Thirteenth Annual Reunion of the Association of Graduates of the United States Military Academy*, pp. 17 ff.
2. Freeman, *R. E. Lee*, I, 156.
3. Vicksburg *Daily Herald*, May 6, 1879, Pemberton Collection.
4. Richard Taylor, *Destruction and Reconstruction* (New York, 1879), p. 116.
5. Letter dated April 23, 1861, written to Caroline Hollingsworth Pemberton, original in Pemberton Collection.

CHAPTER V. RICHMOND AND CHARLESTON

1. Pemberton MSS.
2. Pemberton MSS; Vicksburg *Daily Herald*, April 19, 1874.
3. *Report of June 12, 1882, of the Thirteenth Annual Reunion of the Association of Graduates of the United States Military Academy*, pp. 17 ff.
4. John W. Thomason, Jr., *Jeb Stuart* (New York, 1930), pp. 82-83.
5. Freeman, *R. E. Lee*, I, 607, 616-17.
6. Jonathan Daniels, *A Southerner Discovers the South* (New York, 1938), p. 327.
7. Rowland, *Jefferson Davis* (Jackson, Miss., 1923), V, 282, 310-11, 319-20.
8. Marquis James, *Andrew Jackson, The Border Captain* (New York, 1938), pp. 230-35.
9. Pemberton to the Richmond, Virginia, *Enquirer*, February 22, 1865, Pemberton Collection.
10. Pemberton Collection.
11. Freeman, *R. E. Lee*, I, 624.
12. *Ibid.*, 625.
13. Pemberton MSS.
14. Richard Taylor, *Destruction and Reconstruction*, p. 235.
15. Swiggett, ed., *A Rebel War Clerk's Diary*, I, 388.
16. Letter of Pemberton to Richmond *Enquirer, supra*, n. 9.
17. Letter to Pemberton from William Preston Johnston, Pemberton Collection.

18. Rowland, *Jefferson Davis*, V, 311.
19. *Ibid.*, p. 319.
20. Letter from George W. Randolph, Pemberton Collection.
20ª. Freeman, *R. E. Lee*, I, 607.
21. Eckenrode and Conrad, *James Longstreet*, p. 138.
22. The Charleston *Mercury*, September 29, 1862, Pemberton Collection.
23. Letter from A. J. Gonzales, Pemberton Collection.
24. Freeman, *R. E. Lee*, I, 306-8.

CHAPTER VI. BACKGROUND OF THE VICKSBURG CAMPAIGN

1. Pemberton MSS; also Rowland, *Jefferson Davis*, VI, 203.
2. Lieutenant General Robert L. Bullard, U. S. Army, Retired, to the author, February 12, 1941.
3. From a letter from Colonel Matthew F. Steele to the author, November 27, 1937.
4. New York *Herald*, August 17, 1881, Pemberton Collection.
5. Henry, *Story of the Confederacy*, p. 218.
6. *Ibid.*, p. 496.
7. Rowland, *Jefferson Davis*, V, 347.
8. Pemberton Collection.
9. *Ibid.*
10. *Ibid.*
11. Freeman, *R. E. Lee*, I, 231, 418, 602.
12. *Ibid.*, II, 240.
13. Pemberton Collection.
14. Freeman, *R. E. Lee*, II, 85.
15. *Ibid.*, I, 607.
16. Henry, *Story of the Confederacy*, p. 416.
17. *Ibid.*
18. Freeman, *R. E. Lee*, II, 562-63.
19. *O.R.*, XXV (Pt. 2), 790.
20. *Ibid.*, p. 843.
21. *Battles and Leaders of the Civil War* (New York, 1888), III, 639.
22. The correspondence referred to in the following quotations can be found in Rowland, *Jefferson Davis*, Vols. V and VI, according to the dates given.
23. Freeman, *R. E. Lee*, II, 34.
24. *Ibid.*, p. 230.
25. *O.R.*, XXVII (Pt. 3), 931.
26. Pemberton MSS; also *O.R.*, XXIV (Pt. 3), 890.
27. *Jefferson Davis*, by His Wife (New York, 1890), II, 421.
28. *Ibid.*, p. 422.
29. Statement made by D. S. Freeman to the author, December 13, 1938.
30. *Jefferson Davis*, by His Wife, II, 413.

CHAPTER VII. GRANT'S FIRST ATTEMPT TO CAPTURE VICKSBURG

1. *O.R.*, XXIV (Pt. 1), 287-92.
2. Major R. W. Memminger, "The Surrender of Vicksburg," *Southern Historical Society Papers*, XII, 352.
3. Henry, *Story of the Confederacy*, p. 218.
4. *Ibid.*

5. Sherman's *Memoirs* (New York, 1875), II, 25-26.
6. Pemberton MSS.
7. Henry, *Story of the Confederacy*, p. 219.
8. Grant's *Memoirs*, I, 356.
9. Dorsey, *Henry Watkins Allen* (New Orleans, 1866), p. 174.
10. B. H. Liddell Hart, *Sherman* (New York, 1929), p. 159.
11. *Ibid.*, p. 162.
12. Pemberton MSS.
13. Swiggett, ed., *A Rebel War Clerk's Diary*, I, 197.
14. Liddell Hart, *Sherman*, p. 163.
15. *Ibid.*, p. 165.
16. Pemberton MSS.
17. Liddell Hart, *Sherman*, pp. 165, 171.
18. Sherman's *Memoirs*, I, 290, 292, 294-95.
19. Freeman, *R. E. Lee*, II, 329.
20. Pemberton MSS.

CHAPTER VIII. GRANT'S SECOND FAILURE

1. *Mississippi: A Guide to the Magnolia State* (New York, 1938), p. 269.
2. Henry, *Story of the Confederacy*, pp. 228-29.
3. Freeman, *R. E. Lee*, I, 550.
4. Liddell Hart, *Sherman*, p. 179.
5. Memminger, *Southern Historical Society Papers*, XII, 356.
6. *O.R.*, XXIV (Pt. 1), 289, 290.
7. Memminger, *Southern Historical Society Papers*, XII, 352, 356, 358.
8. *Ibid.*
9. Liddell Hart, *Sherman*, p. 180.

CHAPTER IX. GRANT TRIES AGAIN

1. Grant's *Memoirs*, I, 384.
2. B. H. Liddell Hart, *Great Captains Unveiled* (Boston, 1928), pp. 257, 258.
3. Henry, *Story of the Confederacy*, pp. 128-29.
4. Pemberton MSS.
5. *Ibid.*
6. Henry, *Story of the Confederacy*, pp. 40, 41; Col. G. F. R. Henderson, *Stonewall Jackson and the American Civil War* (New York, 1936), p. 496.
7. Pemberton MSS.
8. *O.R.*, XXIV (Pt. 3), 681. (Much of the correspondence quoted here from the *Official Records* can also be found in the Pemberton MSS and in Dorsey, *Henry Watkins Allen*.)
9. *Ibid.*, p. 687.
10. *Ibid.*, p. 791. Italics supplied.
11. *Ibid.*, p. 689.
12. *Ibid.*, p. 730.
13. *Ibid.*, p. 689.
14. Pemberton MSS.
15. *O.R.*, XXIV (Pt. 3), 741-42, 747.
16. Pemberton MSS.
17. *O.R.*, XXIV (Pt. 3), 752.

18. *Ibid.*, pp. 685-86.
19. Henry, *Story of the Confederacy*, p. 253.
20. *O.R.*, XXIV (Pt. 3), 760.
21. Pemberton MSS.
22. *O.R.*, XXIV (Pt. 3), 751-52.
23. Henderson, *Stonewall Jackson*, p. 660.
24. Pemberton MSS, Dorsey, *Henry Watkins Allen*, p. 173.
25. Pemberton MSS.
26. *Ibid.*
27. This is the opinion of Colonel Matthew F. Steele, U. S. Army, Retired.
28. Dorsey, *Henry Watkins Allen*, pp. 205-6.
29. Pemberton MSS.
30. *O.R.*, XXIV (Pt. 1), 253.
31. *Ibid.*
32. *Ibid.*
33. *O.R.*, XXIV (Pt. 3), 778.
34. *O.R.*, XXIV (Pt. 1), 255.
35. *Ibid.*
36. Henderson, *Stonewall Jackson*, p. 689.
37. Freeman, *R. E. Lee*, III, 139, 140, 147, 148, 160, n. 123.
38. *Ibid.*, II, 308.
39. *O.R.*, XXIV (Pt. 1), 250.
40. *Ibid.*, pp. 251, 252.
41. *Ibid.*, pp. 255, 256.
42. *Ibid.*
43. *Ibid.*
44. Henry, *Story of the Confederacy*, p. 254.
45. *Ibid.*

CHAPTER X. COULD GRANT'S CROSSING HAVE BEEN PREVENTED?

1. A. G. Paxton (Colonel, 114th Field Artillery, Mississippi National Guard), *The Vicksburg Campaign* (Vicksburg, 1939), p. 11.
2. Freeman, *R. E. Lee*, II, 410.
3. *O.R.*, XXIV (Pt. 1), 252, 256; Dorsey, *Henry Watkins Allen*, pp. 188, 189.
4. *O.R.*, XXIV (Pt. 3), 769, 776.
5. *O.R.*, XXIV (Pt. 1), 252, 253; Dorsey, *Henry Watkins Allen*, pp. 177, 182, 183, 184.
6. *O.R.*, XXIV (Pt. 1), 252.
7. *Ibid.*, p. 328.
8. *Ibid.*, p. 257.
9. Pemberton MSS. Telegram, April 28, 1863. Pemberton to Davis.
10. *O.R.*, XXIV (Pt. 1), 257.
11. *Ibid.*
12. Henderson, *Stonewall Jackson*, p. 488.
13. Liddell Hart, *Sherman*, p. viii.
14. *Ibid.*, p. 182.
15. Dorsey, *Henry Watkins Allen*, p. 205.
16. Vilas, *The Vicksburg Campaign*, p. 30.
17. Lieutenant Colonel Royal E. T. Riggs, U. S. Infantry Reserve.

CHAPTER XI. ACROSS THE RIVER: PORT GIBSON

1. Harris Dickson in *Collier's,* March 19, 1938.
2. Grant's *Memoirs,* I, 396.
3. Vilas, *The Vicksburg Campaign,* p. 34.
4. *Ibid.*
5. *O.R.,* XXIV (Pt. 1), 257.
6. According to the opinion of Lieutenant Colonel Royal E. T. Riggs, United States Infantry Reserve.
7. *O.R.,* XXIV (Pt. 1), 257.
8. Pemberton MSS, Dorsey, *Henry Watkins Allen,* p. 192.
9. *Ibid.*
10. *O.R.,* XXIV (Pt. 1), 257.
11. Grant's *Memoirs,* I, 401, 402.
12. Pemberton MSS, Dorsey, *Henry Watkins Allen,* p. 192.
13. Pemberton MSS, Loring's report.
14. *O.R.,* XXIV (Pt. 1), 258.
15. Pemberton MSS, telegram from Bowen on May 1, 1863.
16. Pemberton MSS, telegram, May 1, to Johnston and to Davis.
17. Pemberton MSS, report of Brigadier General W. E. Baldwin to Pemberton.
18. Vilas, *The Vicksburg Campaign,* p. 35.
19. Pemberton MSS, report of Brigadier General W. E. Baldwin to Pemberton.
20. Pemberton MSS, report of Brigadier General John S. Bowen to Pemberton.
21. *O.R.,* XXIV (Pt. 1), 329; Dorsey, *Henry Watkins Allen,* p. 198.
22. *Ibid.*
23. *Ibid.*
24. *Ibid.*
25. Grant's *Memoirs,* I, 400, 401.
26. Dorsey, *Henry Watkins Allen,* p. 213.

CHAPTER XII. AFTER PORT GIBSON

1. Dorsey, *Henry Watkins Allen,* pp. 196, 207; Henry, *Story of the Confederacy,* p. 255.
2. Dorsey, *Henry Watkins Allen,* pp. 205, 207, 211, 213.
3. Liddell Hart, *Sherman,* p. 186; Henry, *Story of the Confederacy,* pp. 255, 256.
4. Pemberton MSS; Dorsey, *Henry Watkins Allen,* p. 200.
5. Pemberton MSS; *O.R.,* XXIV (Pt. 3), 814-15.
6. *O.R.,* XXIV (Pt. 1), 259.
7. Henry, *Story of the Confederacy,* p. 256.
8. Liddell Hart, *Sherman,* p. 186.
9. *O.R.,* XXIV (Pt. 1), 269.
10. *O.R.,* XXIV (Pt. 3), 839.
11. *Ibid.,* p. 844.
12. *Ibid.,* p. 842.
13. *Ibid.,* p. 845.
14. Dorsey, *Henry Watkins Allen,* p. 213.
15. B. H. Liddell Hart, *Through the Fog of War* (New York, 1938), p. 202.
16. Henderson, *Stonewall Jackson,* pp. 707-8.
17. *O.R.,* XXIV (Pt. 1), 326.
18. Pemberton MSS.

19. Armand de Caulaincourt, *No Peace with Napoleon!* (New York, 1936), pp. 16n, 18, 23, 25, 26, 29.
20. Henry, *Story of the Confederacy,* p. 257.
21. *O.R.,* XXIV (Pt. 3), 838.
22. Henry, *Story of the Confederacy,* p. 256.
23. Freeman, *R. E. Lee,* III, 15, 18, 50. Italics supplied.
24. *O.R.,* XXIV (Pt. 1), 269.
25. *O.R.,* XXIV (Pt. 1), 259.
26. Pemberton MS. See *infra,* Appendix B.
27. Vilas, *The Vicksburg Campaign,* p. 40.
28. Paxton, *The Vicksburg Campaign,* p. 14.
29. Henry, *Story of the Confederacy,* pp. 254, 255.
30. Grant's *Memoirs,* I, 410, 411.
31. Henry, *Story of the Confederacy,* p. 261.
32. Swiggett, ed., *A Rebel War Clerk's Diary,* II, 38.
33. Liddell Hart, *Sherman,* p. 192.

CHAPTER XIII. THE BATTLE OF RAYMOND, THE FALL OF JACKSON

1. Pemberton's Official Report, *O.R.,* XXIV (Pt. 1), 269, 324; Grant's *Memoirs,* I, 415.
2. Dorsey, *Henry Watkins Allen,* p. 195.
3. *Ibid.,* p. 208.
4. *O.R.,* XXIV (Pt. 1), 324-25.
5. *Ibid.,* p. 325.
6. Paxton, *The Vicksburg Campaign,* p. 14.
7. *O.R.,* XXIV (Pt. 1), 260.
8. Vilas, *The Vicksburg Campaign,* p. 42.
9. Grant's *Memoirs,* I, 415.
10. Liddell Hart, *Sherman,* pp. 188-89.
11. Dorsey, *Henry Watkins Allen,* p. 222; *O.R.,* XXIV (Pt. 1), 261, 323.
12. *O.R.,* XXIV (Pt. 1), 261.
13. Dorsey, *Henry Watkins Allen,* p. 210.
14. *O.R.,* XXIV (Pt. 1), 260.
15. Freeman, *R. E. Lee,* III, 68.

CHAPTER XIV. BATTLE OF BAKER'S CREEK OR CHAMPION'S HILL

1. *O.R.,* XXIV (Pt. 1), 323.
2. *Ibid.,* p. 326.
3. *Ibid.,* p. 261.
4. Pemberton MSS. See *infra,* Appendix B.
5. Henderson, *Stonewall Jackson,* p. 646.
6. *O.R.,* XXIV (Pt. 1), 323.
7. *Ibid.,* p. 261.
8. Dorsey, *Henry Watkins Allen,* pp. 215-16.
9. Napoleon's maxim LXV, Colonel Matthew F. Steele to the author.
10. Henderson, *Stonewall Jackson,* p. 707; Freeman, *R. E. Lee,* II, 89, 108, 274, 275.
11. Rowland, *Jefferson Davis,* V, 485.
12. Telegram, Pemberton to Davis, May 13, 1863, Pemberton Collection.

13. Henderson, *Stonewall Jackson*, p. 272.
14. Ludwig, *Napoleon* (New York, 1926), pp. 74, 75, 132, 410.
15. *O.R.*, XXIV (Pt. 1), 262.
16. Pemberton MS. See *infra*, Appendix B.
17. Grant's *Memoirs*, I, 423.
18. Dorsey, *Henry Watkins Allen*, p. 216; *O.R.*, XXIV (Pt. 1), 262, 263.
19. Pemberton's Official Report, *O.R.*, XXIV (Pt. 1), 270.
20. *Ibid.*, p. 327.
21. *Ibid.*, p. 263.
22. *Ibid.*, pp. 270, 323.
23. Pemberton MS. See *infra*, Appendix B.
24. Pemberton's Official Report, *O.R.*, XXIV (Pt. 1), 323, 330.
25. Liddell Hart, *Sherman*, p. 188.
26. Pemberton's Official Report, *O.R.*, XXIV (Pt. 1), 326.
27. Grant's *Memoirs*, I, 426-27.
28. Henderson, *Stonewall Jackson*, p. 483.
29. Pemberton MS. See *infra*, Appendix B.
30. *Ibid.*; Grant's *Memoirs*, I, 427.
31. Letter from Grant to Pemberton, dated February 11, 1874, signed by the President's secretary, Levi P. Luckey, Pemberton Collection.
32. Grant's *Memoirs*, I, 425.
33. Sherman's *Memoirs*, I, 321.
34. Pemberton's Official Report, *O.R.*, XXIV (Pt. 1), 263.
35. Grant's *Memoirs*, I, 427, 428.
36. Pemberton's Official Report, *O.R.*, XXIV (Pt. 1), 263.
37. Grant's *Memoirs*, I, 429-30.
38. Pemberton MS. See *infra*, Appendix B.
39. *Ibid.*; Dorsey, *Henry Watkins Allen*, p. 217; Pemberton's Official Report, *O.R.*, XXIV (Pt. 1), 263, 264.
40. *Ibid.*
41. *Ibid.*
42. Pemberton's Official Report, *O. R.*, XXIV (Pt. 1), 263, 264.
43. *Ibid.*
44. *Ibid.*
45. Dorsey, *Henry Watkins Allen*, pp. 217-18.
46. *O.R.*, XXIV (Pt. 1), 322.
47. *Ibid.*, p. 325.
48. Henderson, *Stonewall Jackson*, pp. 146-47.
49. Grant's *Memoirs*, I, 433-34.
50. *O.R.*, XXIV (Pt. 1), 263.
51. Grant's *Memoirs*, I, 434.
52. Pemberton MS. See *infra*, Appendix B.
53. Pemberton's Official Report, *O.R.*, XXIV (Pt. 1), 265.
54. *Ibid.*, p. 320.
55. Grant's *Memoirs*, I, 434.
56. Sherman's *Memoirs*, I, 323.

CHAPTER XV. BATTLE OF BIG BLACK RIVER AND RETIREMENT
TO VICKSBURG

1. This description is taken from Pemberton's Official Report, *O.R.*, XXIV (Pt. 1), 266-67.

2. Grant's *Memoirs*, I, 437.   Italics supplied.

3. *Ibid.*, pp. 439-40.

4. Sandburg, *Abraham Lincoln: The War Years* (New York, 1939), II, 111, 118, 119, 120, 345.

5. Sherman's *Memoirs*, I, 323-24.

6. Pemberton's Official Report, *O.R.*, XXIV (Pt. 1), 267.

7. Dorsey, *Henry Watkins Allen*, p. 225.

8. *Battles and Leaders of the Civil War*, III, 487-88.

9. Freeman, *R. E. Lee*, III, 297, 298 n. 39.

9ᵃ. *Ibid.*, IV, 55; III, 268.

10. Ludwig, *Napoleon*, p. 526.

11. Grant's *Memoirs*, I, 440; *O.R.*, XXIV (Pt. 1), 320.

12. *O.R.*, XXIV (Pt. 1), 269.

13. Grant's *Memoirs*, I, 442, 443-44.

14. Henderson, *Stonewall Jackson*, p. 708.

15. W. E. Woodward, letter to the author, dated June 15, 1931.

16. Pemberton MS.

17. Pemberton's Official Report, *O.R.*, XXIV (Pt. 1), 270-71.

18. *Ibid.*

19. Henry, *Story of the Confederacy*, pp. 259-60.

20. Major R. W. Memminger, letter to the Richmond, Virginia, *Sentinel*, October 24, 1863, *Southern Historical Society Papers*, XII, 358.

21. Pemberton's Official Report, *O.R.*, XXIV (Pt. 1), 287-92.

22. *Ibid.*, p. 271.

23. *Ibid.*, p. 272.

24. *Ibid.*

25. Freeman, *The South to Posterity*, p. 96.

CHAPTER XVI. THE SIEGE

1. Pemberton's Official Report, *O.R.*, XXIV (Pt. 1), 272-73.

2. *Ibid.*

3. Pemberton MSS.

4. Liddell Hart, *Sherman*, p. 193.

5. Grant's *Memoirs*, I, 443.

6. Sherman's *Memoirs*, I, 325.

7. *O.R.*, XXIV (Pt. 1), 274.

8. Vilas, *The Vicksburg Campaign*, pp. 50-51.

9. Paxton, *The Vicksburg Campaign*, p. 16.

10. *O.R.*, XXIV (Pt. 1), 274.

11. Johnston's Official Report, *ibid.*, p. 248.

12. Paxton, *The Vicksburg Campaign*, p. 16.

13. *O.R.*, XXIV (Pt. 1), 274.

14. *Ibid.*, p. 275.

15. Sherman's *Memoirs*, I, 325-26.

16. Stevenson's Official Report, *O.R.*, XXIV (Pt. 1), 275.

17. Forney's Official Report, *ibid.*, p. 276.

18. Smith's Official Report, *ibid.*

19. Sherman's *Memoirs*, I, 326, 327, 328.

20. Grant's *Memoirs*, I, 446.

21. Liddell Hart, *Sherman*, p. 195.

22. Pemberton MSS.

23. Grant's *Memoirs*, I, 449.
24. Sherman's *Memoirs*, I, 328.
25. Grant's *Memoirs*, I, 452.
26. *Ibid.*, p. 451.
27. *O.R.*, XXIV (Pt. 1), 276.
28. Pemberton MSS.
29. Henry, *Story of the Confederacy*, pp. 260-61.
30. *Ibid.*, p. 356.
31. *Ibid.*, p. 363.
32. *O.R.*, XXIV (Pt. 1), 276-77.
33. Pemberton MSS.
34. *O.R.*, XXIV (Pt. 1), 277.
35. Henry, *Story of the Confederacy*, p. 261.
36. *O.R.*, XXIV (Pt. 1), 290.
37. *Ibid.*, p. 277.
38. *Ibid.*
39. *Ibid.*, p. 278.
40. *Ibid.*
41. *Ibid.*
42. Pemberton MSS.
43. *O.R.*, XXIV (Pt. 1), 278.
44. *Ibid.*
45. Wolseley's Introduction to Henderson, *Stonewall Jackson*, p. xiii.
46. Henry, *Story of the Confederacy*, p. 263.
47. Grant's *Memoirs*, I, 455-56.
48. Taylor, *Destruction and Reconstruction*, p. 139.
49. Pemberton MSS.
50. *Ibid.*
51. *O.R.*, XXIV (Pt. 1), 278.
52. Pemberton's Siege Diary, Pemberton Collection.
53. *Ibid.*
54. *O.R.*, XXIV (Pt. 1), 278.
55. Dorsey, *Henry Watkins Allen*, p. 225.
56. *O.R.*, XXIV (Pt. 1), 279.
57. *Ibid.*
58. Pemberton's Siege Diary, Pemberton Collection.
59. *O.R.*, XXIV (Pt. 1), 279.
60. Pemberton Collection.
61. *O.R.*, XXIV (Pt. 1), 280.
62. *Ibid.*, p. 279.
63. Pemberton's Siege Diary, Pemberton Collection.
64. *O.R.*, XXIV (Pt. 1), 280, 286.
65. *Ibid.*, p. 281.
66. *Ibid.*, p. 287.
67. Henry, *Story of the Confederacy*, pp. 262-63.
68. Grant's *Memoirs*, I, 460.
69. Freeman, *The South to Posterity* (New York, 1939), p. 96.
70. *O.R.*, XXIV (Pt. 1), 280-81.
71. *Ibid.*, p. 281.
72. *Ibid.*, p. 287.
73. Grant's *Memoirs*, I, 462-63.
74. Liddell Hart, *Sherman*, p. 196.

75. *O.R.*, XXIV (Pt. 1), 281.
76. *Ibid.*, p. 287.
77. *Ibid.*, p. 281.
78. *Ibid.*, p. 282.
79. *Ibid.*, p. 283.
80. *Ibid.*, pp. 285-86.
81. Henry, *Story of the Confederacy*, p. 488.

CHAPTER XVII. THE SURRENDER

1. Pemberton's Official Report, *O.R.*, XXIV (Pt. 1), 283.
2. Grant's *Memoirs*, I, 465-66.
3. Freeman, *R. E. Lee*, III, 118.
4. The Pittsburgh *Evening Chronicle*, July 14, 1863, Pemberton Collection.
5. *O.R.*, XXIV (Pt. 1), 283-84.
6. *Ibid.*, p. 284.
7. Pemberton MSS.
8. James, *Andrew Jackson, The Border Captain*, p. 194.
9. Grant's *Memoirs*, I, 467.
10. *Ibid.; O.R.*, XXIV (Pt. 1), 284.
11. *Ibid.*
12. *O.R.*, XXIV (Pt. 1), 285.
13. Pemberton MSS.
14. *O.R.*, XXIV (Pt. 1), 284.
15. Dorsey, *Henry Watkins Allen*, pp. 226-27.
16. Vilas, *The Vicksburg Campaign*, p. 52.
17. *O.R.*, XXIV (Pt. 1), 281.
18. *Ibid.*, p. 286.
19. *Ibid.*, p. 285.
20. *Ibid.*
21. Grant's *Memoirs*, I, 468-69.
22. Contemporary newspaper and eyewitness accounts.
23. Letter dated August 20, 1863, Pemberton Collection.
24. Grant's *Memoirs*, I, 472, 473, 475, 477.
25. Newspaper account, Pemberton Collection.
26. Grant's *Memoirs*, I, 480, 481.
27. Freeman, *R. E. Lee*, III, 18, 19.
28. Grant's *Memoirs*, I, 479; Pemberton's Official Report, *O.R.*, XXIV (Pt. 1), 292.
29. The Pittsburgh *Evening Chronicle*, July 14, 1863, Pemberton Collection.
30. *Ibid.*
31. *Ibid.*
32. *Ibid.*
33. Vicksburg Military Park folder.
34. *Home Letters of General Sherman*, edited by M. A. DeWolfe Howe (New York, 1909), p. 269.
35. Freeman, *The South to Posterity*, p. 14; Freeman, *R. E. Lee*, III, 154, 154n.

CHAPTER XVIII. AFTERMATH OF SURRENDER

1. This description of the meeting between Pemberton and Johnston is taken from the account of an eyewitness as told to Dr. L. Minor Blackford, Atlanta, Georgia.

2. Grant's *Memoirs*, I, 476.
3. Major R. W. Memminger, *Southern Historical Society Papers*, XII, 359.
4. Rowland, *Jefferson Davis*, V, 568.
5. Henry, *Story of the Confederacy*, p. 263.
6. Pemberton MSS.
7. Freeman, *The South to Posterity*, p. 45.
8. Letter from Pemberton to Mr. ——, Pemberton MSS.
9. *Ibid.*
10. Pemberton's Official Report, *O.R.*, XXIV (Pt. 1), 285.
11. Grant's *Memoirs*, I, 472, 473.
12. Pemberton Collection.
13. Swiggett, ed., *A Rebel War Clerk's Diary*, II, 195n; Sandburg, *Abraham Lincoln: The War Years*, II, 111.
14. Pemberton MSS.
15. Clippings from Southern newspapers, Pemberton Collection.
16. Letter from Pemberton's Assistant Adjutant General, William H. McCardle, Pemberton MSS.

CHAPTER XIX. THE VICKSBURG CAMPAIGN IN REVIEW

1. Colonel Matthew F. Steele to the author, letter dated November 27, 1937.
2. Freeman, *R. E. Lee*, I, 559; II, 45.
3. *Ibid.*, III, 430, 433, 459.
4. *O.R.*, XXIV (Pt. 1), 248.
5. Sherman's *Memoirs*, II, 39.
6. Freeman, *R. E. Lee*, III, 259, 266, 461, 462.
7. *Ibid.*, II, 428.
8. *Ibid.*, IV, 475.
9. From the original letter, in the possession of Colonel William Couper, Executive Officer, Virginia Military Institute.
10. Freeman, *R. E. Lee*, III, 440-41.
11. *Ibid.*, p. 155.
12. *Ibid.*, p. 150.
13. Lloyd Lewis, *Sherman, Fighting Prophet* (New York, 1932), pp. 261-62.
14. Pemberton MSS.
15. Liddell Hart, *Sherman*, p. 158.
16. Liddell Hart, *Great Captains Unveiled*, pp. 266, 267, 269.

CHAPTER XX. NEW DUTIES

1. Rowland, *Jefferson Davis*, letters listed in index volume.
2. Pemberton MSS.
3. Rowland, *Jefferson Davis*, VII, 321.
4. *Ibid.*
5. Henry, *Story of the Confederacy*, p. 315; Eckenrode and Conrad, *James Longstreet*, p. 246.
6. Henderson, *Stonewall Jackson*, p. 601.
7. From the original letter, in the possession of R. S. Wilkins, Esq., Boston, Massachusetts.
8. Pemberton MSS.
9. *The State*, Columbia, South Carolina, January 23, 1908.
10. *Jefferson Davis*, by His Wife, II, 424.

11. Pemberton Collection.

12. Swiggett, ed., *A Rebel War Clerk's Diary,* II, 210.

13. Colonel William Couper, *One Hundred Years at V. M. I.* (Richmond, 1939), II, 71.

14. Pemberton MSS.

15. Swiggett, ed., *A Rebel War Clerk's Diary,* II, 437.

16. Grant's *Memoirs,* II, 88.

17. Rowland, *Jefferson Davis,* VII, 74-75.

CHAPTER XXI. THE LAST YEARS

1. Anecdotes of the family's frontier and Warrenton days were furnished by General Pemberton's daughter, Mrs. Patty Pemberton Berman; and by his granddaughter, (Miss) Rowland Baylor.

2. Pemberton Collection.

INDEX

INDEX

Adams, Colonel Wirt, commands Mississippi cavalry and state troops assembled as cavalry, 104, 291; in battle of Baker's Creek, 155-56, 158, 315

Allentown, Penna., Pemberton and family move to, 275 ff.

Aztec Club of 1847, formed among U. S. Army officers serving in Mexican War, 15

Badeau, Adam, author of *Military History of U. S. Grant,* gives version of surrender different from Pemberton's, 281 ff. *passim*

Baker's Creek, battle of, 144 ff., 291 ff. *passim;* consequence of Johnston's order, 304; Pemberton's refutation of Johnston's statement concerning, 312 ff.

Baldwin, Brigadier General William E., only one of Pemberton's officers advising against accepting Grant's terms of surrender, 231

Banks, General Nathaniel P., could not get to Port Hudson when expected, 134

Barton, Rev. Mr., bears Pemberton's letter (Aug. 28, 1866) to Davis, 265

Bayou Pierre. *See* Grand Gulf

Beauregard, P. G. T., at West Point, 10, 10 n.; popularity of, 27, 34; on Pemberton's construction of Fort Wagner, 31; wanted by Charlestonians as commander, 34; in command at Charles-

ton, 35; sent little aid to Pemberton, Davis says, 53; praises Pemberton after surrender, 248

Bible, stories of told by Pemberton to children at Harleigh, 268-69, 270

Big Black River, battle of, 166-71

Bigelow, John, mentioned, 227

Big Sunflower River, in approach to Vicksburg, 78-80

Blair, General Frank P., letter of testifying to betrayal of dispatches between Johnston and Pemberton, 288, 306-7

Bolton, Miss., Sherman at, finds copy of U. S. Constitution with Jefferson Davis's name on it, 164-65

Bowen, Brigadier General John S., at Pemberton's orders fortifies Grand Gulf, 106; in battle of Port Gibson, 120 ff.; informs Pemberton of landing of Federal troops at Hard Times, 111-12; at Grand Gulf, 113; held off Porter at Grand Gulf, 118 ff.; in battle of Baker's Creek, 158 ff. *passim;* after retreat to Vicksburg, 173 ff.; in siege of Vicksburg, 180 ff. *passim;* in surrender of Vicksburg, 226 ff. *passim,* 282 ff. *passim*

Bradford, Gamaliel, quoted on Pemberton's hitherto unpublished answer to Johnston's charges, 319

Bradley, Captain L. D., in siege of Vicksburg, 188

Bragg, General Braxton, at West Point, 10, 10 n.; unable to send reinforcements to Pemberton, 51; Davis orders some of army of to Pemberton's forces, 54-55; army of inspected by Davis, 66-67; receives reinforcement of cavalry needed by Pemberton, 89-90; Pemberton recommended to by Davis after surrender of Vicksburg, 258-60

Brooks, William M., Davis writes letter to in praise of Pemberton, 52-53

Brown, Joseph E., Governor of Georgia, attitude of toward Confederate government, 49

Bruinsburg, Grant lands troops at, 108, 118-19

Buckner, Simon Bolivar, unable to send Pemberton cavalry, 90-91

Buford, General Abraham, in battle of Baker's Creek, 161 ff. *passim*

Bullard, Lieutenant General Robert Lee, quoted on Davis's strategy in ordering Pemberton to hold Vicksburg, 40

Bulwer-Lytton, read at Harleigh, 273

"Burial of Sir John Moore, The," recited by Pemberton to little daughter, 273

Caulaincourt, General de, on Napoleon and defense of Paris, 131-32

Cavalry, importance of in securing military information, 90; Pemberton's fatal lack of, 89-90, 103-4, 134, 142-43; Johnston takes three-fourths of Pemberton's, 89, 290-91

Century Magazine, Grant-Pemberton correspondence concerning surrender published in, 281-88; Grant's letter to General Wright on surrender published in, 285-86

Cerro Gordo, Pemberton at, 13

Champion's Hill, battle of. *See* Baker's Creek, battle of

Chapultepec, storming of, Pemberton in, 13

Charleston, Pemberton in command at, 27-35; attitude of toward Lee, 27, 35; attitude of toward Pemberton, 27-38

Charleston *Mercury,* quoted on Pemberton, 35-36

Chickasaw Bayou, abandoned after defeat at Big Black River, 172-73

Chickasaw Bluffs, 62, 63, 67, 68, 71

Chilton, Robert, at West Point, 9

Churchill, Winston (American novelist), quoted, 14

Churubusco, Pemberton at, 13

Cincinnati, Union iron-clad in siege of Vicksburg, 197, 200

Cockrell, Colonel F. M., in battle of Baker's Creek, 159 ff.; in battle of Big Black River, 169 ff. *passim*

Colquitt, Colonel Peyton H., letter by expressing confidence of self and command in Pemberton after surrender, quoted, 236-37

Columbus, Ky., Grant's main base for overland movement, 62

Columbus, Miss., Davis writes to citizens of on Pemberton, 54

Concentration, principle of applied to Pemberton's problem, 109 ff.

Confederacy, hampered by attitude of Governors, 32; hampered by insistence on States' rights and civil rights, 48-49; position of in spring of 1863, 117-18

Conkling, J. C., Lincoln's letter to, 3

Cooper, General Samuel, 5, 5 n., 10 n., 41

Cotton, Confederate government places embargo on trading with enemy in, 30

Couper, Captain J. M., bearer of letter from Pemberton to Johnston on evacuation of Vicksburg, 215

Court of Inquiry, Pemberton asks for, 4; always postponed, 261; failed to materialize in Montgomery or Atlanta because of military exigency, 248-49; Pemberton's anxiety for, 316

Cowan, Lieutenant L. B., Pemberton used residence of during siege, 239

Crocker, Brigadier General Marcellus M., Division of in battle of Raymond, 140; in battle of Baker's Creek, 315

Cumming, General Alfred, in battle of Baker's Creek, 162; Georgia Brigade of in siege of Vicksburg, 216

Custard, Rev. S. Franklin, rector of Grace Episcopal Church, Allentown, 275-76

Daniels, Jonathan, quoted on South Carolinians, 28

Davis, Jefferson, attitude of toward Pemberton and Gorgas, viii; quoted, after

Queen of the West, ran past Vicksburg batteries safely, 85; captured by Southerners, 86

Quinby, Brigadier General I. F., counseled retreat from Fort Pemberton, 77, 78

Railroads, in defense of Vicksburg, 82; Grierson's raid on, 101-3; Pemberton's use of, 126

Randolph, George W., letter to Pemberton quoted, 34

Raymond, battle of, 137 ff.; Pemberton considered fight at unnecessary, 137, 300-1

Reagan, Postmaster-General, considered holding Vicksburg more important than invasion of North, 238

Rebel War Clerk's Diary. See Jones, John B.

Resaca de la Palma, battle of, Pemberton in, 13

Reynolds, Colonel A. W., tried to reach Bowen at Port Gibson, 121; brigade of cut off from battle of Baker's Creek, 314

Rhett, Dr. George, of Charleston, and Pemberton, 29-30

Richardson, William H., Adjutant General of State of Virginia, quoted in praise of Pemberton and criticism of Johnston concerning Vicksburg, 252-53

Ripley, General J. W., mentioned, 27, 36

Roddey, Colonel P. D., not where Johnston said he was, 293

Roebuck, J. A., in London proposes recognition of Confederacy to House of Commons, 227

Ross, Brigadier General L. F., attempt of to reach Vicksburg by way of the Yazoo, 75-77, 78

Sandburg, Carl, in his *Lincoln* tells incident of Sherman at Vicksburg and the Confederate bouquets, 246

Sanders, Captain, carried messages between Pemberton and Johnston during siege of Vicksburg, 208, 209, 216

Schaadt, Mrs., remembers Pemberton at Allentown Grace Church, 276

Scott, Major Taylor, friend of Pemberton, 275

Scott, Winfield, tries to hold Pemberton in U. S. Army, 21; attitude of toward abandoning communication and supply line, 64

Seddon, James A., Secretary of War, Lee writes to on relative importance of holding Virginia and holding the Mississippi line, 49; Davis writes on aid to Pemberton, 51; telegraphs Johnston to aid Pemberton at all costs, 57-58; asks Longstreet's advice on Vicksburg situation, 132-33; on Loring's failure to comply with Pemberton's orders at Baker's Creek, 162; and siege of Vicksburg, 184 ff. *passim;* letter of confidence to Pemberton quoted, 242-43; has conference with Pemberton, 252-53

Sedgwick, John, at West Point, 10

Sevastopol, Sherman declares position at less difficult than Vicksburg, 190

Seward, William Henry, Secretary of State, mentioned, 227

Sherman, William Tecumseh, at West Point, 10; in background of Vicksburg campaign, 39; part of in Grant's first plan to take Vicksburg, 60 ff.; repulsed by Pemberton at Chickasaw Bluffs, 63-64; believed control of whole river more important than back country in taking Vicksburg, 65; quoted on advance down river in December, 1862, 67; attack of on Chickasaw Bluffs failed, 67 ff.; quoted on Pemberton's successful repulse of Grant's first attempt on Vicksburg, 71; on Grant's plans for second attempt at Vicksburg, 74; comes to Porter's aid in Steele's Bayou experiment, 80; in Porter's naval feat of running Vicksburg's gauntlet, 96-97; in position above Vicksburg, 100; at Haines's Bluff during Grant's crossing of river below Vicksburg, 111; attitude of toward Grant's strung-out march down river, 115; in march toward Jackson, 127, 133; congratulates Grant and gives him "every bit of credit for campaign," 136; enters Jackson with Grant, 141; on capture and betrayal of

Johnston's Clinton letter, 155; in battle of Big Black River, 168 ff. *passim;* in siege of Vicksburg, 180 ff. *passim;* and the Confederate bouquets, 246; and Johnston, 252; in battle of Baker's Creek, 298 ff.

Shoup, General Francis A., in siege of Vicksburg, 189

Shreveport, La., railway center important to Confederacy, 59

Siege, chances of its being raised, 184-85

Sioux Indians, at Fort Ridgely, 18

Smith, General A. J., in battle of Baker's Creek, 163; receives Pemberton's emissaries previous to surrender of Vicksburg, 226; present at surrender, 229, 284 ff. *passim*

Smith, General Edmund Kirby, in Confederacy, 10 n.; promoted Lieutenant General, 35; unable to send reinforcements to Pemberton, 51; asked by Pemberton to cut enemy's supply line across river, 101-2; and Grant's crossing of river, 110; senior general west of Mississippi River, and Pemberton's appeals to during siege of Vicksburg, 202 ff. *passim,* 216, 220

Smith, Extra Billy, Major General and Governor of Virginia, friend of Pemberton, 275

Smith, Major General Francis H., superintendent of Virginia Military Institute, 252

Smith, Major General Martin Luther, in retreat to Vicksburg, 173 ff. *passim;* and siege of Vicksburg, 180 ff. *passim*

Smith, General Sooy, in siege of Vicksburg, 205

Snyder's Mill, importance of to defense of Vicksburg, 129; abandoned after defeat at Big Black River, 172-73, 179

States' rights, doctrine of, Pemberton a believer in, 22; operated against Confederacy, 48-49

Steele, Major General Frederick, in siege of Vicksburg, 189; in surrender of Vicksburg, 237

Steele, Colonel Matthew F., author of *American Campaigns,* quoted on Johnston at Vicksburg, 250

Steele's Bayou, Union experiments in, 78-81

Stevenson, Major General Carter L., Pemberton secured Division of from Bragg, 96; ordered by Pemberton to be ready to go to Bowen's aid at Grand Gulf, 113, 119; position of on May 7, 1863, 127-28; in battle of Baker's Creek, 157 ff. *passim;* in retreat to Vicksburg, 173 ff. *passim;* in siege of Vicksburg, 185 ff. *passim;* mentioned, 221, 222; report of on battle of Baker's Creek, 313 ff. *passim*

Stockton, Colonel Philip, arms sent to, 53

Stuart, J. E. B., attitude of toward the cavalry, 26; absence of at Gettysburg prevents Lee from getting necessary information, 105

Supply lines, contrasting attitudes of Grant and Lee toward, 63-64

Surrender, Terms of. See Terms of Surrender

Taylor, Lieutenant J. C., in battle of Baker's Creek, 157 ff. *passim;* quoted on battle of Baker's Creek, 314-15

Taylor, General Richard, son of Zachary Taylor, quoted on Pemberton, 22; quoted on Southern violation of embargo on trading with the enemy, 30; and Grant's crossing of the river, 110; in attack on Milliken's Bend and siege of Vicksburg, 202-4

Taylor, General T. H., in battle of Baker's Creek, 161

Taylor, Zachary, Grant served under, 13; mentioned, 30

Terms of Surrender, 243-45, 281-88

Thackeray, read at Harleigh, 273

Thomas, Brigadier General Allen, quoted on Pemberton's imperative reasons for surrender, 232-33

Thomas, George, at West Point, 10

Thomas, Inspector General Lorenzo, arrives in Memphis, 93

Thomason, Lieutenant Colonel John W., Jr., U. S. Marine Corps (J. E. B. Stuart's biographer), quoted on Stuart, 26; quoted on Johnston, 250-51 n.

Watts, Captain, in battle of Port Gibson, 122

Waul, Colonel T. N., Texas Legion of, in retreat to Vicksburg, 173 ff.; in siege of Vicksburg, 180, 188, 201-2

Webb, Confederate ship, in capture of Union's *Indianola,* 86, 88

Weeks, Lieutenant George H., at Fort Ridgely, 18

West Point, in time of Pemberton, 9-10

"West Point of the South." *See* Virginia Military Institute

Wharton, T. J., cited on choice of Pemberton to command at Vicksburg, 40-41

Wilkerson, Lieutenant Harris, burns *Cincinnati,* 200

Williams, General Thomas, started the canal across peninsula in front of Vicksburg, 74

Wise, Captain G. D., Pemberton's courier to Johnston near end of siege, quoted on his adventure, states that Johnston authorized Pemberton to surrender, 211-14; bearer of intercepted dispatch from Johnston to Pemberton, 220

Wolfe, James, siege of Quebec by compared with siege at Vicksburg, 256-57

Wolseley, Field-Marshal Garnet, cited on Bedford Forrest, 43; quoted, 159

Woodward, W. E. (author of *Meet General Grant*), quoted on Pemberton's duty to hold Vicksburg and on Johnston's lack of cooperation, 171-72

Worth, William J., Pemberton aide-de-camp of, 13, 36

Wright, General Marcus J., agent of war department for collection of Confederate records, receives letter from Grant on surrender, 285

Yazoo Pass, Grant's experiment at, 75 ff.